ON DOWN THE ROAD

Forewords by
Larry Mahan
and
Walt Garrison

ON DOWN THE ROAD

The world of the
RODEO COWBOY

by Bob St. John
Special Photography by Lewis Portnoy
Designed by Allan Mogel, Rutledge Books

Prentice-Hall, Inc. Englewood Cliffs, N.J.

For Katherine, who could dance at Bandera

Copyright 1977 in all countries of the International Copyright Union by Prentice-Hall, Inc., and Rutledge Books. All rights reserved. Designed and produced by Rutledge Books, a division of Arcata Consumer Products Corporation, 25 West 43 Street, New York, N.Y. 10036. Published 1977 by Prentice-Hall, Inc., Englewood Cliffs, N.J. 07632. Printed in Italy by Mondadori, Verona.

Library of Congress Cataloging in Publication Data
St. John, Bob.
  On down the road.
  1. Rodeos. 2. Cowboys. I. Title.
GV1834.S25   791.8   76-49472
ISBN 0-13-637272-4

About an hour before the Mesquite Rodeo started one summer, I was moving along the grounds in back, talking to some of the cowboys, when a man seemed to appear from nowhere. He had a round, ruddy face and closely cropped carrot-colored hair and smiled out the corner of his mouth. He was dressed somewhat like the other cowboys, though there was more newness to his blue jeans. His hat was tilted to one side, and a paunch was at odds with his belt. There was an elastic bandage wrapped around his knee, outside his jeans.

Though I had never seen him before, he approached me and said his name was Red and that he was glad to have me out. He then began telling me what a fine bull rider he was and how he'd scored an 84 on ol' No. 10 the previous night, though the bull had caused him to injure his knee. "Listen," he said, "let me know if I can help you. Enjoy yourself." He walked away, limping, toward a group of giggling camp followers. I could never find anybody who knew who he was and have not seen him since.

B. St. J.

FOREWORDS 9

Chapter 1:
WEST OF THE PECOS 11

Chapter 2:
NINE DAYS OF CHEYENNE 35

Chapter 3:
THE NEW BREED 99

Chapter 4:
SKIPPER VOSS AND A TALE OF THREE CLOWNS 133

Chapter 5:
STOCK AND MAN 157

Chapter 6:
DAKOTA KID AND AN OKIE 173

Chapter 7:
A MEETING OF CHAMPIONS 195

EXPLANATION OF EVENTS 240
GLOSSARY 243
RODEO RECORDS 245

FOREWORDS

I can personally vouch for some of the things you read about in this book (and some you don't), because Bob was with me a lot of the time. Unlike some of the other writers I've met over the years, he fit in well, which I think you'll find evident in this book. Sometimes he fits in too well and is about as crazy as some of the rest of us.

Statistics and things like that bore me, so this book didn't. It's one of the best examples I've seen of getting people off paper and making them real. I found myself laughing out loud at times and feeling a little sad and nostalgic at others. It's a long way from Pecos, Texas, to Oklahoma City, but I found it difficult to put the book down until I got there.

Maybe you have never seen a rodeo or really gotten into the kind of people who participate in the sport. You will when you read this book but, perhaps even more so, I think you will have gotten into people.

—LARRY MAHAN

I'm tickled to death to see a book like this come out. It's certain to turn more people on to rodeo and that'll help the cowboys get the appreciation and credit they deserve. I've been around cowboys all my life—I don't just mean Dallas Cowboys. They're good people. Rodeo cowboys compete against you but still help you the best way they can. If more people were like cowboys, this would be a better world.

This book takes you through some of the hardships and frustrations they go through and also the good times and the natural high that comes from competing and winning. When I read it, I found myself experiencing some of those feelings all over again. I figure if this happens to you, then it's pretty well written. I've known Bob St. John for a dozen years now and think he's a pretty dern good writer, though I wouldn't want him to know I said so.

I understand he's about ready to try and ride a bull now. Well, about all I can say about that is if he does, they better bar women and children from watching.

—WALT GARRISON

Chapter 1:
WEST OF THE PECOS

The river looked old, tired. Blackish green, it was little more than a stream, moving in a steady but slow pace under the bridge outside town. There was difficulty in imagining that this had once been the treacherous, winding river Indians had named Pecos, meaning "crooked." But they say that in the old days the river was a hundred feet wide, wild and fast, and could be crossed in only a few places, not only because of its sweeping waters but also because of its quicksand.

Cattle drives—moving along the Chisholm Trail, the Goodnight-Loving Trail—crossed the river, and then settlers in covered wagons came, and outlaws, hearing there was no law west of the Pecos, escaped to the area. Some went on into Mexico. Some made new lives. Some were hanged. A man named Roy Bean migrated, set up a courthouse in his saloon, declared himself a judge, and, using his six-gun as a gavel, formed his own brand of law—Law West of the Pecos.

Progress has shown little historical respect for the Pecos River, near the town of the same name. On the bottom inside wall of a bridge on the road to Monohans, somebody has written, "This to be used for worms." Another scribble, in red paint, says, "I love CB." Crushed beer cans and empty containers are scattered along the river's banks under the bridge.

Barney Hubbs shook his head, disgustedly, and said, "When I was a kid, we used to come to this spot and go swimming. Why, normally, the river flowed eight, ten feet deep." Stiffly, he bent over and picked up an empty beer can, looking around for a trash container. When he found none, it seemed he might just stick the can in his pocket, but then he just dropped it back on the ground. "These people got no respect," he said. "We got to get out here and clean this place up. Ought to put a kind of a park around here."

Barney Hubbs is tall with white hair. He gets around well for a man in his eighties and is partial to string ties. He came to Pecos with his father at the turn of the century, moving a herd of 400 head from Tom Green County in sixteen days. He borrowed money and started a printing office, which he still owns, in 1910. In 1920 he bought out the local newspaper and was later to own newspapers in Odessa, Midland, and Big Spring. He's retired now, though Barney Hubbs is the historical catalyst of Pecos, a town that cannot or will not let go of its past.

The original settlement had been on the east side of the river, a crossroads for the overland stage and wagon train routes. A flood wiped out the settlement, but it sprang back, almost overnight, when the railroad came in 1881. The T&P Railroad used Pecos as a stopover and the town became a trade center, a shipping center for the large, successful ranching industry. It maintains an impressive museum of the past and has a replica of Judge Roy Bean's saloon, though Bean never lived in Pecos but rather in Langtry, 200 miles to the southeast. "I understand the only time he came around here was to freight salt," said Hubbs. Hubbs will talk for hours about history, one of his favorite subjects being Clay Allison, the famous gentleman gunfighter who had a ranch near Pecos. Allison, who has been depicted in history and on television (not necessarily in that order), was said to have killed fifteen to twenty men. He died tragically when, while very drunk, he fell off a heavily loaded wagon he was driving and was crushed by the wheels.

"This is awful," added Hubbs, looking again at what had been the great Pecos River. "Imagine how it was when they had the world's first rodeo here in 1883. There was a tough breed of men then.

Top *and* above: *Most rodeo events have evolved from the actual workaday world of the cowboy: steer roping was hard work and serious business, and chuck wagon meals were far from glamorous.*

They'd stay on the range for a month, come into town, and raise all the hell you could stand. These cowboys here now, these rodeo cowboys, hell, they can't even build a campfire."

Been a rodeo bum, a sonuvagun,
And a hobo with stars in his crown.
Hey, ride me down easy, Lord, ride me on down;
Leave word in the dust where I lay,
Say, I'm easy come, easy go,
And easy to love when I stay.
—"Ride Me Down Easy," by Billy Joe Shaver

Claude Groves ought to have been born back in the days of the Old West. I tell you Claude's a professional heathen. —Randy Oliver, rodeo clown and bronc rider

Claude Groves is one of those guys who might be on the work list. He just kinda goes from day to day, not making a damn cent. But he's not all that bad a bronc rider. —Tommy Steiner, stock contractor

Claude don't give a damn. He wants to do whatever it is he wants to do on his own terms. And he will. —Paul Mitchell, bronc rider

Yeah, but if it wadn't for the Claude Groveses of the world, there wouldn't be any Larry Mahans. —Randy Oliver

There is an almost frightening suddenness when rains come to West Texas. Perhaps it has to do with the vastness of unobstructed sky, the open spaces, which make you feel so small. But a sudden stillness comes, the sky gets dark, and rain, which a short time earlier seemed to have no chance of falling, will come down in sheets. Pecos, sitting at the edge of far West Texas, is dry, barren, and gets only about twelve inches of rain a year. So about an inch and a half fell during the annual West of the Pecos Rodeo over the Fourth of July weekend, an event that celebrates the beginning of rodeo as a spectator sport. On all but one day of the four-day event, the sun would shine in the morning, but by mid-afternoon the rains would come, turning the rodeo grounds into a mud hole. And yet, as if on key, the rains would usually stop just before the evening performances.

Claude Groves didn't care one way or another. "One time," he was saying, "I rode when hail was coming down big as golf balls. Damned near knocked me out. When I fell off my horse I told them judges the hail had knocked me off and I ought to get a reride."

Claude and two other cowboys were standing around a late model car, maybe two years old, which belonged to his girl friend. An open beer

cooler was in the trunk. It was about an hour before the rodeo was to start but they were already at the grounds. Claude had found out he was up on a horse named Miller's Special and that it might run on him if he wasn't careful.

"Claude," said one of the cowboys. "You live in San Antonio now, I hear. You speak Spanish?"

"Yeah . . . *Sí*," said Claude, grinning, swigging a beer. His face was flushed and he was having a good time.

"You know," said Jerry Lawrence, a bronc rider, "they keep saying cowboys are low-life sons of bitches, heathens, rank types. Well, you hear about that singer, Alice Cooper? She—I mean he—comes on stage, see, and bites the head right off a chicken. You imagine that? And *we're* heathens!"

"Claude's probably bit the head off a chicken before," said Paul Mitchell, whom they call Smallpaul. "Hey, I got it, Claude. You hang onto that bronc and hold a live chicken in your other hand. Then, just before the buzzer sounds, bite the sonuvabitch's head off. They'd give you at least an eighty-five for that."

"I got to quit drinking so much beer," said Claude, patting his stomach, which was at odds

Above left: *Two cowboys, getting on down the road, sharing the weight of a rigging bag.* Above right: *Rodeo, like most sports, has its share of female fans.* Left: *Tools of the trade.*

Top: *An early bronc rider out on the range.* Above and right: *At the early Pendleton Round-Up—Studnick on saddle bronc in 1923, and Mable Strickland, having tied her steer, in 1925.*

with his belt. Claude is about five feet, seven inches, weighing some 185 pounds, though he says it wasn't long ago when he weighed over 200. Long hair, straw-colored, hangs out from under his hat, a weather-beaten black with an Indian band around it. A handlebar mustache crosses his mouth, turning up slightly at the corners. This, with bushy blond eyebrows, gives him a mean yet slightly whimsical appearance.

"Used to work three events, bulls, broncs, barebacks," said Claude. "But I got so fat I decided to stay with one. Last year, when I was weighin' about two hundred, I got thowed, and after I hit the ground I couldn't get my breath right for ten, fifteen minutes. I lost weight after that [he draws in his stomach], becoming this slim, trim, handsome figure standing before you." They all laugh. They like Claude. They like his beer.

We watched the girl walking through the mud. She stepped hard, firm, determined. She wore a high-crowned Western hat, plaid shirt, jeans, and roughout boots. I do not know what else she wore. She looked neither right nor left as she passed, but she turned in our direction once and spat tobacco. We noticed she had a can of Skoal in her back pocket.

"How'd you like to kiss her?" I asked Claude.

"Be worse than biting a chicken's head off," said a cowboy.

"Bet she had hair on her legs," said Claude.

Girls and women from town and the area walked past the line of cowboys, now gathered outside the grounds and busy taking gear out of cars or drinking beer with Claude. They were like floats in a parade. A girl that I'd seen with Claude that afternoon at poolside of a Holiday Inn rode toward us on a horse. The girl, whom we'll call Nancy, was holding a drink and weaving from side to side as the horse moved closer. "Claude, you'd best get her off that horse 'fore she falls off," said Smallpaul.

Claude swigged a beer and stared at Nancy. "Leave her," he said. "She signed on to be tough."

"Yippeeee," said Nancy, waving as she moved past. People got out of her way.

Claude, Nancy, and other rodeo performers had gathered at poolside that afternoon while the sun was out. Claude didn't have a bathing suit so he took a knife and cut the legs off a pair of jeans. Instant bathing suit. They'd drunk beer, joked, laughed, and the world had become a soft, easy carpet. When they saw Randy Oliver, a fringe bronc rider and rodeo clown, they threw him into the pool. Randy flailed his arms wildly, kicked out his legs, and made everybody laugh as he hit the water.

Randy Oliver doesn't drink. Though only twenty-two, he has traveled the back road of rodeo as a bronc rider, but he wants to be a clown. He dried off and went to his room but came back out later, sat near the pool, and drank coffee.

"I like this clowning," he said. "It makes me somebody. When I grew up in Weatherford, I was always real little and everybody joked about me. I was nobody. Just pushed off. I want to make a name for myself in this business and go back there. Maybe I'll sign autographs for those people who thought I was nothing." He looked at the pool, blankly, and added, "Then maybe again I won't sign my name for them."

Oliver had traveled the circuit with Claude, five to a car, three to a bed, two on the floor. "Claude's had lots of girls—one in every town, as they say. He must have set a record staying with this one, but I hope she don't plan on settlin' in. She'll look up one of these days and Claude will be gone on down the road."

The afternoon drinking pace had gotten to Nancy, and by the time they reached the rodeo grounds that night, she had been transformed from a school teacher to an experienced horsewoman—if she could only find a horse. Claude found her a sober horse, and we watched her pass around the arena at ten- to fifteen-minute intervals, either leading or following a parade.

Opposite top: *Buckle from West of the Pecos Rodeo.*
Opposite bottom: *Cowboys at Cheyenne catching up on the results from Calgary in* Rodeo Sports News.
Below *and* below right: *Waiting in the back and watching from the top at Cheyenne.*

"Lookee here," said a cowboy, watching a girl approach. She had originally started for the bleachers but spotted the group around Claude's car, turned around, and came over. "Hi," she said. "You just get here?"

"Reckon," said Claude, trying to look suspicious, but grinning under his mustache. "I'd offer you a beer 'cept you probably under age."

"Under age! I'm eighteen years old. And well, I'm soo drunk. My roommate is soo mad at me. I was supposed to be back and pick her up at our apartment but got to drinking." She eyed the cowboys, all looking at her. She was tall, dark, dressed in jeans with a red shirt, outside, its tail tied in a knot in the front. She had little in the way of a chin but was somewhat attractive, despite pimples of adolescence. And she did not have a can of Skoal in her back pocket.

Claude took off a knit shirt and got a starched denim out of the trunk. He put it on and tucked it into his pants, trying to keep his belt buckle from being covered by his stomach. He put on a black vest, tied a blue bandanna around his neck, and yanked his rigging bag out of the car. The girl watched him. "I am soo drunk," she said. "Who you, anyway, Gene Autry?"

"I'm a Hacksaw Indian," said Claude. "I'll cut anything."

"Well, you shore don't look like no Indian to me," said the girl, becoming serious. "And if that's your girl friend, you'd best get her off that horse 'fore she falls off."

"She's soo drunk," said Claude, laughing out loud.

Claude had won the first go-round with a 69. He was feeling good after that and now hoped to place high again and maybe win the average. He had a chance to win over $400. He wanted at the least to make expenses. The beer was included in expenses. "I like this ol' town pretty good," he said. "They treat you alright. Lot of these little towns we go to, the daddies they lock up their daughters, keeping them away from the cowboys.

"Got thowed in jail here just onc't. We had a

little brawl, and they slung me in the jail with a bunch of niggers. I got in there, and those niggers told me to wash their dishes. I told them to screw theirselves. Well, they jumped me in that cell and beat the shit out of me. Yeah. I washed their dishes."

Claude Groves is out of his time, his period. Many cowboys at the far edge of rodeo are. Sure, they like to compete, but most do not make expenses. More than anything, they seem to be trying to recapture a life of the previous century, a kind of tough romanticism when there were cattle drives, saloon brawls, gunfights, and a freedom of space, an open range. For some the quest is almost quixotic, funny and sad. But perhaps the feeling of wanderlust is the same now as it was then. And, as then, many must stay on the move because places tend to close in on you, make you steady, nine to five.

But Willy he tells me that doers and thinkers say movin's the closest thing to bein' free.
 —"Willy, the Wandering Gypsy, and Me," by Billy Joe Shaver

Claude tries. The Professional Rodeo Cowboys Association likes—in fact insists—that its membership adhere to a dress code of jeans, boots, Western shirt, hat. Nothing more. Nothing less. So Claude Groves showed up to judge a PRCA rodeo in Mercedes, wearing a Mexican sombrero, with gun belts crisscrossed over both shoulders, Pancho Villa style. Another time, during a rodeo in Big Spring, Claude and a friend won a diamond ring shooting pool. They hocked the ring, bought a gun, and drove through town shooting into the air and yelling.

"Yeah," Claude said, "I do wished I lived in the old days. You could have a little fun then and life was exciting. You live on a horse, which I love. You go into a saloon, drink, have a good clean fight. Nowadays, you got to watch it. Some sonuvabitch'll pull a knife or a gun on you. You can't trust nobody these days, especially hippies."

Rookie bronc rider trying it on for size.

"How 'bout that time you spurred that ol' boy," said one of the cowboys.

"That was different," said Claude. "It wadn't no knife. I just took off my spurs and swatted some across the face. But they was beatin' up on this friend of mine. Shee-it, I had to do something, didn't I?"

Claude Groves was raised in New Deal, Texas, a small town just outside Lubbock that has few stores, churches, service stations, schools. His grandfather was a horse trader. His father helped with stock and now runs a wrecking yard. Claude

and his older brother, Sammie, grew up around horses and learned to ride, as they say, about the same time they learned to walk. Sammie got into rodeo and Claude wanted to follow. Eventually. For a while Claude was a jockey at Sunland Park, near El Paso. Then he got too fat. He's also driven heavy equipment, trucks, and worked in construction.

Claude has been in rodeo for about twelve years, off and on, though he's only twenty-five. He's ridden broncs, barebacks, bulls, and tried being a clown. Pay was steadier but he didn't particularly like that image of himself. It is the romantic image he's seeking, though I doubt he knows it. But the image is important. Mostly, he's had a good time, though times have not always been good to him. A bull once stuck its horn into his mouth, knocking out his teeth. He has torn up a knee falling off a bronc, he has separated a shoulder, and he has been stepped on by a bull, which shattered his ribs and punctured a lung.

He has scars around both eyes and his mouth. They did not come from rodeoing. Claude has a reputation around Lubbock, around the circuit.

A few years ago he was drinking at the Saddle

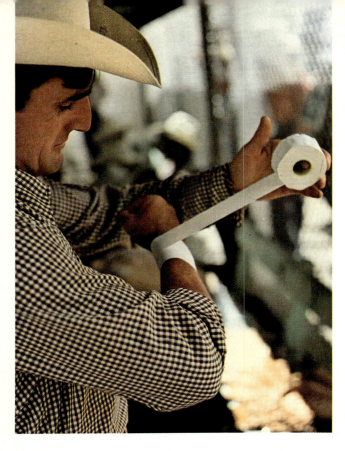

Bronc Bar in Lubbock. He had only a few bucks, but he felt at ease with the loud jukebox, hard neon, beer-smoke smells. He glanced up and saw a man who owed him eighty dollars at a nearby table. Claude picked up his beer and walked to the man's table. He needed the money to get on down the road.

"Hey, you got that money you owe me?" asked Claude. "It's about time you paid."

"Maybe not," said the man. "Anyway, just fuck off."

Claude, grinning, said, "Then maybe we better go outside and talk."

The thing you do not do when you're walking out of a bar with trouble is go out the door first. They walked out together and Claude had that feeling, which is a little bit of fear, excitement, and danger, but a high of a kind. He started to ask for the money one more time when the guy swung, catching him just below the ear as he turned his head, causing a dull, ringing sound in his head, which he ignored. Then the madness took over. It's a madness when you fear nothing, nobody. Claude charged into the guy, tackled him around the waist, and they fell to the ground, each wrestling to get on top. They were on their knees, then on their feet, and Claude had a headlock with his left arm and was trying to get enough leverage to slug the guy with his right.

He didn't know about the knife, never saw it. Somehow the guy had gone into his pocket, flicked open the switchblade, and slipped it into Claude's side, causing a sharp, burning pain that made him cry out and let go. Holding his side, he backed away. The guy, this time with the advantage, moved after him, swinging the knife in a low arc, twice slashing Claude on the neck. "Okay, okay, I quit," said Claude. "Keep the goddamn money." But the feeling was stronger, the madness. As the guy lowered the knife, Claude lunged at him, swinging wildly, and hitting something solid. The face. The man dropped the knife, staggered, and then fell. Claude, bending down over him, smashed at his face with his fists. Then he stood up. The man, his nose and mouth covered with blood, was still.

Claude went back into the bar, into the rest room, and put wet paper towels on his side and neck. He splashed cold water on his face. People told him to go on to the hospital and get sewn up. As he left the bar and started for his car, the man came out from behind a car, holding a gun. Claude swung for the gun as it fired, taking off part of one of his fingers. But, suddenly, the man began to run. "I'll get you, you sonuvabitch!" yelled Claude. "I'll get you sooner or later—and my goddamn money!"

Claude, nostalgic, was saying, "Yeah, we had some good times in Lubbock.

"I was back there at the Saddle Bronc a few months later, drinking with these two guys I'd met from Dallas. I saw that ol' boy I had the big fight with come in again and started figurin' out what I was going to do with him. One of those Dallas dudes said not to worry, they'd take care of him. He asked me how much I'd pay.

"I said, 'Well, get him fifty bucks' worth.'"

Above: *Ben Calhoun taping his wrist before a bareback ride.*
Opposite: *Chris Le Doux helping a friend tape up a shoulder.*

When the guy left the bar with his wife, Claude and his new friends, fifty dollars richer, followed. There was a car chase through Lubbock, and they finally cornered the guy on the outskirts of town. Suddenly, he began to fire, knocking out the windshield in their car.

"Yeah, I remember those ol' boys was sure mad," said Claude. "One of them reached under the seat and got out a pump gun. He started firing, blowing out the windows of that boy's car, shooting holes in the gas tank, and just destroying the car. The ol' boy jumped out and started running across a field, leaving his wife there. We didn't even say nothing to her. We just drove off, laughing. I mean, what would you say to her anyway?

"Anyway, that ol' boy phoned my daddy and told him his son Claude was tryin' to kill him. I just told my daddy I couldn't believe he'd say a thing like that."

Claude's girl, Nancy, came back around on her horse. She looked sick, and she tilted slightly and slid off the horse into the mud. "Yiiii," she said. "Wheeeee." Claude, spitting tobacco, said, "Well, boys, there she goes. Les' put her in the car." She was completely limp and was left, out cold, in the front seat of the car as Claude got his rigging bag and walked toward the chutes.

Jim Moore, a bronc rider who has a spread near Balmorhea, south of Pecos, had already been up, so he was there that night as an observer. "Ol' Claude," he said. "Everybody calls him Claude Balls. I think he's a little crazy and got a lot of guts, too. His ol' gal sure is drunk. I don't drink. Anything I hate it's drunk women. They get drunk on me and I just get up and walk out."

Moore got some notoriety once when a certain weed called marijuana was discovered growing near his spread. It caused some stir around the

Above left: *A rookie in the saddle.* Above: *Ivan Daines just about at the end of his rope.* Opposite: *Claude Groves riding Socks, at Oklahoma City in 1971.*

area, which is generally quiet except during the annual rodeo. "Well," said Moore, "they say publicity's good, even the bad kind."

"Hey, Jim," yelled a girl who had driven up. He went over to talk to her. They drove off. He did not see the rodeo that night. But he had already been up.

Claude was sitting on his saddle, on the ground, stretching out the stirrups. He'd rear back, kick out one leg and then the other, loosening up, loosening up his equipment. He was getting a little excited now, anticipating. "I guess I think sometimes about getting hurt," he said. "But it's odd. I love to do this, too. I worry about getting thowed, hung up, and not winning. But you win or get a rank one and do it and it's like a high. I do pretty good sometimes. People say, how can you ride a bronc, being fat as you are? I just grin and say, 'Want to.' That's how—want to."

Claude found his horse, climbed up on the gate, and slung the saddle, old and worn, over the horse, Miller's Special. The horse moved slightly, nervously. "Better watch her," said a cowboy. "She'll run on you, Claude." Cowboys standing on the chute helped him strap on the saddle. "What'd you give her?" asked Claude. A cowboy held up a thumb and forefinger, showing the distance he should measure the rein, a braided hemp that had been fastened to the halter. If the rein is too short and the horse dips its head, it can throw you over the top. If too much rein is given, you can lose leverage.

Miller's Special was nervous in the chute, moving uneasily as Claude got on. "Easy, easy," he said, patting the horse on the neck. The horse kicked the back of the chute. "Easy," said Claude. It had started raining again. Smallpaul, in the next chute, said, "Dammit!" Claude, adrenaline almost choking him, said, "Well, goddammit, we signed on to be tough and we damn sure gonna be!"

"Must be about time," said Smallpaul. "I gotta pee."

"I gotta puke," said Claude, and they both laughed nervously.

Claude jerked out hair from the horse's mane, tying it on his rope as a marker for his grip. The horse shook its head and kicked the back of the chute again.

I was standing on the chute over Claude and he said, "Hold him for me. Grab his head just like you was gonna manhandle him." I did. "I respect this animal more than anything when I'm in this chute," said Claude. "In here, I'm his. When that gate opens, he's mine. I try to imagine my ride, how it'll be for the first couple of jumps. 'Course," he grinned, "it don't always work out that way."

Claude was concentrating now. There was nothing but him and the horse. We were soaked. Just before Buck Jackson announced that Claude would be the next rider, the horse jerked suddenly. I lost my balance and almost fell into the chute, on top of the horse. "Gawd," said Claude. "Get off my horse!" I regained my balance and later imagined what might have happened. The gate would have opened and Claude would have gone out riding like a wild man, with me hanging onto the horse's neck. The PRCA would have frowned on that.

". . . and ladies and gentlemen, this next cowboy is Claude Groves from New Deal, Texas. He's the brother of Sammie Groves, one of the leading bronc riders in the RCA. Now Claude's an excellent rider in his own right, and here he is on Miller's Special!"

Claude took a deep breath, nodded, and the gate was jerked open. As required to qualify, he got his spurs over the break of the horse's shoulder on the first jump out of the chute. Miller's Special leaped and kicked, once, twice, three times, and then ran for the center of the arena in a series of mini-jumps. Then it began jumping again, and Claude, sweeping his spurs in a rocking motion, timed his body almost perfectly with each move the horse made. The eight-second buzzer sounded and Claude jumped off before the pickup men got to him. One almost ran over him but Claude reacted without thinking and got out of the way. He

was listening for his score as he walked back toward the chutes. The judges gave him only a 61. This wasn't good enough. It would knock him out of the average.

"Goddammit," said Claude, walking over to a judge. They talked briefly. Claude shook his head and walked back through the gate.

Smallpaul's horse was much more active. He rode well, scoring a 69. "Shee-it," said Claude. "I done all I could. But there went the average. Sonuvabuck didn't have any gas out there."

Claude moved back through the mud to the car, got a beer from the cooler, and drank it quickly. "My ambition," he was saying, "is to make the National Finals. I been trying for twelve years. I'd just like the glory of it. I won about three thousand dollars so far and the cutoff ought to be about fifty-two hundred. I got my shot."

He was quiet for a while and then reflected, "I guess I thought about doing something else. But then I'll ride good and get up for it again. My trouble is I like to have a good time. And we *do* have a good time. I got to stop drinking so much beer, though." He drew in his stomach.

Nancy woke up, making noises in the front seat. "Never again," she muttered. "Never again." Claude laughed. "Well, guess I better take her back to the motel. I don't imagine we'll be going to the dance tonight, least ways her."

"Shee-it," he said, getting behind the wheel. Then he drove off.

The mud was ankle deep. When the rodeo ended that night and Buck Jackson had said, "Y'all come back tomorra," Claude Groves was back at the motel. A young girl, with not much of a chin and pimples but without a can of Skoal in her back pocket, was walking toward a pickup with a bull rider. "I am soo drunk," she said. "Soo drunk."

You could hear the music a block away from the Sheriff's Posse Barn, a large hollow building where dances were held each night of the rodeo.

Opposite top: *Saddling a bronc in the chute.* Opposite bottom: *Sitting one out at Cheyenne.* Above left: *Saddle bronc rider getting a lift.* Left: *After the ride.*

The town was there—dudes; storekeepers becoming cowboys for a night; the women, old and young; and cowboys. Always the cowboys. The Country and Western band was playing a slow one as dark shadows, some wearing hats, slid across a sawdust floor, tightly wound, wound tightly. The male vocalist, strumming his guitar, not playing it, sang to the moving shadows, "I'm crazy, crazeee for feelin' so lonely, I'm crazy..."

Many would feel crazeee. Many would be helped to make it through the night. Why not? It was a special night, a special week. "... Crazy for feelin' sooo blue."

Buck Jackson was there, smiling, shaking hands. "Hey, Buck," somebody would say. "Hi. How y'all doin'," Buck would answer, extending his hand here and there, robotlike. Buck, an ex-cowboy, ex-sheriff, and rancher, has announced practically every Pecos rodeo since 1928–29. During the early years he carried a megaphone and announced from horseback. When the band exploded into a wild, loud "Mexican Joe," Buck took his partner to the floor. Local dancers gave him room and he stomped his feet and swung his partner. The bull rider and the girl with pimples, dancing nearby, didn't notice.

A group of young girls from Angelo College were dancing with cowboys. Known as the Six White Horses, they'd entertained during the rodeo, doing precision drills on white horses. They rode in a circle, then moved into patterns, much as a high school band at halftime. Except they had no trombones or drums.

"It might look easy to you, but it's real hard," said one, a short, pretty, well-scrubbed brunet. "We work all the time, just like a football team. We are athletes. And we travel to rodeos around here. My, you certainly drink a lot of beer. I used to drink beer until I got on this drill team. But it hurts your body, alcohol does. I also found it affected my riding. So I just stopped. I don't need that stuff."

"It kills brain cells, too," I said.

"I believe it does," she continued. "I read something about that in *Reader's Digest*."

"Then it must be true."

"My, my, you *do* drink a lot of beer. I think you'll find it affects you, too, if you don't stop." She looked at the shadows on the dance floor. "You *could* ask me to dance."

"Music's too fast. The beer has affected my feet, too."

The vocalist, the leader of the band, told the audience it was getting near closin' time, "But y'all come back, hear? . . . I knew that you'd love me as long as you wanted/And then someday you'd leave me for somebody newwwww..."

Half the population of Pecos is Latin. Their ancestors migrated across the Mexican border, some 135 miles away, to work on the ranches and later to work on farms or pick cotton. Because Mexico is so close, they have remained bilingual, and among themselves they prefer their native tongue. About two miles from the Sheriff's Posse Barn is Rosa's Place, which is patronized mostly by the Mexicans, with only a smattering of gringos.

At Rosa's, the Mexican man, about twenty-five, was saying he couldn't find a proper job in Pecos. "I served my country," he said. "I was in Vietnam, wounded, and I come back here to nothing. What have I to do, dig their ditches?"

His friend, about the same age but much fatter, said, "When I played Little League Baseball, they put me in right field. Why do you think this? Because I am Mexican. That's why. They put the gringos in the better positions. Made them the pitchers though I was the better pitcher. Why do you think this? Because I am Mexican. That's why. You have always treated us badly."

"They. Not me."

"You, all of you, whether here or in Dallas or where."

"Right. All gringos look alike."

"Well, you cowboys come in and take over

now. It is hard to go anywhere because you fight, try and take the girls."

"I'm not a cowboy. I'm a writer."

"Jes'," he said, leaning over the table, "a bull rider. You look like the bull rider, the hat, boots, the look of a bull rider."

"No. A writer. Well, maybe a bull writer."

"See . . . *sí*," he said, looking at his friend. "It is as I told you. He's a bull rider."

Barney Hubbs did not go to the rodeo or dance or go to Rosa's Place. He stayed at home, watching television. Early the next morning he was in his printing office. He rocked back in a swivel chair behind a large mahogany desk and said times were wild back then, in the old days when the Pecos River was difficult to cross. "The cowboys would be out on the range for thirty days," he repeated. "It was rough then. They wouldn't let the Meskins into some of the bars, but they had their own places, of course, near the edge of town."

He paused. "In 1921 the world's first rodeo was thirty-eight years old," he continued. "I was running the newspaper here then and kept hearing old-timers talk about it. I'd hear this story or that story about the rodeo, so I started interviewing witnesses and participants, such as Trav Windham and Henry Slack. I got affidavits from everybody concerned and had them notarized. We ran a story in my newspaper and the people from the *Encyclopedia Britannica* wrote me and asked for the information and affidavits."

Other towns claim the first rodeo: Deer Trail, Colorado; Prescott, Arizona; and North Platte, Nebraska. But through Hubbs's efforts and the proof he found, the *Britannica* credits Pecos with staging the first rodeo. In part, the encyclopedia reads, "The first public cowboy contest wherein prizes were awarded to the winners of bronc riding and steer roping was held on an open flat adjoining the courthouse in Pecos, Texas, on July 4, 1883, but no admission was charged spectators."

Saddle bronc rider in good form—toes east and west.

In 1883, bands of Apaches, stripped of the last vestiges of human dignity, were still roaming the plains. William Bonney, alias Billy the Kid, had been in the grave for two years, stopped by a bullet from the gun of Sheriff Pat Garrett. The railroad, the Iron Horse, was drawing the country closer, tying together east and west.

The ranches were generally self-sufficient, raising what they needed, though ranch hands would have to make occasional trips to town for sugar, flour, and coffee. Ranchers also used Pecos as the railroad shipping center for their cattle. Railroads and the cattle boom drew the usual riffraff: the painted ladies of the night, the gamblers, the drifters. One drifter considered especially dangerous was Jim Milders, who was run out of Pecos by the Citizen's Committee and later hanged in Fort Worth.

Movies, television, and pulp classics have distorted the cowboy. In reality he was, like the vast

majority of rodeo performers of today, a man who lived with his pockets empty. In the end he would inevitably be as he was in the beginning—broke. His bed was the ground or occasionally the corner of a plank bunkhouse and his food was beans, sourdough biscuits, gravy, dried food, and steak served from a chuck wagon. He'd spend his days on a horse, working for twenty or thirty dollars a month, and the only things he was likely to own were his saddle, the clothes on his back, and an extra shirt tucked away in his saddle roll.

In the early days of the cattle industry there were no fences to divide the range, and cattle from various spreads intermingled, crossing the boundaries marked only on maps or in the mind. So ranchers of the area would often pool their cowboys for a giant roundup to separate cattle. During some of these roundups, arguments would often develop as to which ranch actually had the best cowboys or the fastest horses, and there would be impromptu competitions on a lonely range without audience other than their own.

Joseph F. Glidden, inspired by the thorned shrub, invented barbed wire in 1873. Ranches were fenced off and the worst job a cowboy could have was mending fence. That meant he'd have to get off his horse, a loss of dignity. A cowboy had the benefit of endless space, the open sky and range. He was, then, a part of his own theater. Some of the more popular men were not just the best ropers and riders but the top storytellers. They'd entertain around isolated campfires, spinning yarns, real and imagined. Yet there had to be more. After a month or two on the range, cowboys would get their wages and ride fifty or sixty miles to towns such as Pecos, where they'd cut loose, womanizing, fighting, and drinking liquor such as Hill & Hill, $1.50 a quart.

One summer afternoon in the Bar 7 Saloon a group of cowboys from ranches such as the NA, Lazy Y and W were drinking and talking trade. Perhaps, after a time in town, they were missing the range, which was simple, without the complica-

tions of city life. As usual, arguments ensued about this or that cowboy, about who was the best rider, the best roper. Each hero became more proficient, taller, as the arguments continued and wagers were offered. Finally, someone suggested they settle the issues right there in Pecos. The town was getting ready for the annual Fourth of July celebration and they could hold competition right there before anybody who was interested in watching.

Townspeople liked the idea. Merchants offered cash prizes to winning cowboys. Women began baking for the big celebration and deciding on a particular gingham dress, high collar and starched, of course. Word spread along the Pecos Valley and ranchers picked their leading cowboys to compete,

Opposite and above: At a small rodeo in Snow Mass, Colorado—though not part of the PRCA circuit, its bulls are mean and the broncs buck hard.

cowboys such as Trav Windham, Fate Beard, Jeff Chism, Morgan and Jim Livingston, Bill Coalson, Charlie Goedeke, and Henry Slack, who was to recall before his death, "It was not a wild and woolly affair but conducted in an orderly and quiet manner."

Contests were held on an alkali flat adjoining the courthouse. A line of wagons and a plank fence enclosed the area and estimates were that 500 to 1,000 people attended. They were townspeople, storekeepers, railroad workers, ranchers, and cowboys, carrying money in their hands for wagers they were ready to pay but planned to collect.

Windham, a tall, lean man who was later to become foreman of the T Ranch, didn't particularly care for the crowd watching his every move but soon forgot them when his steer was loosed. He spurred his horse, getting an excellent start, and

soon closed in on the darting, scared animal. His lasso found the mark, jerking the steer to a standstill and then into the air and over backwards. In seconds Windham was off his horse and on top of the stunned steer, taking a strand of rope from his teeth and wrapping it around the animal's legs. His time: 22 seconds. Slack, one of the favorites, followed. But just after his rope found its mark around the steer, it broke, causing his horse to rear back suddenly and throw him to the ground.

A few years ago Mrs. Evelyn Mahoney, a Pecos realtor who was Slack's daughter, recalled, "People were always talking about Trav Windham winning. One time I said, 'Pappy, they're all dead now anyway, so why don't you tell everybody you won it?'

"Well, he grinned and said, 'Oh, sister, I couldn't do that. You see by the time I woke up after being throwed Trav was already getting drunk on the prize money at the Bar 7 Saloon.'"

In the other event officially recorded, Morgan Livingston won a matched roping contest against Windham. Old-timers also remember riding events, but roping was most important, the most coveted talent on the range.

When competition ended that day the spectators and cowboys all joined in the celebration of the independence of our country. Little did they know that on that summer day of 1883 they had also laid the foundation for what was to become one of the nation's most popular spectator sports: rodeo, a sport that still brings us closest to the romantic days of the past, of the cowboy.

The rain had gone Sunday morning, and the Pecos area, attempting a return to normalcy, was clear, dry, hot. Rodeo performers were gone or leaving, and the town seemed in a semihangover state after four days of the forty-sixth annual event. Gasoline prices were back down to normal but visitors found on leaving town that beer was not sold on Sundays, not even for medicinal purposes.

Claude Groves was up early and left with Nancy. He planned to drive to Lubbock, see his folks, and then head back to San Antonio. He had won $160.06 for his first go-round victory. Bill Beaty, with a pair of 68s that netted him $180.06 day money, took the average and an extra $160.06 for $340.12 earnings. Claude had spent about $200, counting an entry fee of $25. But it was over. Done. The road led somewhere else.

"I don't think about money that much, but I should because I need some to get me to the winter rodeos," Claude said. "I thought about trying to save, but not that hard."

Two months later Claude Groves was driving a truck. He was ineligible for the PRCA competition because he couldn't pay a $40 turnout fee. His total earnings had been just over $4,000. He had a falling-out with Nancy, who yelled that she never wanted to see him again. Claude left for a few days, then returned, and they made up. "Yeah," he said, "I talked her into letting me back into the house. We made love that same day and then I told her I'd changed my mind and decided to go for good. *Adiōs!*" She yelled, screamed, and then cried. But Claude didn't hear her. He was gone.

About the time the National Finals were held, Claude Groves was down in a small Mexican town riding wild stock. A promoter there had given Claude and a couple of his friends $80 each, plus expenses, to perform in a bullfighting arena. They also got all the extras they could handle. Claude drank, spent his money, and headed home. Wherever that was. Wherever that was.

The highway seems hotter than nine kinds of hell,
The rides they're as scarce as the rain,
When you're down to your last chuck with nothing
    to sell
And too far away from the train.
Hey, ride me down easy, Lord, ride me on down,
Leave word in the dust where I lay.
Say, I'm easy come, easy go,
And easy to love when I stay.
    —"Ride Me Down Easy," by Billy Joe Shaver

Steer roping—sometimes a sport, sometimes a business, sometimes just for the hell of it; here, at an early rodeo.

Chapter 2:

NINE DAYS OF CHEYENNE

Wyoming, despite vast mineral resources, remains an area that has not been choked by the times, by progress. It is a progressive state, but the time-honored vocation of ranching remains one of the top industries. Eighty percent of the state's land is still used for grazing, and over 1,700,000 cattle roam the area. So Wyoming continues to pay homage to the cowboy, such as he is, such as he was. The figure of a cowboy adorns state license plates, and the state university's athletic teams are called Cowboys. And rodeo, with its last vestiges of the romantic cowboy of the Old West, has an impact in the state unequalled by any other sport and, perhaps, any other event.

Cheyenne, the low, sprawling state capital, epitomizes this feeling and pride, not only for Wyoming but for people of the nation who follow the sport. There are other large, well-run rodeos with big payoffs, including those held in Calgary, Houston, Fort Worth, Denver, Phoenix, San Francisco, and Pendleton. But few have the tradition, the history, of Cheyenne Frontier Days, a celebration that began on a September day in 1897 and has continued every year since, making it the sport's longest continually held event. So big-time rodeo, as we know it today, began in Cheyenne. Over the years it has attracted many dignitaries not connected with the sport, such as President Teddy Roosevelt, who attended in 1903. Outside the Yellowstone National Park, Frontier Days is the state's biggest tourist attraction, annually drawing more than 200,000 visitors and pumping some $3 million into the city's economy.

There is nothing quite like the nine days of July for Frontier Days. It is a fine madness of carnival, of letting go, a kind of cult celebration of the past and rodeo, a rodeo that normally draws more than 850 contestants and has the circuit's highest payoff—$128,282 in 1975.

Frontier Days does not simply come to Cheyenne but literally dominates the city, causes it to shake, to vibrate. This could not happen as totally in a place such as Houston, for example, which is just too big, with too many varied interests and groups to be dominated by a single event. But Cheyenne can be, and every one of its some 40,000 citizens is touched in one way or another by Frontier Days and its rodeo—rightly called "the Daddy of 'Em All."

It is Cheyenne, the Frontier Days Celebration last year, this year, next year. Some 8,000 tourists and residents line Capitol and Carey streets in mid-morning, as the downtown parade begins from the domed, sandstone capitol building, tallest in the city. Banks close. Business stops temporarily. Parades are Americana, as marches are Germanic. They are a part of our past, of a fanciful childhood interest, as are the circus, the magic show, cane fishing poles, and men who can juggle or walk on stilts.

But I find myself almost transfixed, straining to look around a man holding a small boy on his shoulders to see the movement of the parade. At first the parade is so far away that it is noiseless movement, like a silent movie. But as it approaches there are the clatter of horses, the rigid stomp of marchers, the sound of horns, and the big brass drum carried by a teenager half its size. He is wearing a huge tasseled hat, which seems to cover his eyes. He puffs air from reddish cheeks in rhythm with the drum beat. The parade is a kind of pilgrimage to history, with more than 100 floats symbolic of the past, bands, various queens on horseback, a posse, Indians, and what they call the "world's largest collection of horse-drawn vehicles." Dusted off and polished are an original Yellowstone Stage, surreys, Buckhorn buggies, an old fire engine. The sign on the carriage reads "God Loves a Good Rodeo."

Opposite: Early Frontier Days at Cheyenne. Top: Billy Jones (mounted) won the bronc riding at the first Frontier Days, in 1897; Elton Perry's horse, Warrior, won him $100 as the best bucking horse— Elton won the bronc riding in 1902. Center: Burl Mulkey stayed on Buck Shot. Bottom: Chuck Lasswell flew off Magic, in 1947.

Clowns run through the crowd, releasing balloons of red, yellow, blue, purple, and sometimes sneak up behind and scare people who are hypnotized by the parade. Small kids pull wagons through the crowd, selling ice cream bars from Styrofoam boxes. Venders, pushing carts, hawk film for self-focusing cameras, urging spectators to purchase their product and "Capture a little piece of history! It might be your last chance!" Some have captured a little piece of history the night before, and there is some irony on a sign in the final float, reading, "Dr. Sam's Cure All."

More than 7,000 people had risen earlier in the day to attend what was billed as a "free and authentic chuck wagon breakfast." Outdoor stoves were fired up at 4:00 A.M. and a breakfast of pancakes, ham, milk, and coffee was cooked by one civic club and served by another to people sitting on bales of hay. Cheyenne's sanitation department has a lot of extra cleaning up to do during Frontier Days.

When breakfast is over and the two-hour parade ends, people migrate to Frontier Park, an area of some twenty acres on the north side near the airport. Hotels and motels along the way have "No Vacancy" signs and all of the rent cars are rented. The taxi driver, zooming along an artery leading to the park, pays little attention to stop signs and makes pedestrians dodge and run from his path. He reminds me of mad taxi rides I have taken in Mexico City, but the driver says, "It doesn't matter now. This is Frontier Week. Cops don't pay much attention this week."

Tepees stand in the Oglala-Sioux Indian camp, in a village near the entrance to the park. If a crowd forms, the Indians dance and play drums, once a haunting sound, but diminished by the daylight of today. Sometimes they huddle in groups talking. Sometimes they sleep. They've been coming from the Pine Ridge Agency in South Dakota to Frontier Days since the turn of the century.

Frontier Park has small lakes, tree-lined paths, and the rodeo arena, which seats about 19,000. In the maze of campers, cars, and horse trailers the less eager seek momentary tranquility under trees near one of the lakes. But they are not distant enough to muffle sounds from the midway, adjoining the rodeo arena. Fast, bouncy music off a scratched record comes from the Ferris wheel, which still makes girls scream. Barkers yell from inverted boxes at entrances to plank half-buildings, urging passersby to try their luck at throwing a softball, shooting a basketball, or pitching a ring, to win Teddy bears, authentic colored glass rings, and necklaces. I step on discarded, half-finished candy. Hot dogs, hamburgers, sno-cones, tacos. It is short-order heaven—or hell. "Hurree! Hurree!

Above left: *Cheyenne begins with a parade.* Above right: *The longest line of horse-drawn vehicles in the world.* Opposite: *The neon glow of the carnival.*

Hurreeeeee!" Midways look better at night, neon sprayed. But it is early afternoon.

There was trouble between hispanos and blacks around one of the beer tents. They traded insults, racial and otherwise. They shoved each other. Finally, carnival workers joined the hispano forces to run off some of the blacks, whom they believed started the trouble. Or wanted to believe. Later, the blacks returned, firing pistols into the air and yelling. They disappeared again when the police arrived. Observers felt Cheyenne might be taking its Frontier celebration too seriously.

The actual rodeo is in the afternoon, with other special events and entertainment held at night. The rodeo begins with a procession of queens, holding flags: Miss Wyoming, Miss Rodeo, Miss Cheyenne, and lastly, Miss Navajo Rodeo. The governor follows, then rodeo directors, other dignitaries, and a precision riding group of young lovelies called "Dandies." Walt Garrison cautioned me a long time ago, "When you're in the arena, the most danger you face *isn't* being hit by a stray bull or horse but being run over by a riding club." Indians end the procession. Lastly "The Star-Spangled

Banner" is sung. The grounds are decorated in red, white, and blue. It is the big rodeo, the glamor rodeo, the star-spangled rodeo.

Ridin' out on a horse in a star-spangled rodeooo . . . Gettin' cards and letters from people I don't even know . . . And offers comin' over the phone.
—"Rhinestone Cowboy," by Larry Weiss

I tell you those rodeo champions would trade every saddle they've won to get a silver buckle at Frontier Days. —R. G. Kekich, steer wrestler

Usually, you find Larry Mahan by the people. They surround him, sometimes engulf him. They are cowboys who know or want to know him, crowding as near as they can as if to discover some of the magic or hear a clue as to what his success is all about. They are hangers-on, shiny people from show business and women and girls from the stage, screen, centerfold, backyards, local cantinas, and whatever who continually offer him a glass slipper. They are those who have escaped the philosophical martini of suburbia to befriend him and find out where it's at, Mahan mostly being It. But Mahan's followers are not like those of a champion boxer, waiting for a crumb, a cull, a bourbon and branchwater. Mahan talks to these people, grooves with them, with everybody. As he has often said, "I get off being around people." And as much if not more so than any athlete I've met, including Muhammad Ali, Mahan has charisma and exudes a solid, not hollow, confidence.

So on Thursday, the sixth day of Cheyenne, Mahan looked almost undressed, unadorned, when he was momentarily alone as he got his gear out of the back of a borrowed car and began the walk through the grounds to the chutes. Tracy Ringolsby, who works for United Press International in Kansas City but is from Cheyenne and takes his vacation each year to return home and help with the media during Frontier Days, said, "There goes

Above right: *A movable hoedown, supplied by a sponsor.*
Right: *If you get up early enough, you can eat a "free and authentic chuck wagon breakfast."*

Mahan. Mr. Rodeo. I met him here last year, but he wouldn't remember me."

Mahan, walking past, looked over and said, "Tracy! How's it goin'?"

When you first meet Mahan he seems almost too outward, with too much personality and too handsome, really, to be what he is, what he had been as the rodeo cowboy of his time. He looks more like a cinema star dressed to portray a rodeo cowboy in the annual epic interpretation. He will do the talking, kiss the girl or horse (nobody kisses a bull), and the stunt man will take the chances, do the falls. But of course nothing could be further from the truth. Mahan is an athlete, the fanatical competitor who takes his own chances. In the rodeo arena he is transformed into 155 pounds of balance, talent, and extreme toughness, mentally and physically. Young, conventional, unbaptized cowboys might wonder about his flashy clothes, the outgoing and friendly way he relates to everybody from longhairs to cowboys, but once he gets on a bronc or bull they find he can outride and out-tough just about anybody. So they stand back and believe what they've heard, what they've read.

Perhaps it is the indoctrination of our times, with giant football and basketball players, but you expect Mahan to be bigger, even though you know he's about five feet, eight or nine inches tall. Perspective distorts. Mahan has dark features, modishly long curly black hair with a balding spot at the crown, and mischievous, alert eyes. His face is lined with time he's spent on the road, and run-ins with bulls have left him with a slightly crooked smile and a scar on his lip. But dimples keep his face from looking worn and make it seem young and at times almost impish. To a pro football fan, Mahan resembles Craig Morton. To a rodeo fan, Craig Morton resembles Mahan. He has no regional accent, having grown up in Oregon and lived in Arizona, Texas, California. In his later years, John Steinbeck expressed the fear that some future generation would grow up without colloquial speech

because children grow up listening to television announcers and commentators who have no accents. Mahan sounds like a television commentator, which he's been. He could not stop at "Yep."

Mahan decided he'd try to win the All Around title a seventh time, though the odds are not good for a part-time rodeo performer. But Mahan will keep trying. Before he came to Cheyenne, he missed six weeks when a nervous horse fractured his hand in the chute; he was absent again while working on a movie called *Six Pack Annie*, and then missed more time when he went to Europe and then Moscow for the Russian premiere of the Academy Award winning documentary *The Great American Cowboy*, a film showing the life of the modern-day cowboy and specifically the race for the 1972 All Around title between Mahan and Phil Lyne. Mahan seemed so natural, at ease moving around in front of the cameras, that the motion picture industry realized that he had screen presence, potential as an actor. He had also been working on a deal to take a rodeo to Russia and had been moving around the country to promote his Western clothes line, "The Larry Mahan Wild West Collection." In four days he'd leave Cheyenne and go to Guthrie, Texas, where he'd work in a Roy Rogers film called *Mackintosh and T. J.*

Mahan, closing in on All Around leaders Leo Camarillo and Tom Ferguson, wasn't Larry Mahan the actor or promoter, but Larry Mahan the cowboy, trying to make up for time that wouldn't wait. He'd won the saddle bronc in Odgen, Utah, on Saturday, picking up $1,238; missed out on money at Deadwood, South Dakota, Saturday night; got thrown by a bull in Salt Lake; and had a 69 on a bareback in Cheyenne on Monday.

"I'm actually enjoying rodeo more now," Mahan was saying. "I don't do it for money, just the competition and the sport. If I could win the All Around this way, with the other things I've got going, it would mean a lot."

"Hey, Bull," said a cowboy, "where'd you get that hat?"

Mahan tipped the worn, beaver-fur Western hat and said, "Found it."

"Looks like a grape-picker's hat to me. You been pickin' grapes out there in California between movies?"

"Well, you got to be ready for any change in life-style you undergo."

As he neared the chutes, he continued, "I'd like to get to the finals about two or three thousand behind and make it in two, three events. Then I'd see how my competition reacted."

Frontier Days is a lot of color, a lot of beauty, and a lot of tradition. Above, left to right: Oglala-Sioux have been coming to Frontier Days since the turn of the century; the reigning Miss Wyoming; lesser royalty. Opposite: Carrying off the flags of the United States and Australia.

Left: *Justin Huffman, with his bareback gear, putting some rosin on his riding glove.* Below: *Larry Mahan, with his saddle bronc gear, walking past the chutes.*

A girl saw him and came over, yelling, "Larry! Larry!" She was a free-lance writer doing a story on what rodeo was really like and placed herself between Mahan and the entrance to the area behind the chutes, where he'd sit and limber up his gear. He smiled and made small talk; leaving, she turned and said, "Larry, I know you won't remember this, but I'm in room two-thirty. Please call. I have something important to tell you. Larry, I know you won't remember . . . two-thirty . . . two-thirty!"

"It just occurs to me that she could get a much better story than I can," I said, watching her walk away.

A man, leading a small boy, had been watching Mahan. He came over and Mahan signed the kid's program and then put his rigging bag down and let the man take his picture holding the kid. The kid laughed, thanked Mr. Mahan, and said he wanted a Sno-cone.

Mahan sat on the bench in the fenced area under the grandstand, behind the chutes, and got out his rigging, a small, worn, leather pad about twenty inches long, in a semi-arc, and half that distance wide. He held it by a kind of D-shaped rawhide handhold, placed slightly off center. The handhold would be the only direct link between Mahan and the bareback horse he'd ride. He put some rosin on the handhold, to better his grip.

"Well, this isn't such a bad life," he said, obviously getting more excited. "You get in your eight hours in eight seconds." He stood, did deep knee bends, twisted from the waist, then began to jog in place. He'd drawn a horse named Milligan's Wake. "Listen," he continued, "I'm psyching on this horse from my ears to my feet. Some cowboys keep a book on horses. There's too many for that. But you remember some things, pick up some others. This one's strong. *Wow, is he strong!* He usually jumps out, goes to the right. I like his looks, though. It's like being with a woman: lack of knowledge creates fear." He sat down again, taped his fingers with borrowed tape, got out his riding glove, and doused it with rosin. He had cut out the welting on the glove, trimming off the excess to make it like another skin. He put his hand into the handhold, which squeaked as he pulled and jerked. Then he took his hand out and tore a small piece of leather from the rigging handle, put his hand back in, and announced, "No way that sonuvabitch can get this out of my hand now."

He stood up, said hello to a couple of cowboys, and made his way through the gate into the arena, walking along the chutes until he found Milligan's Wake. "I don't think about anything but winning, competing and winning, when I'm around this," he said. "Competing and winning. That used to be the two most important things in my life. Now I've got other interests, but when I'm here, it's the same feeling.

"Everybody out here wants to win, but the most important thing is how badly you hate losing. It makes me feel fuckin'-a-sick to lose. Just sick. Sure, I believe in the luck of the draw, but after that it's nobody but you. I mean it. I get sick when I lose. I never, never think about anything negative when I get up."

Mahan climbs up the gate of the chute, as easily as walking up stairs, then places his rigging on the horse. He puts on his glove. Another cowboy, on the inside of the chute, reaches under the horse with a hook, grabs the strap, and ties it loosely over the horse's withers. "I see in my mind what's going to happen before I get on," said Mahan. "I see myself riding and everything I do is positive. You don't have time to think out there, but if you've run it over enough, strong enough in your mind, you just react. It's experience, in a way, because you've faced just about all situations before. But I've seen myself on replays, films, and I'll react a certain way and don't even remember doing it. It's your subconscious at work. Information is stored there and it comes out."

"Little more," says Mahan, scooting the rigging a few inches up the horse's shoulder. A cowboy slowly tightens the rigging, and Mahan eases down on the horse, which moves uneasily with his weight. It is difficult to see how he can concentrate in the chutes. A photographer is there, snapping flashes in his eyes. Others are making idle talk and he'll answer questions, but he doesn't see the flashbulbs and can't tell you what his answers were. He pulls at the rigging. "No way," he repeats. He pulls his grape-picker's hat down tightly on his head, puts his left hand on the chute, and lifts his spurs high on the horse's shoulders, locking his ankles. He nudges up, almost on top of the rigging, and nods. The gate is jerked open and a cowboy yanks the flank strap. Milligan's Wake, a big, strong sorrel with a streaked face, bolts to the right, kicking, leaping. Mahan, rocking on the anchor of his hand, is flailing his legs, spurring high and wide, and as the horse bolts, he jerks and is jerked so hard backwards that his head almost hits the horse's haunches. Then his body goes forward and it's almost as if he's being yanked, alternately, by ropes from opposite directions. But he has purpose, a controlled yet reckless timing with the animal.

Milligan's Wake, with a new trick, changes pattern and, in his madness, jerks to the left, and Mahan tilts slightly, almost losing his timing, then almost instantly regains his rhythm. The crowd,

some 9,000, loves it. Loves Mahan. Loves Milligan's Wake. Being in Cheyenne. Being there. When the buzzer sounds, Mahan brings his left hand down to help hang on until the pickup men get him. He reaches for the one on the left, grabs the man's shoulders, and swings down, shaking his head.

"Listen, that sonuvabitch gave me one helluva whip," he said, when asked if he'd almost lost his balance. "Remember that little piece of leather I jerked off the riggin'? Well, that was the difference in hanging on or being bucked off. I knew he was strong, but he was stronger than I thought. The horse wasn't showy. But boy, was he strong."

Later, a reporter from the local newspaper asked him about his ride and he said, "That's the first time I've been on him and I hope it's the last." The reporter laughed. But, for Mahan, it isn't fear. Mahan can control fear and has conquered it about as much as a man can, though somewhere in a corner of his mind he knows there's reason to be afraid. That bull that stepped on his head in 1961 broke his jaw in five places. In 1964, a bull cracked his jaw. In 1965, he suffered three cracked vertebrae in his back when he was thrown from a horse. In 1971, his hand hung in the rigging and before he could get loose, he had a spiral fracture of the tibia when the bronc stepped on his leg. In 1972, he was jerked so hard by a bull it tore the ligaments in his right arm that hold the biceps to the forearm. He has had other cracked bones, sprains, and fractures, and probably he will suffer more.

"There's no way you can go out there and compete if you're worried about getting hurt," he said. "You learn to conquer fear in your mind, blank it out. A guy worries about injuries and he pulls up short on what he can do. It stops him. There is a fine line. You must know how far you can possibly go and go no farther. Sometimes that little extra blast can make the difference in winning, but if I see the point where I'd be foolish, I'll stop. You must know the difference."

The difference. Later that year, in Dallas, Ma-

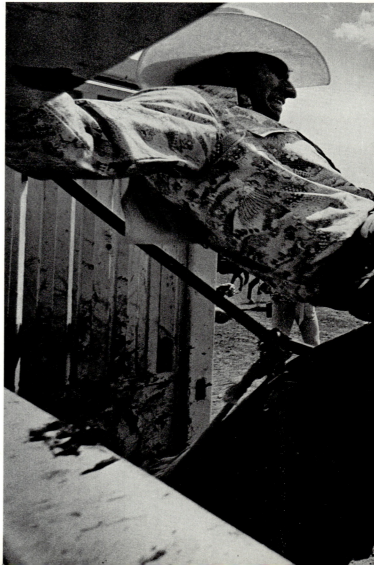

Preceding pages: *Pulling the flank strap tight to make him buck.* Clockwise from top left: *Bareback riders in the chutes: tying down the glove; easing up on the grip; spurring him out.*

There's more of him off than on, but he's holding tight.

han, up on a bull, not only tied the rope around his hand but between his fingers for extra grip. Had the bull bucked him off, he likely would have lost fingers. But he rode the bull, spurring him all the way. It was the extra blast, the confidence.

Larry Mahan scored a 71 on Milligan's Wake, tying him with Lonnie Hall for the day's top bareback ride and moving him into a fourth in the second go-round. Mahan, feeling good, flew his plane back to Denver that night.

"That horse, ol' Milligan's Wake, dooo jerk you," says Rusty Riddle, as we sit among the crowd of rodeo officials in Chute Ten. There are actually nine chutes in the rodeo arena at Cheyenne. Chute Ten is a lounge, a bar on the grounds, a chance to relax. But you ordinarily don't get in unless you are somebody or know somebody.

"When I used to come here, they wouldn't let me in Chute Ten," he continues, sipping a Budweiser. "I was never invited. Then I guess I got to be a little more important, and they asked me to come on in. When I got in, I gave them a piece of my mind about that.

"Yeah, this one and Cal-gary are the biggest 'uns. But, really, this one is best for the cowboys. I mean at Cal-gary you don't always know what to expect. Hell, you spit on the sidewalk and the Queen walks past and they'll throw you in jail."

People—the bartender who knows his name and the woman sitting on the soft Naugahyde couch—speak to Rusty. They wouldn't have spoken to him a few years ago. Rusty is a little out of uniform, which draws some stares. He has on boots and jeans and has a can of Skoal in his back pocket, but he's not up that day so he's wearing a red golf shirt.

Earlier in the afternoon, he'd had an autograph session at one of the special tables set up for that purpose between the grandstand and the arena. As he'd started for the table, a rodeo official had stopped him and said, "Rusty, you need to put a

51

shirt on before going over there. You know that."

"Well, sorry, but this is all I got with me today," said Rusty. The official nodded for him to go ahead and he sat there for forty-five minutes signing autographs in a shirt Jack Nicklaus might wear. But he's the now Rusty Riddle, instead of being the then Rusty Riddle, and it's okay. Actually, he's almost the best man in his event, bareback. Four straight times he finished second to Joe Alexander, whom he and other cowboys call Alexander the Great.

We move out of the crowd, magnetically drawn to the bar, and talk by the window. "I look at it this way," he continues, "number two ain't as bad as number three. I'll catch Joe one of these days. Maybe this is the year. Maybe next year. Anyways, I ain't doin' too bad [he grins], I'm in Chute Ten, ain't I?"

Rusty looks cowboy, all right. Small, with a

heavily muscled upper torso, he has a face that Mark Twain or somebody imbedded in my mind as associated with holding a fishin' pole on the bank of a slow moving, sleepy river or watching a frog-jumping contest. His hair is reddish, his complexion is freckled, and his eyes are faded blue.

Admittedly, he was one of the hell raisers at one time, but he has mellowed. "It used to be a six pack down the road and good times," he says. "Now, I got me a good wife and a nice place, about one hundred and thirty acres outside Weatherford, Texas. I tell you, I been a lucky sonuvabuck. The way I got started as a kid I might of ended up in jail somewhere."

Perhaps the oddest twist to his life is that he now owns the spread from which he once ran away. Rusty, twenty-eight, had been on his own for fourteen years. "My daddy worked our tails off," he recalls. "We hauled and baled hay, worked in the dairy there. He used to whip me all the time. Just beat the hell outa me. I couldn't do nothin' right. One day, when I was fourteen, he got mad and really clobbered me around. When he left that day, I just said to myself, That's it. No more. I got my riggin' bag and hid out in the brush. Then when I got the chance, I hitchhiked for Forth Worth.

"I was lucky. I ran into some good people or no tellin' what would have happened to me. I went to work for this stockman and learned all about the rodeo business. Then I just got myself into it. Those were tough days. A bunch of us would pile into a car and head down the road. But everybody was helpin' everybody else and I learned a lot in those years.

"Then," he grins with satisfaction, "an odd thing happened. One day my momma phoned me to come on back home and run the place. She said the man [his father] had left. I just ups and goes back and buys it. Yeah, sometimes when I'm out there I think about when he caused me to run off. But it's my home now.

"Yeah, I been mighty lucky in life."

Left: *At home in the saddle, maybe, but he's not really asleep.* Opposite: *Lyle Sankey taking center stage—he's made it past the first jump.*

Rusty likes Cheyenne; he likes Wyoming. Cowboys still talk about the time he almost was killed in the state.

Rusty, Pete Gay, and Shawn Davis had gone elk hunting in Wyoming and took time off to help a friend find stray sheep that had wandered up a mountain, some 500 feet above them. That was 1972, when it appeared Rusty just might win the bareback title. Pete and Rusty, slowly, carefully, rode up the mountain. Suddenly, Rusty's horse slipped and horse and rider tumbled down an incline. "When I finally got to him I thought he'd broke his neck," said Pete. Rusty was skinned up and his arm was badly broken. "Well, Pete put me on his horse and walks me about five miles to the house," Rusty said. "Then we got in the car and drove one hundred and eighty miles to Casper to get my arm set. I was feelin' mighty bad. There went my chance for the title." Before the ordeal ended, he was to feel much worse.

It was one of those stupid days. Feeling left out and hopeless, Rusty decided he'd ride along with Pete and Shawn on the long jaunt to San Francisco for the season's last big rodeo, in the Cow Palace. Shawn didn't drink but Pete and Rusty did and along the way, beer flowed. And flowed. Rusty got to feeling better. The influence made them both taller and life became a stage for their own nonsense, which most people can relate to at one time or another—some more times than others. When they got to Evanston, Wyoming, Rusty asked to drive. "Naw, I'll drive," said Pete. "It'll sober me up." Everything was funny. Funny to want to drive. Funny not to want to drive. They got a .38 with blanks and started shooting from the open window, a good way to attract attention in most towns.

As Pete drove the Buick Electra out of Evanston and started up an access road onto the freeway leading to Utah, he saw the flashing red light of the highway patrol closing in behind him. But, distorted, it became a game and he floorboarded the accelerator in a mad dash for the state line. "Hey," said Shawn Davis, in the backseat. "Wait!" The countryside was going by faster and faster, though it didn't seem that way. The Buick hit 90 miles per hour, 100, 120. The freeway had two lanes going in each direction, divided by a shallow ditch.

"There was this truck in our lane in front of us," recalled Rusty. "Needless to say, we were having a little problem judging distance, so Pete swerved to the left too quickly as he got ready to go around the truck."

The Buick went off the road and into the ditch, but Pete hung on and was trying to guide the trembling, shaking car back onto the freeway. There was a culvert ahead, crossing the ditch. "If we'd hit that it would have been like hitting a cement wall, head on," recalled Rusty. Pete fought the car and guided it back onto the highway, but just when everybody was relieved the two rear tires blew out. The car turned over, started flipping, and then everything seemed almost in slow motion, as if they could see themselves, mirrored in numb shock. Movement lost control. Just as Rusty was propelled through the front window he put his arm with the cast in front of his face. He was like a man being shot from a cannon, hitting the ground and then rolling to a dead stop, his face cut and bloody, the cast shattered. The car continued to roll, flipping back into the ditch. Finally, its momentum slowed, ended, and just as it was about to roll over one more time on the driver's side, it rocked, paused, and stayed upright. Pete, his foot caught in the steering wheel, was hanging out the window. Had the car rolled again, it would have crushed him.

There were skid marks for over a mile. Beer cans and glass covered the area. Sirens of police cars, ambulances cut through eerie silence. Davis crawled out of the wreckage. Pete untangled himself and they looked for Rusty. The police, the ambulance attendants, Pete, and Shawn got to him. Twice they took his pulse and found none.

"We all thought he was dead," said Shawn. "Then he moved a little."

Left: *Chris Le Doux screwed down tight.* Above: *Larry Mahan off center over the mud at Cheyenne.*

Chute Ten was filling up fast in the late afternoon. "What saved me," Rusty was saying, "was that cast. If I hadn't put it in front of my face it'd have cut my head near off when I went through the window. I ended up with a bad concussion, injured ribs, and a bunch of stitches, and that was about it."

He laughs. "You know, ol' Shawn don't even drink. Well, he got a knee injury when a case of beer was thowed up against him."

Rusty started for the door. "You see, I'm just a lucky sonuvabuck. I guess that happened about October and I was back ridin' in the finals in December, wearing a fiberglass brace on my arm and also this kind of corset brace on my ribs.

"Well, listen, I got to go meet my wife." When he walked out, some people in Chute Ten watched him and some did not. But they knew he was there.

Early in the week, monsoon rain showers, though short-lived, left the arena slightly muddy but kept the dust down. The infield and the track were somewhat slippery and made the nightly chuck wagon races even more treacherous. There were other effects. One of the Dandies, Kathleen Murray, suffered a dislocated knee when her horse slipped in the mud. Though in pain, she said she'd be back in the saddle before the celebration ended.

Besides the chuck wagon races, the night shows were not particularly calculated to speed adrenaline so much as to soothe, to entertain. Roy Rogers and Dale Evans; Buck Owens and the Buckaroos with Susan Raye; Marty Robbins; and, finally, Mickey Gilley and Barbara Mandrell all entertained for two-night stands on a wooden, portable stage in the arena. Robbins, drawing some 7,000, said he was glad he outdrew Owens and sang "El Paso."

Waiting to go up. It's a little easier if your baby's there.

Chuck wagon races are almost as popular as football in Canada but haven't caught on in the United States. They're one of the most popular events at the Calgary Stampede, which started holding the event in 1923. Cheyenne had about everything else during Frontier Days, so it started holding the races in 1952 and has seen three drivers killed since. Dangers are multiple, and include falling and getting crushed by wagon wheels or tumbling under an outrider.

"Your number's up, it's up, and it don't make no difference," said Orville Standquist. He's a fifty-five-year-old, thin, weather-beaten Canadian, who makes his living racing chuck wagons. Standquist travels the circuit with his family, in a camper, towing sixteen horses in a cattle liner. He explained that sponsors, whose names are on the wagons, were very important because about all you could hope to make a year was $15,000.

"It's hard to keep on the road," he continued. "The wagon we got, for instance, is about fifty years old. Wheels are hard to find and go for about a hundred dollars each. But I like the excitement."

Chuck wagon races are like watching a gold rush created by Cecil B. De Mille. Five heats were run each night during the week, and each was like

an extravaganza, an epic undertaking. Races begin when contestants load a simulated range stove into the wagon. Outriders then mount and the driver, his wagon pulled by four thoroughbreds, must essay a figure eight of barrels before he gets on the half-mile track and races around the arena back to the finish line. They used to have real stoves but now use a box of sand. "Why don't you do a story on what chuck wagon racing is really like," I asked the girl free-lance writer, watching from the press box. She ignored me.

Bill DuBoise ("call me Bill") sat at the VIP table near the track, where he'd watch the Oglala-Sioux Indians dance before Marty Robbins came on. DuBoise acts as publicity chairman for the Frontier Days Committee, which plans and runs the show. He is a proper, straight man who wears glasses and looks like a high school history teacher. He is a high school history teacher.

His grandfather, Col. E. A. Slack, editor of the *Cheyenne Sun Leader*, might have started Frontier Days. Some old-timers and local historians say it was his idea, while others believe F. W. Angier, a Union Pacific passenger agent, got the idea once when he was stranded at a railroad station and watched cowboys try to get a bucking horse on the

Opposite: *Lettin' her hang.* Above: *Mickey Young, a little out of step.*

Howard Hunter, a top man in saddle bronc, hangin' tough bareback.

train. Slack later wrote in his newspaper that Angier had the original idea. But Slack got the wheels turning.

"This rodeo has survived four wars and not missed a performance," said DuBoise, who watched me take notes as we sat at the table, which he called his box. "You might say we work on the rodeo about twelve months a year. We have a tradition to maintain, and there's a lot of civic pride. Oh, I'd say we make about fifty thousand dollars in profit each year, but it just goes back into the pot for the next year."

I had read Cheyenne was very wild in its beginning and that, in fact, outlaws once controlled the town before vigilantes ran them out. "Oh, Cheyenne wasn't as wild a place as people would like to think," said DuBoise. "Sure, it was a rough, frontier town, and you had to be hard and tough to survive." He smiled, laughed aloud, and added, "They used to say Cheyenne didn't get much snow, but it blew through all winter." When I took notes about the Indians, he looked over my shoulder and corrected my spelling.

Indians—the men, women, and children who are descendants of Red Cloud, Crazy Horse, and Sitting Bull—came on the small wooden stage to beat drums and dance. Their names were Max Blacksmith, Richard Elk Boy, Harry Jumping Bull, Mathew Two Bulls, Nellie Two Bulls, Calvin Jumping Bull. The program said the piano on stage was furnished by School District Number One. Before the show, an Indian talked into the microphone

and said, ". . . be happy and contented in this great country of ours. I hope the flag of the U.S. stands forever! Forever!"

It struck me as sad, in a way, that men of the earth had now come to dancing on wooden stages for white men, though it happened a long time ago.

This is the greatest sport and sorriest business in the world.   —Brad Clements, bull rider

On Friday, the seventh day of Cheyenne Frontier Days, cowboys gathering around the chutes before the rodeo began were talking about the weather, what had happened at the Mayflower Bar the previous night, rodeo judges, girl friends, wives, families, and the state of the economy. Scotty Platts, a friendly little guy from Lyman, Wyoming, who pulls his hat down so tight before he rides bareback that his ears are forced out at ninety-degree angles, shook his head and said, "It takes practically every dime I earn to keep me on down the road. You figure it costs at least one hundred dollars in expenses to attend a single rodeo, an average rodeo. To be in contention, you need to go to, say, one hundred a year. Well, that's ten thousand dollars expenses right there, almost minimum. Most guys can't win ten thousand dollars in a year, so they don't break even."

"Gas kills you," said J. C. Trujillo. "It gets worse and worse. Cheapest gas I've seen this year was this little town in Utah. Cost forty-three cents a gallon, self-service."

Platts makes enough to get on down the road, but he's having difficulty making enough to buy the house he wants for his family. He earned over $20,000 in 1975, so he didn't have to spend as much time in the construction business, his fall-back-on profession. But he doesn't make enough to take his family along.

"I used to drive by myself," he said. "I'd put about eighty thousand miles a year on a car. That would wear it out and I'd have to trade it in for another one. Now automobiles are so high and gas is up so much that I can't handle it alone. So three of us bought this van to get on down the road."

He laughed, pushed his hat back, and added, "But this has drawbacks. You can sleep in the van but there's no way to clean up. After a while you get to smelling pretty bad, so we have to break down and rent a motel room to clean up.

"It's hurting us all. Look at Shawn Davis. He had to swap his Cadillac for a Gremlin. Course, we can get by cheap on food. Like me. I only need maybe a hot dog or hamburger a day. I usually eat one of them in the afternoon. It keeps you lean and a little hungry, which is good for riding broncs."

Motel rates in Cheyenne were up because it was Frontier Days. Doug Brown, a former bull riding champion and also a bronc rider, said, "Four of us are staying in this room at the Holiday Inn. It costs thirty-five dollars a day, so that's nine dollars each. But I'd like to have my family here with me. But no way to pay thirty-five dollars a day by myself. Then there'd also be food. Imagine what it would cost to feed them.

"The thing that worries me a little is that this might turn into a rich man's sport."

Larry Mahan, who had attended North Salem, Oregon, High School with Brown, wasn't worried about expenses. Back from Denver that morning, he was up on a bull in the afternoon performance. A cold was bothering him, but because there were 124 entries in the event, Cheyenne was a one-shot deal for the finals and he had to do it right. It appeared he'd drawn badly, but there wouldn't be another chance.

"There are lots of bull riders," Mahan said as he took out his bull rope and began stretching it over a fence, getting any kinks out. "All these kids coming into rodeo go into bull riding. It's cheaper to get started. All you need is a rope with a bell on it and a glove. And you have more of a chance. You just get on a bull and hang on, without doing anything else, and you have a chance to be in the money. You can get lucky and win.

"But it's not always so easy to hang on. You better stay up there close to your hand, using it kind of like a shock absorber. Get away from it and you get the power of the bull and no man alive can hang on. Bulls scare you a little, leave you with that little empty feeling you have to conquer. You look forward to riding a good horse but you don't always feel that way about a bull. You can't go out on a bull and be real aggressive. He jerks and you try to compensate, keep your balance, react to what he does. Just grit your teeth and go."

Mahan put rosin on his rope, stretched it out on the fence, and rubbed it up and down to make the rope tackier. Cowboys walked around, many of them limping. It had been a long week, but as long as it wasn't anything serious, I don't think they mind the soreness. They almost embrace it, as a pro football player likes to wake up with some soreness on a Monday morning, reminding him of Sunday.

Earlier we had been talking about a mutual friend, Craig Morton, and Mahan, who was about to get on top of a 1,600-pound bull that would try to buck him off, stick its horns in him, or try to stomp him, said, "You know, I watched ol' Craig and Staubach out there playing and saw them get blind-sided. I tell you I'm chicken. I could never do that, thinking some old tackle was about to hit me."

The bull is black with short horns. A Brahma, he likes nobody. He doesn't like the man dropping the rope around him, nor the clanging or weight of the bell. He doesn't like the flank strap, though it's

Opposite top and left: *A lot of bareback riders have a lot of hell at Cheyenne Frontier Days.* Opposite right: *Even without a hat, Joe Alexander—"Alexander the Great"—knows what he's doing.*

still loose. Mahan has on an old pair of boots, which he has tied around the tops with leather straps to keep them from being jerked off. He climbs up on the gate, and after he drops the rope, weighted by the bell, down one side, a cowboy on the other side gets it with a hook and brings it back around to tie it up. Mahan pulls his glove on tighter, moves his rope up just behind the animal's shoulders, and starts wrapping it back of his hand, across the palm, leaving a strand sticking out so that he can yank it free with his other hand once the ride ends.

Before the bull riding, more than before any other event, danger seems to take on a solid dimension, a certain smell of its own, like manure, leather, and the sweat of tension all combined. Mahan had first gained fame on the circuit when he won the bull-riding title in 1965. That's when they started calling him Bull.

The gate opens, and the bull immediately tries to rear its head back and hit Mahan. Then it tries to kick him off with its hind feet. Then it runs, pauses, and starts kicking again. Mahan is not just hanging on, he's spurring the animal, but it doesn't make that much difference. When the buzzer sounds, he times his jump with the movement of the bull and clears it, landing on his feet, going down to his knees, and then getting up as the bull chases the clown, Wick Peth. He scores a 67 on a bad draw. "Anybody else would have had a sixty," says a cowboy, as Mahan walks over near the fence to watch the rest of the event. Only two cowboys made eight seconds on their bulls that day.

But the 67 won't make the finals. Cutoff will be 69. "I'm not riding bulls worth a shit lately," said Mahan. A month later he would ride much better, and team roper Leo Camarillo, in a close race with

Mahan and Tom Ferguson for the All Around title, would chide him, "Well, it's about time you started riding those bulls right. The pressure's on." Mahan, looking at Camarillo, would answer, "Pressure hell! I've already been there. The pressure's on you."

Mahan knew he wouldn't make the finals. He had tried but lost on the black Brahma. Cowboys who used to travel with him said he used to have awful downers when he lost, sometimes driving 500 miles without saying a word. "Winning is a fantastic high," he said. "When I lose, my mean streak, if I have one, comes out. It doesn't come out against other people but myself. I just go around for a while kicking my own ass." But he is too turned on to people, to too many different things, for bad downers now.

James Thompson, who handles Mahan's line of clothes in Denver, joined us after the bull riding. Thompson had his pants tucked in red, white, and blue bicentennial cowboy boots and had a Larry Mahan T-shirt over his regular shirt. A writer from the East asked Mahan when he first got interested in rodeoing, and he answered, "The first time I fell on my head." Mahan, sipping a Coke at the concession stands outside the chutes, was called over to a group and introduced to a small, blond singer named Karen Irish. She was entertaining with a group called Frenchy Burke and his Cajun Show in the lounge at the Hitching Post motel. Miss Irish seemed very nervous, but Mahan promised he'd come by and catch the show.

Cowboys were talking about the accident Shawn Davis had had. Karen Irish didn't know who Shawn Davis was, but Larry Mahan went to see him in the hospital.

Opposite *and* above: *Bobby L. Steiner, two hands down, gets help from a pickup man.*

The horse called Joe Buck had been uneasy in the chutes as the saddle bronc competition had gotten under way on Thursday, the third day of Cheyenne Frontier Days. But the suddenness, the uncontrollability of danger, had never been a factor before or the rider would have given it up long ago. So Shawn Davis momentarily eased out of the saddle as cowboys tried to calm the horse. "I rode him before," said Shawn. "He's always a little bad in the chutes, so most don't like him, but he hasn't been that bad for me."

A cowboy grabbed the horse's head, held it tight. It stilled, then twitched as Shawn eased back into the saddle. He raised his spurs, grabbed the rein tightly where he'd marked it, and nodded, "Let him go!" Then it happened. The horse's flank strap was yanked but the man at the gate missed the latch and failed to open it immediately. Joe Buck reared high in the chute, just as the man finally got the gate open. When the horse came down, one front foot hung up on the gate and the other one went over, causing the horse to lose its balance and fall.

"I knew he was going to fall and I was ready," recalled Shawn. "I tried to relax, get ready for the concussion." The horse fell on Shawn, rolled over his right leg and then kicked wildly and got to its feet. Shawn stood up, started to brush off, and then, as he put weight on his right leg, it gave and he fell down. "Oh no," he said. "Think I might have broke my leg." But cowboys helped him up again and there wasn't particularly any pain. Shawn grabbed

Opposite *and* left: *Pickup men at Cheyenne—sometimes the horse just doesn't hear that buzzer.* Below: *Paul Mayo, trying to get his faculties back, after a wreck.*

Chuck wagon races, exciting and dangerous, have been part of Frontier Days since 1952. Opposite: Letting loose on the half-mile track around the arena. Below: Essaying a figure eight marked out with barrels.

a chute hook and, using it as a crutch, hobbled to the side of the chute where he planned to watch the remainder of the rodeo. A doctor in the arena was worried and talked him into going to the first aid room. There was some swelling but not the awful deformed look of a broken bone, a bone that bends and then snaps like a stick. But, on the doctor's suggestion, a friend took Shawn to the hospital for X rays, which showed that his leg was broken in the lower shinbone.

So, a mile from Frontier Park, Shawn Davis was in a hospital room, the familiar drowsiness of pain killers in his head, and the long, white cast on his leg. When Larry Mahan showed up the room filled with nurses and attendants who probably did not know that Shawn Davis had been the world saddle bronc champion in 1965, 1967, and 1968 but did know who Mahan was. "You talk about being tough and making comebacks," Mahan told me. "Well, Shawn wrote the book. He probably should have been dead, much less still competing."

Shawn Davis walks with an unnatural bend in his back, a stark remembrance of a vivid, red nightmare in May, 1969, at Thompson Falls, Montana. A horse jumped so high into the air, with such momentum, that it flipped over backwards on Shawn, all 1,100 pounds smashing him into the ground and snapping his lower back. Doctors, fearing further damage to the sciatic nerve, fused the vertebrae slightly out of position, forward and to the left, permanently out of place. "They told me I'd never ride again after that and that I ought to feel lucky I wasn't killed," he said. "Due to nerve damage, they thought my leg wouldn't be normal, that my foot would eventually turn in, and I might lose feeling in it.

"I was in traction for months. I kept thinking doctors were just over-cautious. I'd never been hurt seriously before and didn't have anything to relate it to. But they kept saying I couldn't ride again, and I guess it was like when my parents told me I couldn't rodeo when I was a kid because it was too

Since it started, chuck wagon racing has seen three drivers killed. The dangers include getting run over by the wheels of a wagon and tumbling under the horse of an outrider.

Above: *Bull and bull rider taking a walk out of Chute 2.* Opposite: *Down in front.*

dangerous. The more they told me, the more determined I was to do it."

Thirteen months after Shawn suffered the broken back, he won the bronc riding event at Gladewater, Texas. But it was as if a gate of accidents had suddenly been opened. He suffered a badly sprained ankle, a broken ankle another time, and then faced death once again. In 1973, he was out in a pasture attempting to rope a bull. After he got the rope around the bull's neck and tied it to his saddle horn, the animal jerked with such ferocity his saddle broke, causing Shawn to fall to the ground. The bull was on him in no time, hooking, trying to stomp him. Its horn drove across his face, knocking his nose loose, tearing and ripping bone and skin and taking it completely off his face. He tried to roll, but the bull hooked him in the tail, sticking its horn up him as it tossed him high into the air.

"The only thing that saved me was some good

dogs we had," said Shawn. "They came running out and chased the bull off me. Some of the hands around the place got me, put me in a truck, and took off to Forth Worth, where a plastic surgeon fixed my face and nose. It took a lot longer to get my rear all right." He laughed when he talked about being hooked in the rear. After all that's happened, what else can he do?

Five months before he came to Cheyenne, a horse stepped on his foot, breaking it again. "When that happened, I said, that's it, I had my share of accidents," said Shawn. "I just keep thinking my accidents were freak things that I didn't cause, except I probably should have been more careful with that bull.

"Rodeo's hard to quit. It gets in you, the people, the competition. You want to be the best at something. A guy might work twenty years to win a few championships and think that's the ultimate. Then three weeks after you've won a championship, everybody has forgotten about it and you got to go out and do it all over again. You win three, you want four; four, you got to have five. I guess it's man's nature."

Shawn Davis still has a young face, though his nose is too straight, too perfect. But when he takes off his hat, baldness suddenly makes him look older, vulnerable. "I dunno," he added. "I'm thirty-three now, and I'm thinking this time I might just quit. This might be about it for me."

Paul Mayo, told that Shawn was thinking of quitting, said, "Shawn quit? Naw, he won't quit. It's like a fever with him, with a lot of guys. It's something in the blood—sounds, smells, competition. Hell, as long as he can crawl out there he won't quit."

Shawn, in obvious pain and on crutches, attended the finals at Cheyenne. Often he'd have to prop his leg up so the swelling would go down and some of the throbbing would ease. Six months after Cheyenne, he was on a saddle bronc at the big indoor rodeo in Fort Worth.

Listen, that Mayflower's boxing matches. You can't mix cowboys, kids, hippies, freaks, and beer.
—Rusty Riddle

There's no place like the Mayflower. I never walked in there that I didn't walk out with a gal. —Mike Bandy

Let's go on down to the Mayflower drinking and eating establishment. —Larry Mahan

Two of Cheyenne's Finest parked the police car a block away, slowly got out, and approached cautiously. It was about midnight, but there's no bewitching hour at the Mayflower Dance Hall, on Seventeenth Street, downtown Cheyenne. As was true during each night of the Cheyenne Frontier Days celebration, the crowd had overflowed onto the street. Some sat or leaned against surrounding buildings and others rested on fenders or hoods of cars parked along the curb. Inside there was the usual shouting, occasionally a scream, and loud, loud music played by a large fat man named Tiny Wellman and his group, The Raindrops.

"Why me?" said one of the cops, a short, heavy man whose hat was slightly tilted, as if he was about to make a funny face.

"Listen, you want to go in there?" asked the taller one.

"Hell, no. Do you?"

"Hell, no. But we're it. It's duty. Like they say, we got our duty to keep the peace."

"Piss on duty."

The Mayflower has its place on the rodeo map. Normally, during the weeks when it isn't Frontier Days, the place seems almost nondescript, another bar. Actually, the Mayflower complex is composed of a cafe, a package liquor store and tavern (complete with long bar and swinging doors), and the dance hall. During Frontier Days, it is an after-hours headquarters, where the action is, an altar to pleasures, real and imagined.

The taller officer hitched up his pants and went

Opposite: *Butch Kirby fixin' to bite the dust.* Below: *Monty Henson.*

in, followed by his partner, who was hitting the palm of his hand with a billyclub, as loudly as he could. *"Vaya con dios!"* I yelled after them. I was standing next to Larry Mahan, who leaned up against a car outside the Mayflower, which we called no-man's-land. Earlier we had stopped by the Hitching Post to catch Karen Irish's act. Mahan talked to her and her agent, who was so good he had gotten her all the way from Southern California to—Wyoming. When she got up to sing, Mahan already had the itch to go. He sat through one or two numbers and then got up to leave. Miss Irish, looking right at him, sang, "IIII been jilted, III been walked on. When will III find love." Larry Mahan, outside the Mayflower, did not know.

We had been joined by the Eastern writer, now decked out in Western hat, jeans, boots, the works; Thompson; and a thin, pale female school teacher, who had said at the Hitching Post she'd appreciate a lift downtown if we didn't mind. Mahan, in his beautiful balloon, didn't mind.

A man, perhaps twenty-six or twenty-seven,

saw Mahan and staggered over, a silly grin under his mustache. "Hey, Larry! Larry, by Gawd, Mahan!" he said.

"Hi, how are you," said Mahan, making a statement, not asking a question.

The man looked at Mahan's fancy shirt and said, "Hey, when did you start putting shirts on your pockets?" Mahan looked puzzled. "Oh, ha, I mean pockets on your shirts."

Mahan smiled and shook the man's extended hand. "Well, I watched you ride and just wanted to tell you I think you're the greatest. You're my idol. Why, you been my idol since I used to watch you when I was a kid."

Mahan, who like most people thirty-one would like to be twenty-nine, looked at the man painfully, managed a weak smile, then looked over at me and said, "God, I feel old." We kidded him the rest of the week about being our idol when we were kids.

Left: *Ride's end.* Above: *Wick Peth (in barrel) watching Too Salty.*

77

Two young men with short hair, the military look, started into the Mayflower with their dates, blonds wearing cutoffs, loose blouses, and sandals. They saw Mahan and came over. Both turned out to be pilots, stationed at a nearby air base, and talked flying with Mahan, who has been moving around in his own Cessna 310 for some four years. "I can't believe I met you," said one of the pilots. "Wait until I get back and tell everybody."

"I'll look you up next time I'm up your way," said Mahan, sipping his beer. Mahan drinks little, mostly a glass of wine here or there, but the Mayflower is not a place to order wine. The young girls were on a short sabbatical from the University of Wyoming, heading nowhere in particular.

"Young lady," the Eastern writer said to one of them, "I'd like to drink a beer out of your sandal." The girls giggled and stared at Mahan, after one of the pilots had whispered who he was.

"That would be great," said the pilot. "You show up and it would blow everybody's mind. Great!" The two couples headed into the bar. *"Vaya con dios,"* I said. About fifteen minutes later the two blonds came back out. Alone. They talked to Mahan, though neither knew anything about flying.

We had also been joined by a female lawyer from Denver, who brought her own Scotch in a fruit jar. It was half empty. She was very drunk and said, "Sure, I always come up here for Frontier Days. Bet half the girls you see [she waves her arm in a semicircle] aren't from Cheyenne. Who cares?"

"Who cares?"

A little boy with a wooden shoeshine kit got on his knees and started shining Mahan's boots, which didn't need it. "Hey, what's this?" said Mahan. "A shine, mizter, one dollar." Mahan took out a coin. "We'll flip. Double or nothing for the shine." The kid took the quarter and flipped. He got the coin just as it hit the ground. "What did you call?" asked Mahan. "Heads, mizter. You lose." Mahan gave him two dollars. The kid also kept the quarter.

We went in. *Vaya con dios.* A guy with a beard, wearing fatigues, said something to a cowboy at the end of the bar. The cowboy, half looking at him, grabbed him by the beard, yanking him around and on down the bar. Another cowboy did the same thing, pulling him even farther. This went on until he was at the opposite end of the bar, where somebody booted him in the seat, sending him to the floor, where he crawled, then got up and walked into the rest room.

"You have to watch coming out of there," said Ginney Storey, a secretary for the Frontier Days Committee. "Last year I was in here with my date and went to the rest room. I came out the door and this guy socked me, knocked me flat. I didn't know if he was trying to hit somebody else and just missed or what. I just all of sudden woke up on the floor and somebody was helping me up."

Mahan, catlike, moved deftly through the crowd along the bar and into the dance hall. I

Above *and* opposite: *Rookies trying their luck at saddle bronc.*

followed and, though I don't know why, turned my head just in time to see a fist coming at me. I leaned back and it glanced off the side of my head, knocking off my hat. The guy who had swung was off balance and I cupped my hands and slammed forward and downward into the back of his neck, knocking him into the crowd. Before he could recover, I grabbed my hat and ducked back into the montage of people, remembering something important about the better part of valor.

"Listen, if you going to start fights around here, just stay away from me," said Mahan, with a grin.

Sometimes the police use German shepherds, big and vicious, to shake up those who go too far celebrating in the Mayflower, though nobody has ever defined what is too far. During one particular German shepherd threat, a policeman was at the swinging door, using all his strength to hold the animal out of the fight going on inside. A cowboy, passing behind the policeman, shoved the officer, grabbed the snarling dog by the tail, and swung it into the bar.

"You never heard such yelling, screaming, and barking in your life," said Rusty Riddle. "Feathers were flying but I don't think the music ever stopped."

Rusty and Paul Mayo, chumming around in Cheyenne one night, "accidentally" borrowed an antique stagecoach, on display in front of one of the city's hotels. It seemed like the thing to do at the time—to drink beer and shove the stage around the area. However, the police didn't agree and soon they could hear sirens. Mayo, quicker on his feet, said, "Listen, Rusty, you can have my half of the stagecoach," and disappeared into the night. Soon, Rusty was surrounded, cornered. One of the officers had a German shepherd on a leash. "All I could see was teeth," said Rusty. "That dog was all teeth." The officer ushered Rusty into the backseat of his car, putting the dog with him. As the officer started to drive away, he turned back to Rusty and

Opposite *and* above: *Trouble in and out of the chute.*

said, "Boy, you make one move and that dog'll tear your arm off. I can't stop him. You hear?"

"Yessir," said Rusty, who began stroking the dog on the neck and back.

When they got to the station the officer looked back at Rusty and the ferocious animal. The dog was curled up against Rusty, licking his hand.

The officer jerked open the back door, grabbed the yelping dog, and yanked him out of the car. "Goddamn you, dog!" he yelled, trying to kick the animal, which took off. "Yeah," added Rusty, "I really did like that ol' dog."

We moved slowly into the dance hall and towards another bar but couldn't get within shouting distance. A giant man, who later said he was six feet, eight inches, 290 pounds, stood in three places at the bar, looking at us. He was with a small, shy woman, who didn't talk but smiled a lot. "By gawd!" yelled the man, whose name was John. "If it ain't Larry Mahan!" John stuck out a giant arm, brushing aside a path to the bar for Mahan. Like the small woman with John, I didn't talk but smiled a lot. "Honey," said John, "meet my fren Larry Mahan. Boys, have a beer on me. Buddy, gimme two more beers for this feller and Larry Mahan."

John said he was in the construction business. If he'd had a beard the cowboys wouldn't have jerked him along the bar, though they'd probably have tried. Twice we attempted to slowly edge

Saddle bronc riding at old Cheyenne. Clockwise from opposite: Jim Kelts, a Canadian, busting a wild one; Garald Eichelberger pulling hard; the end of a ride for Gary Tescher; Dan Filippini hangin' on.

away from John and Honey, but each time he saw us and plucked us back, buying another beer for Larry Mahan and this feller. Once Honey said something and John reached down and picked her up, like a baby, holding her up toward the ceiling. "Now you can talk, Honey," he said. "John, I got to go to the rest room," she said.

John and I talked about the rodeo, the construction business in Cheyenne, and whatever else he wanted to talk about, and Mahan sneaked away and watched from a distance while he stood on the dance floor and visited with Don Graham and a girl dressed in a slinky black dress. Mahan had introduced them. They were dancing and Mahan was standing there talking to them. When I got away from the bar, Mahan said, "That's the biggest human being I've ever seen. What did he keep talking to you about, anyway?"

"Oh, he said he was queer and was in love with you and, if necessary, would take you against your will."

"Fun-nee," said Mahan.

The air outside felt good. We leaned against the car again, drinking beer, when the two officers came out. Both looked somewhat disjointed, hats ajar, the short one with his shirttail out. "Now, Larry," said the tall one, "you know you can't drink out on the street. You got to go back in or put the beer away."

The officers turned away and looked at the people outside drinking. "You know, he could put us in jail for drinking out here," said Mahan philosophically. The tall officer saw a guy sitting up against an adjoining building, holding a beer near his face with both hands, looking into the can as if he'd discovered the secret of life. He said nothing to anybody and was just sitting there as if he spent his life leaning against buildings, holding a beer.

"Him," said the tall officer. They got the guy under each arm and literally lifted him into the air. "You can't drink out here," said the short, heavy officer. "Against city ordinance." The guy realized

what was happening and started dragging his feet. "But—but—," he said. "Shut up, boy, you broke the law." Our group, with the Eastern writer missing, went to the Americana and heard Johnny Western, who wrote "Paladin—Have Gun Will Travel," sing in the lounge. Western had once seen Walt Garrison in the audience and dedicated a special song to him called, "I Offered Her My Ring and All She Gave Me Was the Finger."

I supposed the guy the officers carried off would spend the night in jail. The Eastern writer told me he went with the female lawyer from Denver. Both were very drunk when they got back to his motel.

"We woke up the next morning," he said, "and felt like hell, really hung over. I got up and went to the bathroom and when I came back she was sitting up in bed, looking around the room.

" 'Hey, what's that?' she asked me.

" 'A typewriter,' I said.

" 'A typewriter? What you doin' with a typewriter?'

" 'I'm a writer.'

" 'A writer? You . . . you mean you're not a cowboy?'

"She got up, dressed, and slammed the door as she went out, cussing every other breath. I never told her I was a cowboy."

On Saturday morning Mahan got up around ten, late for him, and had breakfast. He'd drawn a saddle bronc named Billy Bob, which he found amusing. One of his best friends is Billy Bob Harris, a realtor with whom he stays when he's in Dallas. He phoned Harris, pointed out the humor in his draw, and said, "You'd love this horse. He looks like you. Ugly, mean as hell." His cold was getting to him so he'd turned out on rides elsewhere and stayed in Cheyenne.

"This can be a good horse," said Mahan, looking down from the top of the chute at Billy Bob, a dun-colored horse that cowboys say is coming into

From hind legs to forelegs, it's a harder bump than a rocking horse.

its own as a bucker. He put an old, worn saddle on, loose, and wouldn't cinch it until later. The horse stirred in the chute. "He's treacherous in the box," said Mahan, easing back off, shoving the horse, which had momentarily trapped his foot against the gate. "The sonuvagun can break your foot if you let him."

Mahan had a 63 on saddle bronc earlier in the week, giving him little chance to make the finals in that event unless he scored extremely high. Everything had to go just right. It had before when he needed it most. This time it didn't. When the gate opened the horse jumped out the gate and then ran toward the center of the arena before it started kicking. When it did buck, Mahan was in perfect timing, spurring in an arc down from the horse's shoulders and then back up again. "You get out of timing with him and you get his full power, which you can't handle," Mahan had said earlier. There was nothing to do but ride it out and hope. At the buzzer he was given a 67. "Dammit," said Mahan, "if he hadn't run out of the box, I'd have had a seventy-five."

Kids entered in the small-fry bucking contest, a special event Mahan would judge, watched him as he jumped off and walked back to the fence. J. D. Romsa, eleven years old, wants to be a rodeo hand more than anything; he wants to be a Larry Mahan. When he was eight, his father, Larry Romsa, started working with him on bulls and horses around their ranch near Laramie. J. D., who attends all the Little Britches rodeos he can, won

Grandchildren at the granddaddy.

the All Around in Deadwood, South Dakota, leading in bareback riding, bull riding, and goat tying. J. D. won a saddle. His father said, proudly, "After he outgrows Little Britches, J. D. will join the High School Rodeo Association, then maybe enter Intercollegiate Rodeo at the University of Wyoming, and then step into the Professional Rodeo Cowboys Association."

"I see that kid around a lot," said Mahan. "He's always asking advice, getting pointers from cowboys. He's pretty serious about this business, even at his age."

"Even for an eleven-year-old," I said.

J. D. Romsa looked very serious. He hadn't reached puberty, gotten out of elementary school, and his father looked at him proudly and said, "All he wants to do is win."

"I hope the kid has fun when he loses, too," I said, as we stood by the fence and watched the remainder of the saddle bronc event. Mahan was

married and had a kid when he was nineteen, trying to make it on the circuit. He now has a boy, a girl, and what is termed a "legal separation" from his wife, who's a Catholic and doesn't believe in divorce. He sees his kids when he's in Dallas and noted, ironically, "My boy likes to play hockey." He stared blankly at the ground for a minute and then easily moved up on the fence when the pickup man came hoofing near us, leading a saddle bronc.

"The girl free-lance writer was looking for you earlier," I told him. "She said she was at the Mayflower and missed you last night."

"Geeze," he said.

"She wanted to find out what beer drinking at the Mayflower was really like," I added.

I'd paid little attention to what was going on in the arena after Mahan's ride, but it got my attention when a cowboy came out, waving his left arm high in the air, on top of a giant Brahma. I remembered somebody had told me about a photographer who, momentarily hypnotized by an onrushing bull, failed to get out of its path and ended up splattered against the fence. The bull threw its rider, then turned and tried to hook him, but Wick Peth ran in, grabbed the bull by its horns, and diverted its attention, as the cowboy got up and scrambled to the fence. The bull lost interest in Peth, circled, and then charged along the fence as cowboys leaped and climbed to the top. Mahan, somewhat casually I thought in retrospect, got up on the fence, but I froze for an instant longer. I don't know why. When the bull was about four feet away, I couldn't decide whether to dodge, running back toward the arena, or jump on the fence. On my last chance I jumped on the fence, feeling the bull brush my seat.

"He would have run over me, right," I said.

"He would have run over you unless he looked at those bloodshot eyes and got scared off," said Mahan.

At that moment I remembered something I'd learned some ten years ago but had somehow for-

Opposite: *Calf roping requires a well-trained horse, one that knows to stop when he sees the lasso hit its mark.* Above: *It's all over—three legs tied, the roper signals for time.*

gotten, or not thought about: just how awesome a bull can be and how small and insignificant a man is beside the animal, which can make him look and feel like a puppet.

It was Mahan's day to sign autographs and, of course, he drew the biggest crowd, signing programs, belts, shirts, pants, scraps of paper, and skin. He was completely surrounded, but you could see the tall, deeply tanned girl with an Indian band around her head watching him, because she was standing on a box, near the front of the crowd. She was a very pretty girl who turned out to be a ski instructor, visiting from Colorado. "She looks like an Indian, so they'll probably tell her to get to the back of the crowd," I told Mahan.

Later that afternoon they were turning out stock and Mahan put his saddle on a bronc and rode it. "I just haven't been satisfied with my riding," he said. "I've been using my old saddle I got ten years ago but it didn't feel right. The practice will help me." I suppose I never thought of Larry Mahan as practicing.

When he was getting ready to leave the arena he ran into some new rodeo fans, who had become avid in a very short time. Among them were a ski instructor, two young blonds from the University of Wyoming, and a singer from the Hitching Post.

"Tough life," I said.

"They just want to know what rodeo is really like," he said, throwing his gear into the trunk of a car.

Mahan was feeling better Sunday for the finals, which he'd made only in bareback. Finals, competition at the top, always made him feel better or, as he said, got his "motor running faster." He would make money but had only a slim chance to win the average. His total of 140 on two horses put him fourth behind coleaders Jack Ward and Royce Smith, both of whom had 144s. The day was warm, summerlike, for a crowd of over 19,000, which gathered in the arena, spilling over from the grandstand

and standing outside the fence. Mahan had drawn a horse named Devil's Dream, a small sorrel mare with four stocking legs, which had possibilities.

When he gets on, Devil's Dream immediately sits down in the chute. It hasn't been a good week for horses in the chute. "Hey," Mahan yells at stock contractor Billy Minick. "You didn't tell me he'd do that!" Minick, a man who seldom smiles, makes a pencil-thin effort, and shrugs. Prodded by cowboys, the horse jumps up, then kicks at the chute, striking back at its own discomfort. It is time. The final time at Cheyenne Frontier Days. Devil's Dream leaps out when the gate opens, kicking up its back heels, and then almost dives into the ground with its head. The horse jerks quickly to the right, then back in midair as it jumps. Mahan holds fast, reacting to the horse's moves and staying in time. I thought it odd. I couldn't think of another sport where you work against something, man against animal, yet together in order to please the judges—even in rodeo, the fickle logic of man. When the buzzer sounds and Mahan jumps off, a pickup man almost runs over him. Earlier that year one had run over saddle bronc champion Monty Henson, breaking his jaw. "You almost blind-sided me," Mahan tells him. "You know better than that."

The judges gave him a 71, leaving him with a 211 on three rides. This would be good for fifth in the average for $480.66. He'd also made $448.62 by tying for third in the second go-round and $75 on a short go-round, so he totaled $1,004.28 for Cheyenne, but he didn't care all that much about the money, just where it put him in the All Around standings. "Boy," said Mahan, "that SOB does try to ali-oop you. He about jerked me out my own asshole. I always think I should have done better but, realistically, with the stock I drew I'm fairly satisfied."

Mahan stayed in the arena to watch Jim Dix and Royce Smith ride and then part of the bull riding. Smith, with a 72, would win the average

You've got to rope him, throw him, and tie him—as fast as you can.

and total $2,676.50 for his week's barebacks. Both Dix and Smith had paid special attention to Mahan's ride and score. But perhaps the most exciting ride of the week was Jerome Robinson, on bull C-13. The bull came out spinning as it tried to drop Robinson into the well. Then it stopped, spun the other way, and bucked and jerked. Robinson, once tilting slightly, regained his balance, and hung on for an 81. "Super," Mahan told him, "super ride."

It was time to go. Mahan didn't want to stay for the finish but couldn't find a car. I borrowed Ringolsby's car, which we planned to leave for him at the airport. "I knew sooner or later you'd be good for something," said Mahan. The ski instructor wanted a ride to Greeley, Colorado. She didn't talk much but just sat there looking pretty.

While attendants got his plane ready, Mahan made three phone calls. I have never seen anybody make so many phone calls. No matter what he's doing, he'll duck out for a phone call to Harris, his girl in Los Angeles, the guy who handles his line of clothes, a real estate man, another rodeo, movie people, his parents, a hotel. His phone bill must run $500 to $600 a month, and I told him he was certain to end up with a cauliflower ear. The ski instructor said she liked to talk on the phone, too, and I said I hated Alexander Graham Bell and didn't like to talk on the phone except late at night, on those rare occasions when I'd had too much to drink.

"Like after we left the Mayflower the other night," I said. "I felt, about 3:00 A.M., that it was most important that I get in touch with Eva Peron. I felt I had something very important to tell her about her country. With much trouble, I got through to somebody in Argentina. I couldn't catch much of what was said to me other than that the person was very, very mad. They slammed down the phone. So I tried to phone Richard Nixon."

We loaded the plane, then got in. The girl looked at me in a very funny way, then said, "You going to leave your briefcase on the wing?" An attendant yelled at Mahan, "When are you going to

Right: Bob L. Walker, the Marlboro man, hazing for a friend. Opposite top and bottom: The steer must be thrown and then wrestled down flat on its side, all four legs extended.

give me some of those shirts?" Mahan told him soon. Soon.

Cheyenne Frontier Days was winding to a close as Mahan lifted the small jet into the air and turned south toward Colorado. At Frontier Park, awards were being presented to winners of each event and All Around winner Eldon Dudley of Perryton, Texas, a steer roper who'd also won money in the calf roping, making him the only cowboy placing in two events. He'd won $3,400. But Don Smith, of Kiowa, Oklahoma, was the biggest winner, taking $4,075 in calf roping go-rounds and the average. Bareback rider Jack Ward also won a lot of money, almost $2,000. Asked if he and his wife were going to celebrate, Ward said, "Yeah, we're going to the laundromat."

And it was over, the Frontier Celebration, the nine days of Cheyenne. Frontier officials and local people felt a little empty. Antique carriages were put away. Stock was loaded. Rusty Riddle hit the road to try to catch Joe Alexander. Scotty Platts and his pals, freshly showered, jumped into their van and took off. Shawn Davis's leg throbbed. John went back to the construction business. Remaining visitors searched Sunday night for the feeling that had been there before, at beer joints, night spots, the Mayflower. But the feeling was gone now. The cowboys were on down the road.

The Laramie Mountains, to the west, were miniatures in pastel, slowly drifting, almost floating away, as Mahan moved his Cessna, with gold paint peeling off its sides, south toward Greeley. His gear and our suitcases had been piled on various assortments of clothes scattered in the back. There was also a small barbell that Mahan used to do curls when he had the chance or thought about it. Mahan often took cowboys along with him when he was going to rodeos and had a sign posted for those sitting in the back seat. "BMA (Bull Mahan Airlines): Turnout fine $1.00 for obscene odors." But he wasn't going to a rodeo this time but rather to Lubbock, Texas, where he'd leave his plane and get a car and drive to Guthrie for filming of *MacKintosh and T. J.* BMA did not fly directly to Guthrie.

Mahan was a relaxed pilot, which I suppose everybody is after they've flown enough. He said he might just do a loop the loop for me, but, not being proud, I begged that he not or I'd have to pay more than a $1.00 turnout fee. An open flight map was across his lap, and he said, "Listen, this really freaks me out. Roy Rogers was my hero when I was a kid. Now we're in the same movie. I met him once in Cheyenne and that was the only time I can ever remember choking up when I talked to somebody. But, hey, Roy Rogers. Terrific!" I thought for a second the ski instructor was going to ask who Roy Rogers was, and I was glad when she didn't.

After Mahan let her off in Greeley, he promised to fly me to Denver, where I had to catch a flight to Los Angeles. I was supposed to have been at the Dallas Cowboys training camp in Thousand Oaks two days before, and I was worried about AWOL

charges from the *Dallas News*, for whom I worked. When he let the ski instructor off, she said he was wonderful to bring her back, the flight was wonderful, and that she hoped I didn't leave my briefcase on the wing anymore. As he lifted the small jet and turned for Denver, he said, "Tell you what. I don't want to fly all the way to Lubbock by myself. So I'm not going to stop in Denver. I'm taking you with me."

Imagining the problems involved in getting from Lubbock to Los Angeles, I asked him if he knew of any job openings. Traffic crawled along the interstate below. "It must tell on a man's body to drive eighty thousand miles a year rodeoing."

"True," he said, "it's tough for a guy down there to have a chance against somebody flying his own plane. But if you're going for a championship you forget a lot of discomfort. Nowadays, the guys in the championship race drive but they also hop a lot of commercials. But, hell, if you're young you fear no schedule. I know. I've been down that road.

"Even when I was growing up in Brooks [now incorporated into Salem, Oregon] I always had a lot of hustle. It's just my nature. My dad ran a riding saddle club. He had a couple of acres and about eight or nine horses. I'd ride everything. At first I'd go out and get on these two calves we had. Then I'd try and ride our milk cow. I was always riding something and I don't think I ever really thought about being anything but a cowboy.

"I went to the kid rodeos. My dad and mom separated, but when I was about twelve, my mom and stepfather took me to Redmond, Oregon, for a kid rodeo. I won the calf roping and they gave me six dollars and a buckle. I still have that buckle. Funny, I remember that better than some things that happened when I was winning a championship."

He laughed. "There was this ol' feller I used to hang around named Sterling Green. He did a little bit of everything. When I was about sixteen, Ster-

ling bought me an RCA permit. He had this old one-ton truck. He took me to this little town in Oregon where I was going to get into the team roping, bull and bareback riding. I hit it big, won the bull riding, and got about two hundred and forty dollars.

"The deal was that Sterling got a third of my winnings, so there went eighty dollars. I had to pay my entrance fees, so there went about eighty dollars more. Sterling happened to mention he had a chance to buy these calves at eighty dollars each. He said it would be a good investment for me and that he would take care of my calf and I could sell it later for one hundred and twenty dollars.

"Well, one day about a year later, I went to see Sterling and asked him about my calf. 'Son,' he said, 'I ain't seen that calf since I turned it out one day to feed.'"

It did stretch the imagination, but Mahan was once a very conservative young man. He wore a crewcut, looking like a Marine recruit, but obviously had the talent. He earned the $1,000 that enabled him to trade his permit in for a full-fledged RCA card in 1963. He won $5,641 that first year, $12,009 the second, and the bull riding championship the third. The rest is history, sometimes bordering on legend. Mahan took six All Around titles, five in a row, and barring injuries there is no telling how many more he might have won.

"Things were pretty tight financially when I started," he said. "I remember once my wife and I had to stop and work, picking grapes, to make money to get on down the road. I thought right then and there this wasn't for me. I *had* to win." He did win, and winning opened up the world for him; life in a kind of cubicle suddenly became so wide and broad he couldn't see the end in any direction. He let his hair grow longer, changed his life-style. In the process he was very instrumental in opening up rodeo.

"When I started in rodeo I had no other interests," he said. "As I told you before, my life revolved around competing and winning. Then, I started getting a look at the outside world. I met a lot of real people, very interesting people who had nothing to do with rodeo.

Two views of bulldogging: one cowboy's off target, one's on.

"The change started when Jantzen asked me to join the athletes it was using for the clothes commercials. I didn't know anything. But these athletes I met were super; they'd been around. I met people like Don Meredith, Bobby Hull, and Lance Alworth.

"Jantzen sent us to Europe, to Spain, to film commercials. One day we were at this real elaborate hotel and club. I was just sitting there by the pool. No, dammit, I didn't have on cutoffs. Anyway, the last thing in the world I wanted then was to attract attention. But I got up, snuck up on the diving board, and dove in. I missed a little, scraping my back on the side of the pool. It hurt like hell.

"Apparently, this very proper Englishman had been watching me. When I climbed out, all skinned, he came over and said, 'Say, old chap, you seem a bit hurt. Might I help you to the first aid station?' People were looking and I wanted to hide under the grass. I probably had tears in my eyes from the pain but I just said, 'Oh, no. No. No. It's nothing. Didn't hurt a bit, ha-ha-ha.' As he started to walk off, I said, 'Sir, maybe you could tell me where the first aid station is in case I do need it.'

"Well, being around those guys from other sports, it dawned on me that I might turn more people onto rodeo. It would mean so much more not only to me but the sport. I could just see unlimited potential because just about everybody who took time to see a rodeo liked it. Hell, I just loosened up."

Mahan became rodeo ambassador, a publicity agency of one. His hair was stylish, his clothes turned-on. He got around and made friends outside of rodeo. Some people in rodeo had difficulty understanding him. He was authentic but he was also rhinestone. Jim Shoulders gave him a hard time and Mahan laughs about one particular episode, though admits he wasn't laughing at the time.

He was told a couple of reporters wanted to talk to him in this room. When Mahan entered the room three bulldoggers grabbed him and held him down. "I had no idea what was happening," he said. "Then the door opens and in walks Jim Shoulders, grinning. He had a knife and walked over to me. I was scared to death. I had no idea what he was going to do. He laughed and said, 'If you going to wear your hair down to your neck, you ought to wear your pants up to your knees.' Then he cut my pants off at the knees. I went around like that the rest of the day. But I was relieved."

Mahan said Shoulders might be the reason he had the bald spot on the back of his head. "He was always grabbing me by the hair back there," he said. But Shoulders once remarked at a banquet, "If Larry Mahan hadn't come along when he did, rodeo would have been in a lot of trouble." It took others longer to admit this.

"Some people don't think he ought to be doing some of the things he does," Jerome Robinson said. "They might not like him because of it. But I do. Everybody ought to appreciate what he's done for the sport. By promoting himself, he promoted rodeo and made money for us all."

"I've decided once and for all," said Mahan,

checking the air map in his lap. "I'm taking you to Lubbock with me. I won't let you out in Denver."

"I'll jump if you don't."

"Well, maybe I will, maybe I won't. You just have no adventure left in you. Listen, this picture is a cool part. It's not heavy or anything, but a lot of people have been working in the industry for years to get a part like this. I play this college type who figures he knows what it takes to run a ranch. And Roy Rogers. Imagine, Roy Rogers!"

Mahan, because of who he was, got bit parts in movies such as *J. W. Coop* with Cliff Robertson and *The Honkers* with James Coburn and Slim Pickins. Being himself in *The Great American Cowboy* opened doors to being somebody else.

He lives most of the year in Beverly Hills now, taking lessons from Hollywood acting coach Vincent Chase. One day earlier that year he was up at 6:30 A.M. and into his 1963 Jaguar half an hour later. He drives like he lives. He pressed the accelerator, speeding the car to sixty in a thirty-five mile zone, as he headed out Hollywood Boulevard and turned onto the Ventura Freeway. He wheeled around a Mercedes, dovetailing, and said, "These people are crazy out here the way they drive.... You know, I'm very serious about acting. I've talked to a lot of people in different sports and they tell me how tough it is to replace that kick, the natural high you get out there doing your thing on the field. But I get the same high out of acting, the same kick. It's a great head trip to become a character and make people believe you're him, to believe it yourself."

Mahan was driving out the freeway to Thousand Oaks, where Universal Productions was filming *Six Pack Annie*. Often when I'm in Southern California I get disgusted about the way man has screwed it up. The ocean is there, and part of the Sierra Madre mountain range, a natural beauty. But it has all been grayed by smog and sliced by cement and freeways, going many directions. Now, it is real make-believe.

The Jaguar, which Mahan had bought for $2,500, spending another $1,500 to fix it up, edged up to sixty-five, seventy, zigzagging in traffic, which would be bumper to bumper by 9:00 A.M. "A lot of guys," he continued, "say you shouldn't study acting, but I don't agree. Working with Vincent Chase is an experience in itself. He's probably the smartest human being I've ever met, and he has more insight into life than anybody I know. You have to do a great deal of exploring life, of exploring yourself, in acting."

Mahan braked and the tires spun as he pulled into Glenmoor Stables, a 300-acre layout outside of Thousand Oaks. Once many of the big television Westerns had been made there but plans were to turn it into an apartment complex. Television doesn't make big Westerns anymore.

"*Annie*," said Mahan, "isn't heavy. It's the story of this sexy Georgia girl who goes to Miami to try and strike it rich so she can save her aunt's restaurant from going under back home. I play a guy named Bustis, who chases her all over the place and, shall we say, tries to distract her."

The first time they filmed the sequence, calling for a chase in pickups, it was uneventful, so they tried it again. The second time, the girl drove her pickup into a mud hole, spun around, and almost turned over. Mahan swerved to miss her and almost ran into a tree.

"Great!" screamed director Fred Throen. "Use it! Print it!"

Mahan left at 3:30 P.M., drove home like a madman, showered, shaved, changed, and hustled to the CBS studios to film a guest appearance on the Dinah Shore show. The other guests were Lawrence Welk, Judy Collins, and Bill Daly and Ellen Corby (the Waltons). The taping went well and everybody asked him what it was really like being a cowboy. He wanted to know what it was really like being an actor. That day he left the taping at 10:30 P.M., got up at 8:00 A.M. the next day, and caught a flight to Phoenix where his clothes collection was being shown, then picked up his own plane at the airport and flew back to Los Angeles, where he caught a commercial flight to Salem, because he wanted to talk to his mother about a real estate deal.

Mahan wears you out trying to keep up with him, I thought, as we neared Denver. "I don't like to be tied down to any particular world," he said. "I enjoy life more now because I taste so many different life-styles. It's a helluva trip. I keep meeting different kinds of people. I'm in L.A. one day, Cheyenne the next. I like to rodeo as much as ever, but I can pick my shots now. When I do stay away too long I get to missing it. As I said, acting should help me keep from missing it when I get too old.

"Right now I've put myself in a position to make a lot of money. I think I'm going to be able to retire my old man and my mom. My old man lives in Phoenix and all he's ever done in his life is work his ass off. He's been wanting to graze Paint horses, so I'm going into the horse business so he can do it.

"My mom has a good head on her shoulders. She does a good job for me in real estate. I want her to do that or just do nothing, whatever she wants. I want both of them to enjoy the rest of their lives, like I'm doing."

A small plane coming in before us at the Denver airport had problems with a landing gear and scooted on its belly. Mahan was diverted to another runway, so he banked and almost went upside down turning ninety degrees. I leaned toward him as much as I could to keep the plane straight. Finally, the runway was right there and he leveled the wings just before the wheels hit the ground. We bounced, then eventually rolled to a standstill. "That," he said, "is a cowboy landing."

Mahan made three phone calls, ate cheese crackers, drank a Coke while they gassed up his plane. Then he took off for Lubbock. It would be a long time before the cowboys driving out of Cheyenne got to Denver.

After Cheyenne, some cowboys get on down the road a little slower.

Chapter 3:
THE NEW BREED

When I was a kid, everybody played baseball. That's where the hundred thousand dollars was. Kids tried to be like DiMaggio. Now there's money in other sports. There's much more in rodeo, though only a small percentage get their hands on it. Tom Ferguson got his hands on a hundred thousand dollars in one year.
—Jim Shoulders

The way I look at it, we're the kind of guys other guys want to be. I don't mean just in the rodeo sense but in the general sense that we're doing what we want to do and nobody gave us anything.
—Monty Henson

I can remember being in elementary school. When they had "Show and Tell" I'd always bring this picture of me riding a bull. When those kids saw that picture, I guarantee you they wouldn't fool with me.
—Bobby Steiner, bull riding champion, 1974

We had been flying more than three hours, most of the time into a twenty-five-mile-per-hour head wind, but finally, in late afternoon, just before us lay the mountains, majestic and ominous against the darkening sky. The mountain range, a spur of the Rockies, rose from an elevation of 3,670 feet to 8,751 feet, just to our right at Guadalupe Peak, highest point in Texas. Ahead was a natural opening between two sections of mountains, two peaks, that the Mexicans called *El Paso del Norte*, the Pass of the North. I was afraid the pilot, Don Gay, might try to fly his Piper Cherokee directly through the opening between the peaks and was relieved when he veered slightly to the southwest, climbed over a smaller section of mountains, and then turned directly toward El Paso.

Don was considered one of the good pilots among the handful of rodeo performers who fly their own planes; however, he had admitted earlier, when we hit turbulence, "I would show you some tricks up here and try to scare you, but, frankly, it would also scare the hell out of me. This isn't a car and I ain't ready for too much trial and error."

"How long have you been flying?"

"About two years, counting the time with an instructor in the plane. Otherwise, not too long by myself. Actually, outside of taking daddy and my girl up for a little ride, you're my first long-range passenger. Does flying in small planes bother you?"

"Not really that much. But about twelve years ago, I was flying from Dallas to Fayetteville, Arkansas. They were still using the old DC-3s then. That's the same plane that flew the Burma Run. Anyway, one of the two engines went out. The plane dipped, then leveled off again, and was okay. But it was scary. When we landed I asked the pilot about the engine going out. He scratched his head and said he couldn't figure it out. I asked him why. He said, 'Well, that was the good engine.'"

"Well," said Don, "this is our *only* engine."

But the trip from Dallas to El Paso had gone well as we followed the main highway below, setting down once, in Midland-Odessa, for fuel (eaten up more quickly than usual because of the strong head wind). Don was up that night at the annual rodeo in El Paso, the largest city on the United States–Mexico border, lying directly across the Rio Grande from Juarez. I've always liked El Paso, with its blend of old Spanish and modern architecture—a pleasant mixture of the sleepy, restful look with the progressive, the metropolitan.

Don's schedule was hectic, as usual. After the rodeo he had to return to Dallas in order to catch a commercial flight to Billings, Montana, where he was guest speaker at a sports banquet. Then he had to return to Dallas to receive a special award for athletic achievement.

Opposite top: *Canadian champion Brian Claypool about to lose; Wick Peth is closing in.* Right: *Lyle Sankey going after the money.* Far right: *Donnie Gay and Wick Peth discussing tactics.*

100

High winds and storm possibilities were forecast, and there was some question as to whether we would be able to return in the Piper or catch a commercial flight, which was leaving around 2:00 in the morning.

I thought how misleading Don Gay's general appearance of vulnerability was. He is a small, young man, five feet, seven inches, 145 pounds, but he has a reputation for toughness; he was, after all, the World Champion Bull Rider, a man excelling in a most dangerous, rugged event.

Don is a member of the new breed, a group of young cowboys who, though they are making a great deal more money, seem to attempt to emulate the style and success of some of the old-timers, while trying to live down, to underplay, their predecessors' reputation for rowdiness. But trouble, though far from prevalent, still comes at times, and today's cowboys are usually more than able to take care of it.

"Don," bull rider Don Graham told me, "is what we call a bantie rooster. He might be small, but you don't fool with him, because he'll knock your head off."

"Listen, one thing I don't want is the reputation of being a little tough," said Don. "I want to stay away from trouble. But that doesn't mean some dude can push me around because I'm small and wear a cowboy hat."

Cowboys told me a story about a particular time when somebody tried to push Don around in Springfield, Illinois, a story he somewhat reluctantly admitted was true.

"Now, that was one time I tried to walk away,"

said Don. "I honestly tried, but I guess there was no way out."

The bar seemed to be closing in, the atmosphere tightening around them. The three of them had stopped there, near the Springfield airport, to kill time before their flight. When they'd first entered and sat down, conversations stopped as people stared at them, their cowboy hats and boots. The cowboys felt the hostility and knew it wasn't their kind of place. Don Gay went to the rest room, and when he got back to the table, he leaned over the table and told Mike Bandy and Gary Barton, "Now I *know* we better cut out. They're selling heroin in the john."

Each made his way to the exit, but a tall young man, wearing a big top hat with traces of rouge on his cheeks, watched Don and spoke as he went past. "Well, hiii, Tex." "Shut up, fag."

Don started out the door and the tall man grabbed him by the arm and spun him around. "What's your name, Tex?" "My name ain't Tex."

The tall man, gaining confidence, reached out and grabbed the brim of Don's hat and pulled him forward. "You arrrre, toooo. Your name is Tex."

Don jerked his head back, straightened his hat, and drew his right back to slug the tall man, when somebody grabbed him from behind, wrestling him around and shoving him a few steps forward. "You're not going to hit him," said the guy, who then smashed Don with a haymaker, sending him backward against the wall as the tall man clapped his hands, wildly.

For an instant Don wasn't sure what happened,

Opposite: *Champion bull rider Donnie Gay getting ready.* Left: *A bull rider putting in his eight brutal seconds under a cloudy sky. The clown is Wick Peth.* Above: *Donnie Gay and Guy Barth.*

only that the wall stopped him, and he later admitted, "If the wall hadn't been there, I'd probably have been knocked clean out into the street." He shook his head, his eyes clearing enough to see what appeared to be a Crazy coming toward him. The guy's eyes were wide, as if they were about to pop out, and his face was drawn.

Donnie, obviously hurt, wasn't about to let on. "Friend," he said. "You just made a mistake. Because if that's the best one you got, you better get yourself a lot of help."

Planting his feet, Don caught the guy on the left cheekbone with his right, causing him to stumble to the side, momentarily dazed. Just as the guy was regaining his balance Don swung from the floor, connecting at the temple and flipping the guy backward onto the floor. The guy tried to put his hands over his face, but Don was on top of him, pinning him to the floor by putting his knees on the guy's long hair. He slammed him across the face twice as the crowd moved closer. Don was kicked in the side once, twice, but wouldn't let the guy up. Then he thought his head was exploding as a bottle was smashed across the back of it.

Don almost lost consciousness and for an instant didn't really know what was happening, though he kept striking the man he'd pinned to the floor.

"Hey, man, let him up," said a voice behind him. "Let him up."

Don heard the words, which seemed far away and then closer. "Find me the SOB who hit me from behind with that bottle and I'll trade him this guy!" Don said. Suddenly, he felt himself being lifted bodily from the floor, into the air and down on his feet. Recalling the impression later he said, "I look up and there was Godzilla, this huge, hairy man, who looked like an ape."

"Did you hit me with that bottle?" asked Don, hoping Godzilla would say no.

"No. But I'd beat the hell out of you."

"Well, who did hit me with the bottle?"

"Listen, cowboy, I don't like the way you jumped that guy on the floor, but I also don't dig the odds here. You're outnumbered, about to get killed by these people. I better help you outta here."

"I don't know who you are or where you came from, but I agree to that."

"Listen, cowboy, I dig fighting. Maybe another day we'll get it on. But now, you got to get outta here."

They walked outside as the crowd stood in silence. Godzilla went back in, and Don looked for Bandy and Barton. When he found them, he said, "Where the hell you been? I got in trouble in there and couldn't find my backup."

"What?" asked Bandy.

"I like to got killed in a fight in there."

"Oh, we were out here protecting the women and children."

"Sure," Don said, starting a gradual descent into the El Paso area, "I fly off the handle sometimes. Everybody does. But when *we* do it, it sticks in somebody's mind. People have this impression that we all go around in pickups, chewing Copenhagen and staying in dance halls and beer joints. You get off work and you want to relax. We do, too. We just go boogie, not to the Silver Spur Beer Joint.

"It bothers me that a lot of people think rodeo's a circus. Hell, we're athletes just like football or basketball players. Anybody who thinks we're not ought to try it."

Don Gay had started slowly that year, though he would gain momentum as usual on down the road and stay on top of his specialty, bull riding. Larry Mahan once called Don "the toughest bull rider ever to nod for the gate." Certainly, he is a most unusual man for his age—twenty-two—and could surpass even the legendary Jim Shoulders, one of his boyhood idols, who won seven bull riding titles, and Harry Tompkins, who won five.

When he was twenty, Don was runner-up for

Rarely used, because it's rarely needed: the cattle prod.

the bull riding title to Bobby Steiner, losing at the National Finals Rodeo. But he won the championship the following two years, setting an all-time record by winning $34,850 for the event in 1975 (plus $9,000 in Winston bonus money and monies won in saddle bronc, for a total of $48,234). He did this despite missing forty-five days due to a torn groin and thigh muscle.

"That about drove me crazy," he said. "I go mad just staying in one place more than three days. Being around that long I drove everybody else crazy, too."

Success has been a landslide for him at an age where most young men are nearing the end of college and planning what they will do in the future. "I'm twenty-two years old with only a high school education," said Don. "I make from thirty to sixty thousand dollars a year, and I don't know many others my age who make that kind of money. I do what I want to do when I want to do it. I don't have anybody to answer to but myself. Nothing was given to me. I earned it all by myself. So this ain't so bad.

"I always knew exactly what I wanted to do and did it. Now, I want to make as much money as I can as quickly as I can. I want to be able to do whatever I want and buy whatever I want."

He has World Bullriding titles, an airplane, a Lincoln Continental (for which he swapped a red Cadillac he'd worn out on the rodeo road), and he *is* somebody. But there is always more. It is people's nature to want more, and this is especially true with a competitive nature such as Don's. He plans to concentrate more on saddle bronc riding, with hopes of combining this event with his specialty and taking the All Around title. And at his age, the book is open on what he might accomplish, not just because of his age but also his talent, persistence, and durability in an event that often takes heavy tolls.

When Jerome Robinson, another top hand at bull riding, attended 124 rodeos in a single year, observers were amazed. But in 1974, Don attended a record 169 in 365 days. "It was just drive," he recalled. "I was obsessed with winning. Bobby Steiner had beaten me at the NFR the year before, and I was determined to win, to do everything humanly possible to win."

Oddly, the first year he won the bull riding title had started out as a downer, perhaps the low point of his career. "My ass was dragging," he said. "I'd spent every buck I made trying to get down the road and win the title. It all went to no avail.

"Bobby beat me and I got to feeling it wasn't fair because he had the backing. His folks bought him a plane and I was still going along the hard way then. But I look back on it all now and know it wasn't Bobby's fault he had the advantages; and, after all, he still had to get up on those bulls.

"Bobby was a helluva bull rider. If he came back today, he'd still be the man to beat."

(Bobby Steiner retired after winning the bull riding title in 1973, joining his father Tommy in the stock contracting business. But once, when we talked, he said, "I knew I couldn't afford to be bucked off that year, because Donnie was right on my tail. I tell you, though, if I'd stayed active for many more years, with all that travel, they'd have had to put me on the funny farm.

"But I wouldn't trade my belt buckle for the rest of my years.")

"Like I said, I was having a bad time," continued Don. "I didn't do anything early that year and then won the first go-round in Denver. Well, all I needed to do to win the rodeo was ride this ol' bull we used to own. It was one I'd practiced on at home when I was fourteen. I knew him perfectly. Sure enough, he did just what I expected him to do, but he thowed me off. I didn't win any money for two months after that.

"My attitude got to be awful, and I just didn't give a damn. 'You got that attitude and there's not a damn thing I can do for you,' my daddy told me."

Don recalled that he hit bottom during a long drive from San Antonio to Long Beach, California, while there was a gas shortage. He ran out of gas late one night in a small Arizona town and had to spend the night in his car. "Well, what do you know," he told himself. "Now everything's happened. Only way to go is up."

He continued to rodeo and successfully rode Ringeye, the Bull of the Year in 1974. "That made me feel better and I just kept going until I worked myself out of it," he said. "When I'm going good, I go to a lot of rodeos. When I'm going bad, I go to more."

Champions in all sports have a flair, a knack of doing their best against the best. At the 1974 National Finals Rodeo, where the crowd is all aficionados and the stock is the rankest, Don came out of the chutes on Tiger, a small, striped animal that had never been ridden at that time. Tiger was unpredictable; it might turn and spin in either direction. The animal immediately jumped some four feet off the ground and, kicking, jerked to the right. It bucked, then started spinning to the left, perhaps more quickly than any other bull. This strategy had always ridded it of the man on its back. This time it didn't. Don was in control, if indeed one is ever really in control of a bull. He hung on until the buzzer and scored a 94. At the State Fair Rodeo, in Dallas, with his friends and neighbors watching, he stayed atop Number 167, another animal that had not been ridden successfully, for a winning score of 90. And in 1976, he rode Panda Bear in Tulsa for a winning 84. Panda Bear, another Bull of the Year, had been ridden only three times. Don accounted for two of those rides.

"I guess it's like a batter wanting to hit against the best," said Don. "If I played Major League baseball I'd want to face a Catfish Hunter or a Nolan Ryan, not just some humpty that everybody hit."

When Don rides, you can see the dogged determination, which many feel makes him a champion; and yet, there is more. Because of the power of a bull, most riders cannot avoid a jerky motion, but

Opposite top: *James Ward.* Right *and* far right: *One for the bull.*

I have seen Don become one with the animal, which of course is working with all its might against him. This can only be done with perfect timing, coordination, and control.

"I try to ride like that, to almost become part of the animal's movement," he said. "But you can get tapped off quick by taking that approach. I do think you can come nearer doing it when you ride a lot and try to learn something from every bull, a good one, a sorry one, whatever. You learn enough and sometimes everything will just happen, fall together, and you're one with the animal.

"I guess my style is a combination. I admire three guys—Jim Shoulders, Harry Tompkins, and Larry Mahan. Shoulders was around when I was growing up, and I learned a lot from him and my daddy. The thing I got from Shoulders was determination and 'try.' You see pictures of him riding and you can just see all that 'try' in his face. He wasn't about to be bucked off. He never gave up.

"Tompkins was probably as talented as Jim but sometimes he'd check out [jump off] in a jam. He had this fluid motion, though, that I like. Larry had class. You've got to have some class while riding. If you don't, you can get beat by a guy looking good on a worse bull or horse."

Don comes off brash and cocky to some people and also has a great deal of showmanship in him, though it is more contrived than natural.

Jerome Robinson, a college graduate who is six years Don Gay's senior, recalled years ago when he was competing at the Mesquite Rodeo, produced and operated by Don's father, former rodeo contestant Neal Gay. At that time Don was still a kid in school. "Donnie came up to me before I rode and said, 'Let it out on this bull. I'm betting on you.'

"'Don't throw your money away,' I told him.

"'Well,' he told me, 'I been betting with these amateur guys around here. They say you won't last one jump out of the chute; I bet you last two.'"

Don told me he had matured and was still maturing. "I do come off conceited sometimes," he

continued. "I *am* confident. But, say somebody comes up to me and asks, 'Just how good are you? What's your secret?' Well, I'd probably say, 'I'm pretty good. My past record speaks fairly well for me. The reason is that I had the opportunity to learn, growing up at my daddy's place in Mesquite. And I took advantage of that opportunity.'

"But if somebody puts it to me like, 'You're the luckiest SOB I ever seen. How in the hell do you do it?' Well, I'd say, 'Because I'm better than anybody

Clockwise from below: *Wick Peth watching Russell Welch at Cheyenne Frontier Days; Rod Staudinger looking like he's gone; Skipper Voss keeping an eye on things at the Calgary Stampede.*

else.' I wouldn't stand up in front of some TV camera and say that, like Muhammad Ali, but if it's put to me a certain way, I'll do it around people.

"It gets some people's goat. So what? If it makes them mad they'll lose concentration and give me an advantage. Listen, I'm lucky. You have to be. I feel lucky, believe I'll be lucky, and I usually am."

Robinson said Don was the "Ali of rodeo," and others agree. He's a flashy dresser, whether in rodeo clothes or in mod tux for a banquet. But in the arena he favors silk shirts and engraved black leather chaps.

"We need more showmanship in rodeo," he said. "But it's difficult for me because when I show off it makes my girl and friends sick. They know it's a ham job done for the people in the grandstand."

When Don heard his winning score in Lubbock, Texas, he tossed his hat high into the air as fans cheered wildly. His girl friend, Terry, whom he planned to marry, said, "That's sick looking. Everybody'll think you're just a show-off."

"The cowboys know what I'm doing. I don't like to do it either, but in order for people to remember you, you've got to do something different instead of just get off, duck your head, and walk shyly back to the chutes."

Don has been known to leap off a bull after a good ride, then raise both hands in the air, Ali fashion. Actually, bull rider Gary Leffew got him started doing that at his first NFR. It means "hot," a "hot man," or "hot rider."

"Gary was doing it that year and said I should, too," recalled Don. "I was eighteen at the time, and he started calling me Baby Hot. In the 1972 finals Gary broke his leg and I kinda took over the sign. I used to use it every time I made a good ride. Now I save it for super rides."

We were through the mountains and coming down into the El Paso airport, smoothly. After we landed, Don phoned Hertz Rent-a-Car to pick him up at the auxiliary airfield, where they'd fuel his plane and make it ready to go again. He checked on the probable weather for around 11:00 P.M., when we expected to leave, and told me, "Don't know yet. They say it still might be bad. We'll check again."

At the main terminal the girl at the Hertz counter wanted everything but our blood counts. She also could not find a map of El Paso and Don said, seriously, "Okay, I demand to see O. J. [Simpson]."

The girl did not smile but asked what was in his rigging bag.

"Guns," I said.

She looked at Don, at his cowboy hat, and said, "You *will* be checking back in here tonight, sir?"

"Don't know. We're crossing the border with these guns and might not ever come back. But I'm sure Hertz has insurance on this car."

"Sir, you can't do that."

"O. J. could."

"Well, sir, you just can't do that."

"Can't you see me on that TV commercial, like O. J.," said Don. "I'd be running through the terminal, like he does. Then I'd trip over my rigging bag and knock myself out cold."

We drove along the freeway, looking for a shopping center in order to buy a flashlight. Don wanted one so that he could see the instrument panel better in case we had problems flying back. He continued to drive very fast after we got off the freeway, missed a turn into the shopping center, skidded into a service station, bolted back in the other direction, fishtailed as he entered the parking lot, and came to a screeching halt by a drugstore.

It was the first time I could remember buckling my seat belt. "God," I said, "I feel safer in the plane."

Don Gay just grinned, humming along with the radio.

Once, in Georgetown, three girls gathered around a contestant, who was not a big rodeo star at the time. He knew one of them, and they struck up a conversation. Just before he was to ride, the two of them disappeared into his van, parked on the grounds. They came out thirty minutes later. He tucked in his shirttail, ran for the chutes, mounted, and finished second in the event. It was not clear at the time whether the girl finished first or second.

Two young girls, perhaps eighteen to twenty, waited by the refreshment stand at the rodeo arena in El Paso and watched cowboys check into the nearby office to pay their entry fees. It was still early, and only a handful of fans had arrived. But the girls, very carefully, checked each man's buckle, looking for signs of a champion, rather than an ol' boy who just gets on down the road.

"Hey, look at that one," said one of the girls, eyeing Don Gay as he went into the office.

"Gracious. Gracious!" said the other, giggling.

Camp followers in rodeo are like those in most other fields of athletics and music. They are good, bad, ugly, pretty, devoted, on a lark. "Well," one told me, "the thing about cowboys is that they're predictable. I mean, they're here for a night or so, and when you go out you *know* they'll be happy, turned on.

"You see, I've dated some of these football players out here [at the University of Texas at El Paso], and my, my, they can be moody. Sometimes you have a good time and other times they're down or so moody they just sit there, all wrapped up in themselves."

"Yeah," said the other girl, "with them cowboys you know what you'll get."

"Or not get," laughed her friend, looking for that big, ornate championship belt buckle.

Don came out of the office and the girls moved near him as he used a pay phone on the wall, checking to see when he was up at another rodeo. He hung up the phone, tipped his hat to the girls, then walked with me over to the refreshment counter. We stood there, eating cold hot dogs on stale buns and drinking Cokes. The girls edged next to us, obviously trying to get Don's attention or, if you will, see their reflection in his big belt buckle.

"I tell you we were scared to death," said one, talking loudly so that we could hear. "I mean about that bomb scare at our office building yesterday."

"Well," answered the other, smiling at Don, "you know there are some real crazy people in this world, 'specially around here. I mean, they plant a bomb and it blows us all up. Friends and enemies. They might put them anywhere. They are communists, or, what is that crazy Irish bunch—revolutionaries. Why, they put one here in this place and you can imagine what it would do to the people and animals."

"Don't worry about a bomb here," I told her, finishing my hot dog. "I just ate it."

We went over to talk to Phil Lyne as he walked out of the office. Phil, perhaps one of the best all-around performers to ever go down the road, had won the All Around title in 1973, then said he'd had enough travel and went back to his ranch near Three Rivers, Texas, settling down with his wife and baby.

"Well, while the baby is still young," he said, "I decided to come back a little this year and maybe take a shot at the title, if things go right."

Phil can rope, bulldog, ride bulls, and do about anything else he sets his mind to. "He's just liable to win the thing again, despite the fact he's been away so long [two years]," said Don.

There is no pretense about Phil Lyne. Dressed in rough-out denims, his features are dark and clear and his manner is straightforward. "Things are clear to me," he said, when we talked about a particular mounting controversy in rodeo. "There's the honest, right way, and there's the wrong way. People going the wrong way can fool themselves, thinking or rationalizing that something is right."

"Try the hot dogs," I said.

"I'm an expert," said Don. "I've eaten more hot dogs than anybody in America. On a scale of one to ten, I'd rate these about a five—like those two girls over there."

We moved down the hall, into the chutes, through the gate, and into the soft dirt of the arena. A very large policeman was guarding the gate, keeping noncowboys from entering. A cowboy started walking through with a photographer, who was taking publicity pictures.

"Hey, boy, you don't come through here," said the policeman, moving in front of the gate, putting a hand on his pistol.

"Well, officer, we're doing some pictures. I have a badge. I'm a photographer."

"No, you ain't coming through here."

"Listen, he's with me," said the cowboy. "We're doing a rodeo commercial."

"Well," said the policeman, easing off, "all right, if he's with you. But you're responsible for him, not me."

"That officer looks like he'd blow your head off," said Don.

"Or his foot," said Lyne.

We were in the arena, leaning against a gate. Phil said, "Donnie, how's Neal doin'?"

"Oh, fine. Just fine. But Daddy's ornery as ever."

Lyne started laughing. He asked Don if he remembered a cowboy we'll call Sam Hargrove.

"Yeah," said Don, also laughing. "Sam is a mean sonuvagun when he gets some liquor in him, but I guess my daddy'd have taken him apart, if Pete hadn't already done it."

Pete Gay, Don's older brother, is a top bull and rodeo hand in his own right, having twice made the National Finals. He's considered one of the toughest guys on the circuit when he's riled up.

"Sam always riles people up," said Don.

Guys you don't fool around with? Well, don't fool around with Roy Duvall, Bob Perkins, or Pete Gay.
—Don Graham

Above (left to right): *Scotty Platts, Jack Ward, Ben Calhoun, and Chick Elms at Cheyenne, taping up and talking about some good times.*

One time, when we were kids, I got real mad at Pete. So I picked up this two-by-four and hit him upside the head as hard as I could. He just grinned at me.
—Don Gay

Pete Gay and Bobby Steiner hadn't been in the fight at the motel bar during the rodeo in Houston's Astrodome. But now they sat there, over a beer, and mulled over the situation. Pete is a low-built young man, five feet, eight inches, around 180 pounds. He has short legs, but his upper body, extremely muscular, is like that of a man five inches taller and thirty pounds heavier. He has a round face, pug nose, and perpetual grin. Pete laughs easily, is easygoing, and he gets along well with everybody. Unless . . .

Sam Hargrove, six feet, two inches, 202 pounds, and about thirty-two years of age, had been drinking, causing trouble, and yet, somehow, had avoided the police when they came earlier and arrested a number of brawlers in the bar. Sam, who sometimes worked for Neal Gay, had recently joined Pete to win the wild horse races in Fort Worth. He wasn't a bad guy, but, with enough pop in him, it was as if he were under a full moon.

"Hey, Sam, how's it goin'," said Pete. "When you think they'll let those ol' boys out of jail?"

Sam drew back and slammed Pete across the face, knocking him out of his chair and onto the floor. Pete got up, walked back to the table, looked at Sam, and said, "Now, Sam, did you mean to do that?"

Sam let him have it again, catching Pete squarely on the nose with a right cross, mashing it all over his face, and sending him staggering backward four, five steps. Pete walked back to the table, looked at Steiner, and said, "Bobby, I think he meant it."

Pete, swinging upward at the taller Hargrove, caught him under the chin, flipping his head backward. Sam's knees buckled, but he stayed upright long enough to catch a left, which sent him crashing to the floor. He got up swinging, but Pete ducked and charged, butting Sam in the stomach as they both fell to the floor. They got up again, exchanging punches, with neither trying to block the other's fists. Pete, more mechanical, slammed a fist into Sam's side, then followed with another roundhouse, which caught him just below the eye. Sam fell over a chair, hit the floor, and became quiet.

"I just don't know why Sam would go and do a thing like that, Bobby," said Pete.

"Neither do I," said Bobby, "but we'd best get out of here before the cops come again."

Just after they'd gotten into the car and started to drive away, a staggering shadow of a man came out of the bar and waved them down. It was Sam Hargrove, his face and clothes looking as if he'd been attacked by a wild animal.

"I guess we showed those boys who was boss," said Sam, getting into the car. "Let's get out of here."

Pete and Bobby looked at one another blankly. After they'd driven to safety, Bobby noticed Pete's nose was in a mess, crooked, out of shape. "Well," said Pete, "let's fix it." Bobby and Sam each took a pencil out of the glove compartment, put them up Pete's nostrils, and proceeded to straighten his nose. "Listen," said Pete, "I appreciate that." Looking in the car mirror, he added, "Well, good as new."

The following day, at the rodeo grounds, Sam Hargrove thought a storm was in his head. He was sore all over and could barely move his head. Dark bruises were all over his face, and his mouth was so swollen he couldn't chew tobacco—a real crisis as far as Sam was concerned. One eye was closed. Neal Gay had heard about Sam's fight with Pete and had searched the grounds for him. Finally, he spotted him, sitting against a fence, elbows on his knees and his hands holding his face, as though it were fine china.

"Sam," said Neal, moving Hargrove's hat back

so that he could look him in the eye, "I hear you been pickin' on my baby."

"Baby!" said Sam, his mouth hurting when he spoke. "Baby, my butt!"

"Well, I just wanted to tell you one thing, Sam. Before you decide to go jump on one of my kids again, you're going to get some of me. And, Sam, from the looks of you, you had a lot of trouble with Pete, so you shore don't want none of me. You understand!"

Sam, beaten and pathetic, slowly looked up at Neal, nodding painfully.

Sittin' in my easy chair
Takin' in the sun,
Looking back at all my memories,
Looking back at all the fun.
Used to ride the buckin' broncs
And the wide-eyed Brahma bulls,
Chased the gals and drank the country wine.
Hypocrites and fools
Think it's a sin;
But I have no regrets,
Only wish I could do it again.
I'm old and gray but young at heart,
Even got kids on the road.
I wish 'em luck and God's speed,
Hope they give 'em hell.
—"Wish I Could Do It Again," by Don Gay

If you wanted to cast the cowboy in bronze—realistically, not abstractly—he would be in the image of Neal Gay. The man is slightly bent and bowed from more hours on a horse than he could ever remember. His stomach hangs over his belt a bit and and his face is leathery, weather-beaten, and lined from a lot of experiences, some told and some untold.

In his day, I kept hearing, Neal was a tough man to cross; he could be very mean and raised hell with the best of them. But he doesn't talk about those times, preferring to keep them to himself, though you know in your heart they are there, a flick of the memory away.

"Well, first of all he didn't want Pete and me to grow up and look up to that kind of thing," said

Above left: Rod Staudinger finishing a ride at Cheyenne. Above right: Brian Claypool getting a good ride on Head Hunter at Calgary. Opposite: Cheyenne bull rider keeping his eyes on those long horns.

Don. "Daddy knows how dangerous it can be fighting and messing around and didn't want us to be a part of it, though I think he understands that sometimes you can't avoid trouble. Another thing, he doesn't want to say anything that would hurt the image of the cowboy, now or back when he was rodeoing. But I think Daddy had a good time, gettin' on down the road. Yeah, I think he enjoyed himself."

Neal Gay is a stock contractor, sells a line of rodeo equipment, helps stage rodeo schools, and does just about everything else connected with the sport. But mostly, he is the Mesquite Rodeo, and it is he. Neal's rodeo—a small but continuing event held each Friday and Saturday night from April through September—completed its nineteenth year in 1976. And actually, on most any weekend, Mesquite, a suburb of Dallas, will have top hands. Dallas–Fort Worth is not only an airline center but also a gathering place for cowboys looking for a ride elsewhere. They're passing through, so they usually go ahead and compete one night at Mesquite. They also know Neal has good stock and a fine covered arena and that he will treat them fairly.

Even people who don't like Neal Gay grant he is an honest man who goes by the rules. The term went out of vogue some years ago, but "honorable" is a good way to describe him.

"Being honest and going by the rules are great, unless you have to live with it for twenty-two years," said Don, grinning. "It *can* be tough."

He told a story about a Jasper, Texas, rodeo his father was producing. Don was late getting there; he quickly parked his car, grabbed his gear, and

Wick Peth watching as Mike Smith loses his hat but stays on the bull.

rushed for the nearest gate. The guard stopped him and told him contestants had to go around to the other side to enter.

"Traffic's jamming up here, so Mr. Gay told me not to let anybody else in this gate," said the guard.

"Listen, I'm his son and it's a good mile around to the other side," said Don. "I got to hurry and get in and be ready to ride."

"Mr. Gay said not to let anybody in here."

"Buddy, Mr. Gay is my daddy and I'm coming through this gate!"

Don saw Neal walk toward the gate as he was letting the guard have a piece of his mind. Neal came over, stopped, looked Don in the eye, and asked what the problem was.

"Daddy, I'm late and this man is tryin' to stop me from coming in."

"This man has his orders," said Neal. "Now,

you get your tail around to the other side and we might let you in."

Neal got the idea to have a weekly rodeo while competing on the circuit. During a lean time, he began wondering just what would happen when he quit, when he was no longer able to travel from rodeo to rodeo. He talked his buddies, Jim Shoulders, Ira Akers, and Bob Grant, into pooling their money and starting a rodeo at Mesquite, which seemed a good location. Neal, made managing director, quit the circuit and devoted his time to running the entire operation.

"Times were pretty hard for a long time," recalled Don. "I can remember one time debts got so bad that we couldn't have sold out if we'd wanted. My daddy sold used cars, insurance, got a broker's license, worked as a part-time salesman, and I don't know what all, just to keep working capital for the rodeo. But he hung in there."

Neal is very proud of his family and what he has done. He takes a great deal of quiet pride in the success of Don and Pete and also Monty Henson, the saddle bronc champion who grew up around the Gays and learned his trade at Mesquite.

"Donnie was only three years old when I started out at Mesquite," Neal had told me. "He and Pete grew up in this business. They met Monty while they were all playing Little League baseball. Then he started coming around and it's almost like he's just part of the family."

"Daddy worked our tails off," said Don. "When we were eight or nine we tended the rodeo stock. On Saturdays we'd work from six in the morning until nine at night. We did everything. I can remember driving a tractor, discing the arena for a night performance. I think we worked so hard the cowboys who'd come around felt sorry for us.

"I was riding calves at five, six years of age. I got on my first bull at thirteen. I'll never forget it. Jim Shoulders let me get on him and he just ran off. But I thought he was bucking like hell.

"Before my senior year in high school, I was so sure of what I wanted to do that I didn't see wasting another year to get my diploma."

When Donnie told Neal that he planned to quit, Neal said, "Now Donnie, we both know what you want to do and that's fine with me. But, son, I tell you what. You'll get that high school diploma even if I have to take you down to that school every day and handcuff you to a chair. You *will*, understand me, graduate."

Opposite: *Down early*. Above: *Wick Peth and A. J. Swaim after a fall.*

"I will graduate," said Don.

High school graduation was on a Saturday night. Don got his diploma and found his parents in the audience. He kissed his mother, Kay—who barrel races—shook hands with Neal, and left. He competed in Mesquite that night, and then, as he put it, "hijacked Phil Lyne's station wagon and took off." Lyne had left his wagon in Mesquite while he caught a commercial to another rodeo. So Don, Monty Henson, and a couple of pals jumped into the vehicle and drove all night to Du Quoin, Illinois, for the rodeo.

"That Donnie," Henson had said. "He started winning right away, unlike the rest of us. I guess he's never been poor since we took off that day."

At Du Quoin, Don's first rodeo on the road after graduation, he won the saddle bronc and bull riding, receiving a grand total of $442. Excitedly, he phoned home. "Daddy?"

"Yeah, how'd it go?"

"Listen, Daddy, I won saddle bronc and bulls! I'll never see another poor day!"

Neal has the door open for his sons to move one day into the business. It's something they'll have, not worry about getting. The Mesquite Rodeo has begun showing a profit in recent years, and Neal now owns all the stock and equipment, leasing only the actual grounds from the corporation.

"People always used to ask me why Daddy'd do something like this rodeo if he wasn't making any money all those years," said Donnie. "Well, what good is a lot of money if you're not happy with what you're doing?"

I'm sure each year when the Mesquite Rodeo opens, Neal Gay remembers the hard times along with the good. People look back on their lives and sometimes wonder why in the hell they did this or that, when they weren't really making anything out of it. Neal Gay won't.

*But I have no regrets,
Only wish I could do it again.*

Above *and* opposite: *Two cowboys with their bull riding gear: bull rope with weighted bell, riding glove, and tightly wrapped spurs.*

The El Paso rodeo was starting in half an hour and we began to walk out of the arena and back behind the chutes. "My daddy says my hair is too long," said Don. "But I just got a haircut!"

"Wonder what happened to ol' Sam Hargrove?" said Phil Lyne.

"Well, I'd like to see the ol' fart, unless he's been drinking," said Don.

Lyne went to the other end of the arena where he'd soon be up in calf roping. Don and I stood by the gate, looking out into the arena and talking, when somebody grabbed him from behind, wrestling him away from the gate. It was a tired, worn-looking man, with a handlebar mustache and wild hair sticking out from under a black cowboy hat.

"Gotcha, you little SOB!" yelled the man, pinning Don's arms to his waist.

"Let me see, that has to be Ronnie Rossen," said Don. "I can't see you but I can smell you. I thought they'd buried you three years ago."

"Buried me, you little SOB. Ol' Ronnie's about ready to make a comeback and take your title away from you."

Rossen let Don go, shook his hand heartily, and must have slapped him on the back five times during their short conversation. Ronnie had won the bull riding championship in 1961, 1962, and 1964, but seemed a little on hard times. "Comeback time!" he said. "Ready for a comeback!" Then he moved on down the chutes.

A cowboy sat on the ground behind the chutes. The boot and sock were off his left foot, which was swollen double around the ankle. He took a small, round white pill, which I recognized as codeine, out of his shirt pocket and gulped it down without benefit of liquid. I asked him if his ankle was broken and he answered, "No. Sprung."

"If you just did it," I said, "use ice. An ice bag. Freeze it. It'll be much better tomorrow."

"Aw, it's all right."

"Ice keeps the swelling down. It's a lot better than heat, right after an injury."

"Aw, it's just a matter of getting my boot back on before I ride. I do that, and the ankle's all right. I'll prop it up in the car tonight. Thank gawd I ain't drivin'."

"I'm so wide awake from that pill the trucker gave me last night I might not ever sleep," said another cowboy, sitting down and looking sympathetically at the size of his friend's ankle.

"What'd you give him?"

"A buck, a buck for the pill. It was one of them RJS pills."

"What's an RJS?" I asked.

"A Road Jumpin' Sonuvabitch. Ha-ha-ha-ha."

"One time," continued the cowboy with the injured ankle, "I seen this trucker order two cups of black coffee in this all-night place. We was leaving, and when we got outside he had the hood up and the radiator cap off his truck. Well, he was just standing there, talking to his truck. Then he dropped a pill into the radiator and poured in one of the cups of coffee. Then he said, 'If I got to stay awake all night, so do you, you sonuvabitch.'"

"Who you got tonight?" the second cowboy asked.

"That 'un there."

"Watch him. He comes out, turns to the left."

"I know." He had the boot on over his swollen ankle.

I had hoped to see Don Gay ride a bull, but

because of his appearances in Billings and at the banquet in Dallas, he had turned out in his specialty but was up that night in saddle bronc, on a buckskin mare named Nellie Bly.

"I've been doin' better in saddle bronc than in bull riding, lately," said Don. "But I've got to get them both going for me. If I can stay up in the saddle bronc [making the NFR], then I've got a shot at the All Around. Now, this buckskin here can be a good horse if all goes well. He'll circle either way but sometimes also jumps and kicks and then takes off on you."

He had his saddle on the horse, loose, and stood on the gate. "Sure," he continued. "Fear's always in the back of your mind, but more so riding bulls than horses. You never really conquer fear but you just know your business and then you know how to get out of most problems you might run into. Of course, there's nothing you can do about freak accidents, but if the Good Lord figures it's my time, it's my time.

"It's just like auto racing. Richard Petty knows he can be killed instantly. But he's sure of himself, of his knowledge and ability. He doesn't dwell on danger. Neither do I."

"By gawd, Donnie, that shore don't look like no bull to me," said a cowboy from back of the chutes. I thought it might be Ronnie Rossen.

Don laughed and lost concentration momentarily. He had his bronc rein around the horse's neck. A cowboy on the other side of the chute reached a hook under the horse, caught the strap under the saddle, and made it snug.

The announcer was talking about Don Gay, the World Bullriding Champion, who was trying his hand at saddle bronc on a horse called Nellie Bly. As the gate was opened, a cowboy jerked tight the flank strap, reinforced with soft sheep wool, and the horse came out, kicking high. Suddenly it turned, jarring Don a little off balance. He regained his timing and rode until the buzzer. But he got only a 64, out of the money. He'd flown all the way to El Paso, bought gas for his plane, rented a car, paid his entry fee, and come up with nothing.

"Well," he said, taking off his chaps, "one day you eat chicken and the next day feathers. One week I won six thousand dollars. This week don't look like I'll win anything.

"But one of these days I'll make my saddle bronc riding comparable to my bull riding. I'll master saddle bronc, too.

"I better go phone the airport and check on the weather to see if we can get outta here."

"You guys headin' to the airport?" asked Bobby Brown, who enters all riding events.

"Yep. You got a flight? Come on, we'll give you a lift."

"Appreciate it."

As Don came back from phoning, one of the girls we'd seen earlier was talking to a cowboy who did not have a championship belt.

"Okay," said Don. "You want me to tell you about the weather now, or after we get up?"

Don drove away from the arena, onto the freeway, and back toward the airport. "Listen, y'all get up and the weather's too bad, just sit down in Lubbock," said Bobby Brown. "We always got a place for you at my house."

"Well," said Don, "just might do that."

He drove eighty, eighty-five on the freeway. It reminded me of the time Pete and a couple of cowboys were pressed for time to get to the airport but couldn't get a ride. They rushed to a used car dealer adjacent to the rodeo grounds, bought a $75 car, and took off. As they stopped by their airline, an attendant came out to the car. "You got a car?" asked Pete. The porter said he did but his wife didn't. "Well, here," said Pete, handing him the keys. "Now she's got a car." They jumped out of the car and rushed into the terminal.

Bobby got out of the car at his airline and Don drove around the airport to Hertz. The music on the radio was loud. "Everybody figures all the cow-

Three views of Phil Lyne, All Around Cowboy winner in 1971 and 1972. Top: Riding Cloudburst in Sidney, Iowa, in 1970. Left: At Fort Worth in 1973. Above: At the 1973 National Finals in Oklahoma City.

Below: *Neal Gay taking a ride at Phoenix.* Opposite: *Monty Henson— at Pine Bluff, Arkansas, in 1975—performing the Casey Tibbs style of dismounting from a bucking bronc.*

boys are the same, that they like that old time C and W music. I don't. I like rock, progressive country, but not the old twangy music.

"Sometimes, when there ain't no big rush, some of us like to sit around and pick and sing."

Don hadn't been at a particular session of "pickin' and singin'" that I attended in a motel room at 3:00 A.M. after one rodeo, but Monty Henson was there and so was Steve Davis, a sometime bull rider who has an outstanding voice.

There were five of us in the motel room, listening to Monty Henson and Steve Davis pick and sing. We'd decided to meet after the rodeo, and though it was 3:00 A.M., the session was just getting started. Two girls, both models and one with flaming red hair, had attended their first rodeo and were obviously impressed with Davis and especially Henson, a slender, darkly handsome young man who was polite and had a belt buckle that said he was the saddle bronc champion.

Mostly, Monty accompanied Davis with his guitar as Steve sang "Bandy, the Rodeo Clown."

Who was once a bull-hookin' sonuvagun;
Now who keeps a pipe, hid out behind Chute Number
    One.
Who was ridin' high,
'Til a pretty girl rode him to the ground.
Any kid knows where to find me;
I'm Bandy, the rodeo clown.

Henson, son of a policeman, had told me how he'd had to sneak around to compete in the rodeo. "My parents didn't mind me hanging around Mesquite so much, but just didn't want me moving on down the road," said Monty. "We had no rodeo background in our family. But, must have been about nineteen sixty-two, I had become friends with Pete and Donnie, so we all went out to the rodeo. I dug it. The next year I showed up at Mesquite wearing boots and a cowboy hat and started working for Neal in the chutes. Then I started competing in junior rodeos, stuff like that."

When they got back from Du Quoin, Monty was outside his parents' house one day, cleaning out his car. A construction job he thought he had fell through, and he recalled, "I got to thinking, why would I do some kind of work I didn't want to do? I had about seventy-five bucks. That was it. I drove down to the police station and told my dad I was going to rodeo. Boy, was he mad.

"I went back home and told my mom. She cried. I knew I couldn't hang around the house with everybody so upset, so I went over to Donnie's house and stayed for a while. We took off for a rodeo in Gladewater. In a few days I went back home and my folks had calmed down. They just figured, 'He's going to do what he wants to do no matter what we think.'"

The redhead, who had been drinking as much as any of us—with the exception of one person there, a friend of mine who was not in rodeo—sat next to Monty, who was on the edge of the bed playing his guitar. Steve, leaning against the headboard of the bed, continued to sing.

In the ridin' and the ropin'
I was closin' in on number one,
Now in dreams at night
I ride on that silver saddle I never won.
Since she left me, the whiskey
Takes me to the rodeo grounds,
Where the cowboys think I'm handy;
I'm Bandy, the rodeo clown.

"Well," Monty had continued, "they kept after me to go to college in the fall. So after rodeoing all summer I decided to take Stephen F. Austin up on a scholarship it had offered me. But first I had to go to Eastfield College [a junior college] because my grades weren't high enough for SFA.

"You might say I was majoring in pool. I lasted about two weeks. Then I got to thinking about all those guys going on down the road to places like Albuquerque and Denver. I just gave up for the last time and took off for a rodeo in Omaha. I had twenty dollars and wrote a hot check for my entry fee. But I placed in bull riding and made up the check before it went through.

"After that I never did anything else except rodeo, though we do some pickin' and singin' now and then."

I could ride 'em all,
The bulls and the broncs knew I was boss.
But the ride that woman took me on
Broke a whole lot more than this
Old cowboy's bones.
While the tears on my makeup
Melt my painted smile into a frown,
The crowd thinks I'm a dandy;
I'm Bandy, the rodeo clown.
And I could ride 'em all,
The bulls and the broncs knew I was boss....

Clockwise from above: *In saddle bronc riding, the rider and the horse move together—and when the horse falls, the rider falls.*

My friend, drinking Scotch straight out of a bottle, said, "Hey, we gonna have some fun."

The redhead was leaning against Monty as he played, her feet resting on a nearby chair. My friend, who is a nice fellow, noticed her foot and, though he meant to reach down and tickle it, pulled too hard, yanking the girl clear off the bed and onto the floor. She let out a giggle-scream and three of us quickly helped her up, including my friend, who apologized sixteen times. She just giggled some more and sat back down by Monty, who hadn't stopped playing.

"I'm *so* sorry, darlin', did I hurt your foot?" asked my friend.

"No," said the other model, across the room, "you didn't hurt her foot but you'd have hurt her disposition, except it's amply padded."

Monty is utter flamboyance in a rodeo, wearing a black silk shirt, initialed in red, and a black hat with a long, bright feather in the band. The saddle bronc event is the finesse event, the showy event, and he likes it when observers compare him to Casey Tibbs, who was not only one of the greatest performers of all time but also was the biggest ham.

"When I was a kid in the early sixties," Monty had said, "all you heard was Jim Shoulders, Harry Tompkins, and Casey Tibbs. Casey was the real flashy guy, the saddle bronc rider. I have pictures of him on a saddle bronc, wearing a real loud shirt. He was better than anybody else in the event. I also liked that wild style of getting off."

When the buzzer sounds after a ride, the cowboy usually waits for the pickup man. The cowboy will hand him the rein, then wrap his arms around the pickup man's waist and swing down by sliding off the bucking horse, over the pickup man's horse and onto the ground. But Casey liked to rocket out of the saddle, into the air, and land on his feet.

"Yeah," Monty had continued, "I like that. I started doing it and it almost killed me at first. I'd land every which-a-way, including on my head.

128

Opposite: *Larry Mahan coming down hard.* Opposite bottom: *Calgary saddle bronc rider dismounting the hard way.* Top *and* bottom right: *Sometimes the first jump is the last jump.*

Then I learned how to do it. At least, I thought I had."

In 1975, at Oakdale, California, Monty leaped off the horse, Casey Tibbs-style, and the pickup man didn't see him. Just as Monty landed on his feet the pickup man galloped right over him, the horse's back foot striking Monty in the temple, shattering his jaw. Doctors operated and used a wire to put his jaw back together. He rode again about a week later, though admittedly he was nervous.

"Sure, I'm flattered when they compare my style to Casey Tibbs," he said.

Davis got up, stretched, then sat down again, leaned back, and said, "Now here's one I wrote you might like. Call it 'Someday It'll All Be Over.' Monty, you sing it."

Sitting here, drinkin' beer,
Raindrops fallin' down,
I hear a lonesome whistle blow,
Freight train is going through town.
I wonder where you are tonight
And if you're all alone;
I wish that I was there with you,
But I am far from home.

The redhead watched and listened, transfixed. Somebody knocked on the door and asked if we could be a little quieter. "Grab him by the foot," I told my friend.

I've been gone about three months
But I miss you so.
I been true, to the kids and you,
But my heart tells me to go.
I can't sit behind some desk,
It's not the life for me;
I'm used to livin' a life as free
As a rodeo cowboy can be.

Someday it'll all be over
And I'll be home with you;

Going over the luck of the draw.

*It can't go on forever,
Someday it'll all be through.*

"Hey," said my friend to the redhead, "I'm sorry." She giggled and whispered something in Monty's ear. He continued to sing and Davis continued to pick. I admired them because they could pick and sing with people talking and blowing in their ear. Now Monty was speaking the words softly as Davis played.

*I'm in the bull ridin' tonight in Jackson,
Got a bronc tomorrow in San Antone;
And you know just sitting here thinkin' about it,
It wouldn't take but about four hours to get home.
You know I'd love to see you,
And God knows how much I'd like to tell the kids hello;
But I could only stay for about a day,
Then it's back down the road to the rodeo.*

*But someday it'll all be over
And I'll be home with you;
It can't go on forever,
Someday it'll all be through.*

"It was about 1974 when I actually first saw Casey Tibbs," Monty had said. "I was at this rodeo in Inglewood, California. I must have been about twenty years old at the time. I met him, but he was drunk and it really burned me up he didn't talk to me. But I was in the bronc riding that night and got an eighty-four or something like that on a horse named Southern Pride. I won the event.

"After that, Casey came out and talked to me."

We'd drunk all my friend's Scotch. "I wished I could sing," he said.

I asked Steve and Monty if they knew Jerry Jeff Walker's classic, "Mr. Bojangles." After I asked, I wondered if, in another place, it might have sounded like I was saying, "Do you know 'Melancholy Baby'?"

But Steve, thinking for a second, sang:

*I knew a man, Bojangles, and he danced for you
In worn-out shoes,
Silver hair and ragged shirt and baggy pants,
The old soft shoe . . .*

At about 6:00 A.M. the party was breaking up. Everybody headed in a different direction. Except the redhead.

Don Gay lifted the Cherokee Piper into the soft night, leaving the lights of El Paso glittering like strings of diamonds on black silk. He had checked the weather, briefly contemplated catching the commercial, but in the end had decided to fly back himself. "We could hit rain but I think we'll miss most of it," he said.

I held the flashlight, showing him the air map in my lap whenever he wanted to see it. We climbed higher and then leveled off and I looked at the tall mountains on our left, black against the horizon. I didn't talk and neither did Don as we crossed through the mountains and then turned east for Dallas.

The sky was clear at first, massive and dark with stars dangling around. It felt somewhat like floating in our own dreams of slow motion. It was about 1:30 A.M. when Don finally said, "This is my favorite time, up here in the air when the whole world seems asleep. Often when I'm flying alone like this everything seems so much clearer. The stars are out, everything's so vast. It's like up here you can hear your own thoughts."

He talked about his girl, Terry. "She's so great because she understands me and this life," he said. "We decided a long time ago to be completely honest with one another. That way, there's nothing phony about our relationship. I'm gone a lot and she knows there are a lot of temptations."

Suddenly, the stars were gone. The plane began shaking, then jumping slightly as if moving on

a rough ocean. Rain began pelting it. "Let's go back and catch the commercial flight," I said, halfway trying to be funny.

He talked little, concentrating on handling the plane, which I appreciated. "One time," he said, "I hit this hailstorm and it scared hell out of me."

"Rain," I said, "scares the hell out of me."

"Bob."

"Who?"

"Let me see the map."

We passed through the rain, and the ride was calm until about two hours out of Dallas. But the tail wind cut our time. One thing that kept worrying me was that the radar detection device on his plane wasn't working. Voices from airfields along the way kept asking him to turn it on. He tried. It didn't work.

"These things aren't necessary but just good to have," he explained. "The big airports pick you up on what's called a primary. We're just a blip. But with this thing not working they might not know which one [plane] we are."

So we watched for the big jets as we moved into the Dallas–Fort Worth area. I searched closely, all around. But we passed the airport area safely, except that I spilled a Coke in my lap. We had difficulty finding Red Bird Airport, a small private airport where Don leaves his plane. Don flew low when we got into the vicinity of the airport, but the wind was making a yo-yo out of us. Once I looked to my right and saw a radio tower near the wing. It was an odd feeling, thinking we might have hit it had we been twenty feet over.

With little help from me, Don finally located the airport, which was deserted. All the personnel had gone home. He started down, the wing at forty-five degrees to the landing strip. He fought it back level just before we hit, compensating for the strong crosswind. But the wheels found the strip, we bounced back into the air, and came down again to stay. I relaxed for the first time in hours and thought about Mahan's landing in Denver, when Don said, "This is called cowboying in."

After he parked the plane and got into his car, he said, "Now remember, it's safer to fly than drive."

I relaxed, as he zoomed eighty or ninety miles per hour down the freeway toward home.

Chapter 4:
SKIPPER VOSS AND A TALE OF THREE CLOWNS

You get the top fifteen bull riders every year, and they'd vote for Skipper Voss. —Mike Bandy

There's some good ones, but Skipper's the best. —Don Gay

Skipper Voss is in a class by himself as far as savin' cowboys. —Bobby Clark

Skipper's the best. He's got a sixth sense. You'll be out there spinning on a bull and not having any idea where you'll end up when you land. But Skipper's there. I don't know how he knows where to be, but he knows.
 —Pete Gay

The preceding night, at the small, whistle-stop rodeo grounds in Arcadia, Texas, the black muley (short-horned) bull had gotten Skipper Voss on the ground and tried to hook him. But the bull had moved too slowly, and his horns were not long enough. In effect, the bull had been able just to nudge him along the ground. Skipper had fended off the horns with his long arms, then rolled away and bounced to his feet, hightailing it in an exaggerated manner to the fence. The crowd had loved this, and tonight most of them had come back to see the rematch between Skipper, the bull-fighting rodeo clown, and the black muley bull.

Skipper had the great confidence you get when you know you have control of a situation, even one involving a bull that would like nothing better than to hook or crush you for taunting it. After the muley bull threw its rider, the crowd got its wish. Skipper ran in, got the bull's attention from the fallen man, and then stopped abruptly, letting the bull pass very near him. The crowd both laughed and cheered. Skipper ran back at the bull, then swerved in front of the animal, passing it on his left side and admittedly thinking, "Look at me go." The crowd laughed again at the man in the baggy pants making a fool of the dangerous muley bull.

As the bull went past him, and he felt once again the exhilaration of letting the animal come close but miss him, an unseen force jerked him off his feet. Then he was pulled uncontrollably up into the air and on top of the bull. One of the bull's horns, small though they were, had latched Skipper's suspenders as it went past, getting entangled in the reinforcement of his baggy short pants, the ones he always wears over red leotards. Skipper, tall and lanky, with his arms and legs flailing every which way, couldn't get loose, and the bull raced across the arena, at the same time trying to toss him up into the air and making him look like the sort of stuffed dummy that clowns sometimes use.

Each time the bull tried to toss him, the suspenders and reinforcement of his pants would cause him to be jerked back to the bull—a human yo-yo. Eventually, the bull decided it must put the strange object on the ground. It dipped its head and tried to step on Skipper, who scrambled as best he could on the ground, moving to miss the hoofs. The bull jerked him back up, then started running again.

"I couldn't do anything," said Skipper. "I couldn't gain enough control to try and get loose. The whole world was bouncing, jerking, and I was trying to clear my head so that when the bull had me on the ground, it couldn't crush me. Finally, I heard something tear, rip. My pants just came apart at the seams and I was free. Somehow, I landed on my feet, just standing there in my red leotards. So I started jumping up and down and then leaped into the barrel."

The crowd went into a frenzy, yelling, screaming, beside itself. That was some act by Skipper Voss, putting himself on the bull's horns and letting the animal carry him all over the arena. "The contractor came over to me and said, 'That's one of

Wick Peth escorting a bull out of the arena.

the best acts I ever saw, Skipper. Could you do it again tomorrow night?'

"Luckily, all I got out of it was bruises."

Part of the act. Skipper Voss put on that same pair of cutoff Wranglers—actually more patches than jeans—and looked into a rest-room mirror in the office on the Mesquite Rodeo grounds. It was about an hour before the show started, and Skipper was using the office because his trailer was in Fort Worth, being painted. Ordinarily, Skipper dressed in the trailer, which he pulled around the country with a pickup. Only a half hour earlier he had looked like any of the other cowboys moving around the grounds, but the transformation into a clown, by way of greasepaint, had almost been made.

"I keep thinking I'll get me a new pair of short pants," he said, "but it wouldn't be the same. These are kinda rotten. I've had them about eight years and would just hate to have to change them now."

He put white greasepaint around his eyes and colored his nose red. Skipper has a long thin face with a pointed nose, and the paint magnifies his features even more, giving him an Ichabod Crane look. He dipped a finger in black paint and put dots all over his face. When he finished, he stared for a long time in the mirror. The makeup was right and the reflection was of a funny man, a clown, but I doubt clowns ever really see their faces as we do. They see behind the paint, whereas we see only the silly face and probably wouldn't recognize them without it.

As though remembering an inside joke, Skipper stuck out his tongue at the reflection, getting the same response. "Almost lost that tongue once," he said.

At Rocksprings, in West Texas, a bull knocked Skipper Voss to the ground and tried to trample

Opposite: *Skipper Voss kicking up a little dirt.* Bottom left: *To the crowds watching, Skipper looks colorful; bulls, however, seem to see only red.* Bottom right: *Wilbur Plaugher and some fans.*

him. He scrambled, but a hoof caught him right in the mouth, shearing off the tops of his teeth, cutting through his lip, and slashing his tongue. He rolled free and jumped up, spitting blood and parts of teeth. He took the funny red rag out of his back pocket and stuck it in his mouth and finished the performance. That Skipper, some of the crowd thought, he really isn't hurt. Look at the rag sticking out of his mouth. That Skipper.

Skipper Voss finished the rodeo and drove seventy-five miles to a hospital, where the doctor sewed up his lip and tongue but apparently did not sufficiently treat for possible infection, caused, among other things, by the dirty red rag. He got back into his car and drove all night in order to get home to Crosby, near Houston. En route, his tongue turned a blackish color and swelled until the stitches burst. His whole head ached, the original sharp pain becoming a dull, throbbing ache. The next day, he went to see his family doctor. "I walked into his office, and he couldn't believe what he saw," said Skipper. "He told me later I could have lost my tongue. Anyway, he fixed it, gave me shots and pills, and it finally got all right, though I sat around for weeks without being able to close my mouth."

Almost losing his tongue hadn't been part of the act either.

Skipper moved away from the mirror and got a white wig, which looked like a peroxided haystack, and a red miniature cowboy hat. A phone in the rodeo office rang, and Randy Spears, who does about everything possible in the operational end of the Mesquite Rodeo for owner Neal Gay, answered and said, "Skipper, you've got a long-distance call. The operator said it was urgent." Skipper picked up an extension, spoke briefly, and started laughing. "It's Lucia," he said. "He's on the other side of the arena and just wanted to make sure I arrived."

Tommy Lucia is a very funny man with a serious, sad face. One of his better acts is when he becomes El Matador, Elisio Tomaso, and parades

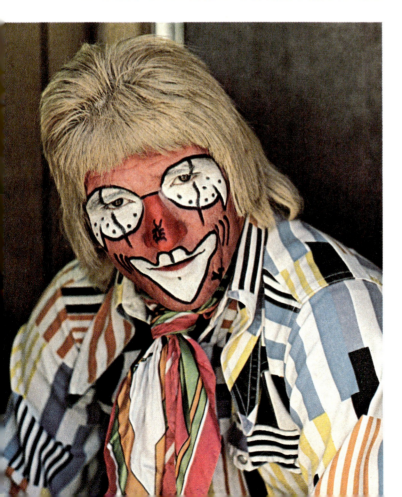

into the arena twirling a cape, accompanied by bullfighting music. He prepares himself for toro's charge, waiting stone-faced. Suddenly, a small dog, toy horns tied on his head, comes charging out, running at the cape. (Lucia has two dogs that charge the cape and uses the one he feels is most apt to perform better on a particular night.) Tommy is not a bullfighter; he's a funny man who'll also jump into a barrel. However, he's still around bulls in the arena, and it is not without irony that he broke his ankle once when, backing out of the arena after his act, he stumbled over one of the dogs. Certainly, he did not want to have to become a bullfighter at Mesquite, so he was making sure Skipper was there.

Bull riders always talk about Skipper Voss, and the man, mostly unknown outside immediate rodeo circles, is a word-of-mouth legend. Without prompting, cowboys will tell about this or that feat Skipper performed, and though I'm sure some have become embellished in retelling and the passage of time, most are probably true: the time, during the 1974 National Finals, when he stepped in front of a rider about to be freight-trained (run over with a full head of steam), taking the brunt of the bull's charge himself; the times he's jumped completely over a bull or let one charge him while he was on his knees; the way he'll leap right into the well (inside a spinning bull) to get a rider clear. Cowboys love Skipper, but some rodeo officials do not. Skipper resents what he feels is the second-class-citizen treatment clowns get and often speaks his mind. Officials believe that clowns are meant only to entertain.

One company gave free jeans to rodeo participants during the NFR. When Skipper showed up, they told him he'd have to wait until all the cowboys got their pants. He told them what he thought of that situation. Belt buckles, with the NFR emblem, are given to participants in the NFR at the championship banquet. But when Skipper asked if the clowns would get their buckles at the banquet, he was told this would be done at a later date.

"Listen, I have a lot of pride in what I do," he said. "I'm proud to be a rodeo bullfighter. But I think maybe I've been speaking up too much about clowns being mistreated. It's cost me jobs. The fact that I call attention to some of these things might help some clown on down the road, but it hasn't gotten me anywhere."

Spears and I both told him he should reiterate his feelings, and he finally warmed to the subject—as I knew he would, and as he knew he would. "All right, I just feel clowns should be treated more like cowboys," he said. "They took the NFR shield off our buckles, which they had no right to do. Then they don't even want us at the championship banquet. Clowns get no credit, but I'd like to see what would happen without us out there. We pay dues like the cowboys, and we're a part of the show and should be treated equally."

"The PRCA pushes cowboys, not us," Bobby Clark, a longtime rodeo clown, had once told me. "But we hit a town and we're the first ones they call to appear at a shopping center or school. I don't believe they think about us that much, though I imagine they would if we weren't there."

Skipper, dressed for the performance, sat on a couch in the office and said he didn't think it would hurt if they'd sometimes put a story about a clown in the *Rodeo Sports News*, the PRCA's official publication. "I guess they're afraid if they gave us some publicity, it might benefit us financially."

A run-in Skipper once had with Mike Cervi, one of the leading stock contractors in the nation, has likely cost him jobs. "He's all right," said Skipper, "but one time I was working for him, see. He'd clowned a few times himself, so he started telling me how I should do things. I let him know I knew what I should do. There went another job."

The phone rang. "Skipper, it's your wife," said Spears. "She says she has to talk to you."

Skipper went to the phone. "It was Lucia again," he said, "wondering if I was about ready."

Wick Peth, fists ready, charging.

Skipper was a rodeo clown for twelve years before he joined the RCA (now the PRCA) in 1973. The next year, cowboys voted him to the National Finals, but he can't go back again until 1979 because the Clown's Association won't let individuals perform in the NFR except every five years. "That rule," said Spears, "obviously benefits clowns who wouldn't otherwise be voted to the NFR."

"Skipper," said Pete Gay, passing through the office, "would go every year if it wasn't for that rule."

The last time I'd seen Skipper Voss perform was at the Southwestern Exposition and Fat Stock Show, in Fort Worth, where indoor rodeo was first held. He was limping badly then, having undergone surgery on both knees in 1975. The first knee injury occurred when a bull, his attention diverted from a cowboy, drove into the side of Skipper's leg, which was planted in the ground. A knee cartilage was torn.

"That one caused me a lot of trouble," said Skipper. "I'd be out there on the ground, pawing in front of a bull. Then I'd try to get up and the knee would lock on me. I'd limp, fall, and get to the fence as best I could, then lift the knee up and it would unlock." Surgery corrected the torn cartilage, but he went back on the circuit after only three months —too soon. He limped through the rodeo in Las Vegas, drove 1,000 miles for a performance in Fort Smith, Arkansas, and then caught a commercial to Reno, Nevada, where he worked with Wick Peth, a fine athlete who's one of the best bullfighters in the business.

Peth, in his mid-forties, has the body and stamina of a man twenty years younger. Wick works out between performances, jogs, and tapes his ankles and thighs before each rodeo. He has quickness, speed, and is constantly on the move, somewhat remindful of a roadrunner or will-o'-the-wisp. Wick will race in through a bull's path, beating the animal to no-man's-land, or run behind a bull, grabbing its tail. "Wick amazes me," said Skipper. "The way he's always moving, there's no way you can keep up with him. I stay inside, trying to maneuver, more than he does."

"I just always try to be ready," said Peth. "By being in condition, I think I can avoid injuries, be more alert. Oh, I think I do about as well as anybody. Skipper's good. He's about the best guy down the road. He's also funnier than I am. I don't even try to be funny."

"I *am* funny," said Skipper, "though of course nobody knows it yet."

Above: *Quail Dobbs isn't completely safe—bulls have been known to stick their horns into barrels.* Opposite: *Wick Peth, out in the open, with nothing between him and clear danger.*

Because Voss and Peth are considered among the very best, there was a natural pressure of rivalry in Reno, whether either admitted it or not. "People at Reno were making a big deal out of Wick and me," admitted Skipper. "We weren't, but they were. My knee just got to feeling better for some reason. I was really back into fighting bulls again. I was jumping over them, doing everything. Then I jumped over both this barrel and bull and came down with all the weight on my good leg. It popped, just collapsed. I'd torn up that knee, too.

I went ahead and stumbled through the year. I *had* to go to Calgary over the Fourth of July because it was too late for them to get anybody else. My first year in the RCA I worked one hundred thirty-five rodeos, one hundred forty-two the next year. But last year [1975] I worked only ten, because of my knees. After Calgary, I had surgery on my other knee."

But in February, he was competing in Fort Worth. There were twenty performances, which meant good money. A clown will usually get $100 to $200 a performance. Skipper now works for $175 to $250, though the most he remembers making in a year was about $19,000. "I couldn't move very well in Fort Worth," he said. "So I got to ducking a lot, just barely going under the horns. That was fine, except every time I did it, the bull would step on me. It thrills the crowd but hurts me. I always say, if you can't fight 'em, thrill 'em."

In one of the early performances, a rider was thrown and the bull ran over him. As the animal turned and started to trample the rider again, Skipper, with no time to get the bull's attention or turn him, jumped over the rider, taking the bull's second charge. "My knee just collapsed," said Skipper. "I tried to move but couldn't. The bull must have run over me three, four times before I could get out of the way. It didn't break anything, though I was real sore."

Don Gay successfully rode his bull, a spinner, during the sixteenth performance. But he got off in the well, falling to his hands and knees. Skipper ran in, grabbing the bull by the head before it could hook Donnie. The bull turned into him, hitting his knee and tearing still more cartilage. Skipper could no longer perform in Fort Worth, and a doctor told him he must undergo knee surgery again, the third time in less than twelve months.

A couple of months later, he was at Mesquite, showing me his knee brace. "This thing helps a lot," he said. "Sometimes I'll have to adjust it, but it gives me a lot more confidence out there. It's like the one Joe Namath wears. Maybe they ought to let me do a panty hose commercial like he does.

"I tell you, after Fort Worth, I almost quit. I've never been so down. I was right to the point, you know, where you go this way or that. Then I got this brace.

"I've had bruises, busted ribs, whatever, but that's been about it, knock on wood"—he hits himself on the head—"until my knees. You can tough it out when you mess up muscles, bones. You just bear down and keep going. But when I tore up them knees, I had to come down. It's not the pain. No, sir. I can take that. But it's just that you can't stand up, can't run. The knees just don't work. I kept falling down.

"Everybody thought it was part of my act."

Skipper appears amazingly relaxed in the arena, almost fearless. I remember watching him calmly stoop down and pick up his hat as a bull snorted and kicked around him. The point is that he remembered he'd dropped his hat, even in the face of a bull. "Yeah, I am nervous," he said. "But I get out there and start thinking about my business, about the bull, and then I just react. The fear passes. Maybe desire just overcomes fear for me. I have a lot of desire to do well at my job. A lot of people up there in the stands, if they're pretty good athletes, could do what I'm doing if they had the desire."

"No," I told him, "they would be too afraid."

"Well, desire overcomes fear. Anyway, situations aren't always the way they look. My deal is fighting bulls close, and I feel safer the closer I am. A bull has such momentum going that it's difficult for him to get at you, unless you just stand there like a dummy. They're going by you so fast it's hard for them to gather themselves quickly enough to get you. By the time they do, you ought to be in another place.

"You've got to learn bulls. They have personalities like people. The better you know one, the less fear you have. A green bull is easiest to fight. I love

Top left and right *and* above left: *Skipper Voss, bullfighter—a legend in his time—putting on greasepaint in his van.* Above right: *A visit from a friend—Wilbur Plaugher.*

to fight Mexican bulls. I went down there once and fought in this little town when temperatures must have been one hundred and five in the arena. The bulls were green." (Mexican bulls are killed during corridas, so they gain no experience.) "I had a lot of control on them. You could lead them around like pups. The people went crazy, screaming *olé, olé*. I loved it. The people asked me up in the stands, and I drank tequila with them.

"Now, you don't hardly see full-blooded Brahmas anymore. They've bred them for meat, taking some of the meanness and buck out of them. But crossbreds still have a mean streak. I don't like those sharp-horned ones. I see one of them out there and I'll tell the stockman, 'Hey, if I want to be a matador I'll go to Mexico for a lot more money.' But the biggest danger is getting stepped on. The bull jumps and kicks out and has his full

power and weight behind it. Man wasn't meant to take a fifteen-hundred-pound hit.

"I saw a bull kick this kid once. They thought he was all right, but he had internal bleeding and died. Those bulls are all muscle, and when they hit you, you get hit and don't have any control.

"Sure, some can fake it, but I ain't mentioning any names. I know several who do it. But what makes me madder than anything is to work with

somebody who'll lay back and lay back and lay back. They'll lay back all week and then, at the final performance, they'll hook up and do something. The committee in town remembers that last performance and thinks the guy is good. They don't remember when he hung back like a log. I like to try to thrill the crowd on every performance. I try to get up for every bull and figure it'll be the one who'll try to hook and stomp a cowboy.

"You get a bull with eight, nine performances behind him, and he gets smart. Some of the veterans are *real* smart. The hardest thing in the world is to fight one which gets experience and just steps up and waits for you. When you run in at him, he doesn't start at you but waits. He'll just turn his head slightly at you and revolve as you go past. Then he drops in right behind you. He has you then. I mean you can't turn and out-butt him, and you sure can't outrun him."

Years ago, Skipper Voss ran into an experienced Brahma bull at one of Sloan Williams's amateur rodeos in Stonewall, Texas, which is in the Hill Country, LBJ country. In fact, a part-time area resident named Lyndon Baines Johnson was in attendance. Skipper often worked for Williams, and at

Left: *A mean one on the loose. While cowboys climb the fence to get out of the way, three clowns—Peth, Plaugher, and Dobbs—run right in.* Above: *Peth staying in close.*

145

this particular rodeo he was the only clown. "Tell you what, Skipper," said Williams. "If you get into trouble, I'll suit up and come out and help you."

The Brahma had wide horns, which, Skipper remembered, "looked like they ought to be on a reindeer." The Brahma tore up one chute and was moved to another. When the gate opened, the rider, sensing the better part of valor, bailed out. The bull turned and set up, pawing the ground as Skipper ran toward him.

"I saw the kid was all right and just ran in there, then gave him a fake to one side and ran past him on the other," said Skipper. "But he didn't take my fake."

The Brahma turned as Skipper ran past and fell right in behind him. Skipper, sensing the bull's move, started pumping his legs for the fence, looking back over his shoulder at the charging bull, getting bigger and bigger. He hit something solid, was momentarily stunned. It was a pickup horse, standing in a corner of the arena. Skipper caromed off the horse, regained his balance, and took off for the fence again. "All I could see," he said, "was two big horns, one on each side of me!"

Each time Skipper would get his feet solidly under him, the bull would hit him, nudging him forward, causing him to stumble for a few steps before regaining balance. Finally, the bull hit him harder and he stumbled, then fell. But knowing his fate if he stopped long enough for the bull to trample him, he kept going on all fours as fast as he could. It wasn't fast enough. Just before he got to the fence, the bull dipped his head and hooked him, tossing him up into the air in a tumbling motion.

"I don't know what happened exactly," recalled Skipper. "But as I was coming down I saw the fence. I was upside down but just instinctively turned my shoulder, hit the fence, and bounced over into the crowd."

Landing on his feet, Skipper, always a master of impromptu, started jumping up and down and yelling, "Sloooaannnneee!"

"I had a helluva feeling not too many years ago," clown Bobby Clark had once told me. "I recognized this bull I'd known three years earlier, too late. That bull stretched his neck longer than any I've ever seen. I was going by him and, just as I got near him, I saw which one it was. There was no time. He just reached out, knocked me over, and trampled me. He broke three of my ribs and punctured my lung. Yeah, I always looked for him after that."

"When I first got into this business," Skipper continued, "I tried everything I'd ever seen or heard of a clown doing. I'd jump on the bull's head, over him, and about everything else. I still do a lot of that stuff, but I got my own thing, too."

Skipper has been known to drop to his knees, taking the bull around him and reminding me somewhat of El Cordobés, the once utterly reckless Spanish matador. When he talks about doing his "thing," he is referring to staying right in with the bull, putting one hand on the animal's head, and then spinning around (turning his back on the bull) and putting his other hand on the bull's head. He appears to make the same movements you would

146

in dribbling a basketball behind your back, except that a basketball cannot hook or trample you.

"I about stopped dropping to my knees," he said. "I did it one time and this bull hooked me in the belly. Like we been talking about, a lot of people think danger's just part of the act. You do this or that and they want you to do more. Always they want you to do more."

We talked about the life-styles of other clowns as opposed to the new kids getting into the profession. "I think the same thing is happening to us as happened to the cowboys," said Skipper. "There used to be a lot more drinking in the old days. Seemed like it was almost required with them, a machismo thing. Now, I'm certainly not beyond taking a drink, but I never do it before a performance. I don't like to work with somebody who's about half drunk. It's too dangerous. I make it a strict rule to have all my senses when I go out there. I don't even take pills. I've taken many a pill to drive all night, even as far back as high school, but not now. They give me a headache.

"But some of the old-timers could do it. Listen, it didn't even effect Kajun. He's something. He must have drunk a fifth before he got out there, but you'd never know."

D. J. Gaudin, the Kajun Kid, is still operating and circulating a business card that reads: "Wars fought, tigers tamed, governments run, saloons emptied, bridges destroyed, orgies organized, uprisings quelled, virgins converted, revolutions started, computers verified, elephants bred."

One clown, who had been at the top of his profession for a couple of years, lost his bout with

Opposite: *Wilbur Plaugher, on a go-round outside the arena, up on his mule.* Above: *Russ Baize about to make his escape with the aid of Skipper Voss.*

alcohol. "Neal stopped letting him work here," said Spears. "He kept showing up drunk, and he didn't want any part of that."

"But he was the best for a while," said Skipper.

Some of the guy's antics were the talk of the profession for a while; but when his performance seemed more like a death wish, nobody wanted to be a part of him.

A cowboy went into a motel room, looking for a particular clown one day, and found a nude girl chained to the bed. After establishing the fact that the clown wasn't around the room, the cowboy asked the girl exactly what had happened. "I was hitchhiking, and he picked me up," she said. "I guess he is just jealous or something because he always chains me to the bed when he leaves."

"Well, I'd say that's mistreating you," said the cowboy.

"Oh, no, he treats me fine," said the girl. "Every day he brings me a Pepsi and a hamburger to eat."

"I'll tell you another crazy one, maybe the craziest of them all," said Skipper. "Buddy Heaton."

Heaton, now retired, was a huge man of 240 pounds who wore hair down his back and a long Buffalo Bill handlebar mustache. Skipper remembered the last time Buddy ever worked the Calgary Stampede. Among the other extra events at the Stampede is a parimutuel horse race with a great deal of money annually riding on the winner.

Heaton had a substantial bet on a particular horse and watched from the infield as his choice faded badly around the final turn. This so infuriated Buddy that he jumped on his pet buffalo, an animal he used in his act, and rode straight onto the track and toward the oncoming horses. It caused somewhat of a commotion. Jockeys and horses scattered in every direction to avoid the wild man on the speeding buffalo. No, they never asked Buddy Heaton back to Calgary again.

"You know, Buddy was also in President Kennedy's inaugural parade," said Skipper. "Nobody knew how he got there, because he apparently didn't even have a permit. But there he was, riding that buffalo, in the parade for the President of the United States."

"Once I saw Buddy eating a barbecue sandwich at the rodeo," said Spears. "I asked him where he got it and he just motioned to the grounds. He'd built his own campfire right there and cooked barbecue."

"You see some guys at the very other end of the scale," said Skipper. "Like Wilbur Plaugher. Wilbur really got religion, which is great as far as I'm concerned." Plaugher, a strong member of the Fellowship of Christian Athletes, speaks at churches as he moves around the country and during a rodeo likes to remind fans what a great and free country this is. "The only thing that bothers me," added Skipper, "is that he runs down hippies and then says it's a free country."

The phone rang again. "Don't answer it," said Skipper. "I'm going." We got into his pickup and drove around behind the arena, where he parked. All the cowboys spoke to Skipper, and two small boys, hovering among the cowboys, asked for his autograph, which he signed. "I always put 'Skipper Voss, bullfighter,'" he said. "A lot of people don't know the difference between a regular clown and a bullfighter."

Generally, there are three types of clowns: comics, or entertainers; barrel men; and bullfighters. Naturally, all avoid the bulls, but a clown who fights them is specifically there to try to get the bull to move a certain way—should it come out of the chutes and stop—and to help the rider to safety after he's thrown or his ride is finished. At times a clown will also entertain the crowd by, say, letting the animal stick its horn into his mouth, knocking teeth out, cutting his lip and tongue. A barrel man dodges the bull and then jumps into what appears to be padded safety. However, bulls have been known to do more than just butt the barrels—such as sticking their horns into the opening and doing

Preceding pages: *Wilbur Plaugher giving Quail Dobbs a ride.*

a great deal of damage to the clown inside. Entertainers try to prevent a lull in the rodeo by using trained buffalo, dogs, chimps, or horses. Bobby Clark, who along with his brother Gene started a number of original acts, has a goose. During the act, it appears that the goose is pulling Clark in a small wagon, though actually Clark's legs, covered by a blanket that reaches the ground, are supporting the wagon and moving it along behind the goose.

Some people enjoy making others laugh, which isn't difficult to understand. But it is difficult to reason why a man would cover his face with paint, dress up like a scarecrow, and attempt to appear as if he's charging a windmill when, in reality, he's putting his well-being, maybe even his life, on the line. This man is paradoxical, almost a foil in the event as a whole. He might take more chances than anybody in the arena, but few people other than the cowboys realize what he is doing, what he has done. His victories are not recorded in a won-lost column, in money winnings, though his losses are usually stated in broken bones. I don't know. Perhaps I see him as a fine rider in a thoroughbred race. Only thing, he is riding a donkey.

"I don't have to do this for money anymore," Wick Peth had admitted. "I'm old enough to be the father of most of the bull riders I try to protect. But I get a lot of satisfaction when they're clear and turn back to me and say, thanks."

"Me, I care more for the bull rider's respect than anything else," Bobby Clark had said. "I care for that more than I do being a hero. If a man wants to fight bulls for the people in the grandstand, he can fake it. You can't fake it with the bull riders."

Skipper walked around the parking lot, looking for Tommy Lucia. "The day I lose the respect of the bull riders is the day I quit this business," he said.

"I guess you might say I'm just a certain type person. When I was a kid, I wouldn't just go swimming. I'd go to a pool, find the highest diving board, and jump off. I just figured to get noticed by the girls more. I played football. I wanted to be noticed. And I wanted the girls to see me out there. Course, I finally figured out that while I was on the field getting my brains knocked loose, the girls were holding hands with the cheerleaders and drum majors."

We walked near the stands, which were filling with people. "Same way with this," he laughed. "We're out there fighting bulls and this dude wearing one of them hats with the crown made of beer cans is up in the stands with his arm around a girl, telling her, 'Aw, I used to do that. It ain't so tough.'"

"Skipper, my man, how's it goin'?" asked a cowboy.

"Lucia's looking for you," said another one.

"Respect is important," continued Skipper. "I like it when I walk into a rodeo and every cowboy knows me, speaks to me. When you got respect from your peers, that's a big deal.

"I *know* I'm important, whether most outside of rodeo do or not. I don't really think about saving lives, though I might have done it a few times. I just think about the ol' boy getting hurt out there and not being able to get on down the road to do his best in the next rodeo. He has to make a living.

"I like to get around the country. I take my wife sometimes. She always wants to go to Vegas when I work there. You sure don't get bored in this life. I have an electrician's license. I tried that for a while but hated it. I'll do anything, anything except get into that eight-hour-a-day grind. Drives me insane. Just living from one weekend to the next. This way, doing this, I keep it going, keep it exciting."

Skipper, raised in Houston and nearby Alvin, home of no-hit pitcher Nolan Ryan, was good enough in football and track to receive an athletic scholarship to Ranger Junior College. He pole-vaulted fourteen feet, two inches, which wasn't bad before the advent of the fiberglass pole. He eventually started using the fiberglass at Ranger and caused a sensation somewhat different than he'd hoped for. "When I started using that thing, people would just stop and watch as I started my run," said Skipper. "I mean, that thing would shoot me off, like I was coming out of a cannon. I'd be flung over the pit, out onto the track, and I think they took bets I would end up in a nearby street sooner or later. I finally mastered the pole, but I'd already flunked some courses and lost my eligibility."

Like other clowns I met, Skipper began as a rodeo contestant, competing in small-town amateur rodeos. His uncle, who was involved in the sport, got him started.

"One day I was waitin' my turn," said Skipper. "I was all ready, even had on my spurs. I was what you'd call a mediocre rider, not really anybody important. But this friend of mine was up before me and got into trouble getting off the bull. He was down and, without even thinking, I just ran out there and started helping him. I grabbed the bull, dodged it, and helped him get out of the way. I didn't even feel afraid, just that I had to help him.

"When I got back to the chutes, everybody started congratulating me, saying, 'Hey, that was great! Just great!' That's all it took. I was somebody. I've been doing this ever since."

He spotted Lucia just as a riding club and local dignitaries were preparing to ride into the arena to start the rodeo.

"You got a long-distance phone call," said Lucia, grinning.

"What would you do if you didn't fight bulls?" I asked Skipper. "What will you do when it's over?"

"I tell you what I really want to do," he said. "I want to be a crop duster. My daddy did that. I know some people in the business, and so I might get into it for a fact. But I don't want to just fly. Just going up and flying around doesn't interest me. I'd like to go up, do some flips, some stunts, and stuff like that."

Skipper Voss tightened his knee guard as he stood by Lucia, just as a recording of "The Star-

Spangled Banner" ended. The parade of riders left the arena. The rodeo started. "You ready?" asked Lucia. "Hey," said Skipper, "I'm always ready!"

I turned back toward the stands and watched a man in a funny hat escort a young woman to her seat. I thought the crown of his hat might be made of beer cans, but he was too far away to tell.

Hey, I forgot somebody. I tell you who was pretty good in his time—Buck LeGrand. He's got to have been the toughest man ever to go down the road. Look at all those hookings he took and got up and come right back the next night. Don't know what happened to him.
—Skipper Voss

And miles to go before I sleep,
And miles to go before I sleep.
—Robert Frost

Above: *Plaugher and Voss all dressed up to go downtown.* Opposite: *At Cheyenne, the bull takes a bow as Wick Peth rushes in.*

There was a slight, unnatural lean to his body, as though he were carrying an invisible weight. He was short, with a ruddy complexion and reddish hair, and a tired but alert face. I kept thinking he looked somewhat like James Whitmore, the actor. He limped as we walked through the grounds back of another rodeo in another town, past cars with in- and out-of-state licenses, pickups, one- and two-horse trailers, campers, and cowboys and would-be cowboys.

"I always limp," said Buck LeGrand. "On both legs. Don't favor one over the other. Broke both ankles before."

The summer night was lazy and warm, though a breeze made it reasonably comfortable. "Yep, that's my real name," continued Buck. "I didn't take it because of being a clown. My father was French and"—he laughs—"my mother was a *short* Irishwoman."

Buck—who is short—T. O. Taylor, and Frank McIlvain, Jr., the seventeen-year-old son of another clown, were working that night. They would smile

for the audience. Buck spoke to a very young woman and small child in the front seat of his car, then went to the trunk and took out baggy pants (five sizes too large) and a small hat (two sizes too small).

T. O., who had dressed earlier, came over. "No sir," he volunteered, "I've been making money other ways. This is my first time back. Guess you'd say I'm in semiretirement. Don't need to keep fighting those bulls. No sir.

"This business just ain't what it used to be. These kids get into this business, and they'll do it for nothing, for twenty-five bucks. Now we get a hundred bucks."

Buck listened, dressing in silence behind his car. "Oh, I guess I been doing this for twenty-five years," he said when asked. "Been slowin' down the last five, six years, maybe doing twenty rodeos a year. Used to do about thirty-five in the old days. Even went to six National Finals."

T. O. said he was thirty-two, had been clowning for eighteen years, and added, " 'Course, you got guys like Skipper Voss. He'll ask one hundred and seventy-five dollars a performance. Well, let him charge that and get the jobs. I just don't like to let a bull charge me. I like to charge it. I won't just stand there. I sure can't understand why some people do."

"Hey," said Buck, "you're talking about me." He paused and added, "I guess it's about like driving down the freeway, being in this business. Same chances to get hurt. I don't think about it anymore. What do you think about driving down the freeway? You don't think about having a wreck."

Buck walked back to the car to talk to the young woman. T. O. came closer and said, "Some clowns like to take a nip. I'd be afraid I might lose some of my reactions if I did. But some of those ol' boys, my-oh-me, maybe drink a fifth of liquor."

Buck went over to T. O.'s Winnebago to put on his greasepaint. He sat in front of a mirror inside, and Mrs. T. O. Taylor asked him how his wife was doing. Buck, a soft-spoken man who speaks matter-of-factly, said, "Well, she got tired of my BS after twenty-four years and left." He smeared white and red paint on his face. "I got me another woman now," he added.

Buck LeGrand had been a bull rider, a rodeo performer, but he had watched clowns, depended on them, and decided to try the work for himself. For a while he worked as a clown and doubled as a cowboy. "Both suffered," he said. "I wasn't that good as a rider. The pay for a clown is steadier. It's not based on competition. You always get paid doing this. Competing, you might not.

"Maybe I was young and ignorant. You have to be. Fill your mouth full of marbles. Spit out one at a time. When they're all gone, when all your marbles are gone, then you're a rodeo clown.

"But I've made some money. Guess in my time I must have made half a million but spent it all. I do have me a place near Sudan. I've got three hundred cows. Them cows used to work for me. Times being what they are, now I work for them."

Frank McIlvain, Jr., came by the Winnebago, spoke, but mostly listened. The previous week, Frank, Jr., had been working with his father. A bull knocked his father to the ground, then stepped on his head, opening a wound near his ear that required thirty-two stitches. Frank, Jr., came running out to help. A bull, escaping near the chutes, hit him from behind, badly bruising his back.

"Daddy's all right," said Frank, Jr. "My back's just a little sore, but that's life."

Outside, Frank, Jr., moved around a lot, doing deep knee bends, jogging in place, stretching. T. O. continued to carry on the conversation; Buck was quiet, moving slowly toward the arena, as if he were looking for a fishing pole.

The first section of the bull riding event opened the program. Frank, Jr., got into a barrel and Buck pushed it at a bull, Mixmaster, that had thrown its rider. Mixmaster hit the barrel and people laughed. T. O. would calculate and then run into the bull's line of vision, escaping up wire netting on the fence as the bull turned to get him.

When the first event ended, T. O. nervously said, "Yessir, I like them muley bulls."

"They all look alike to me now," said Buck. And he meant it.

"If I don't get hit by one, I figure I had a bad day," said T. O.

"If I *get* hit by one, I had a bad day," said Buck.

Buck walked back toward the car, and T. O. said, "Yeah, you're around Skipper and he wants to do it all. Me, I just stand back and let him.

"You know, some like to go to places and have a good time. I take my wife with me. That's why some of the clowns don't like me. But I look at it like this: if I get hurt, she's there. I got my Winnebago, so I save money on motels."

I walked away and found Buck talking to the small boy outside his car. He told me something Skipper had said but Buck had known much longer. "The closer the bull gets to you the better chance you have of getting away," he said. "He gets close, you move quick, and he'll miss you. You want to keep the animal going around in a circle. He'll finally just quit on you that way."

But Buck knows theory is not always animal. He has been hit, stepped on, and has suffered broken bones all over his body and so many sprains and bruises that they don't count—and never did, really.

Once he was almost blown up, which had nothing to do with the bull. An explosion was supposed to go off near him, making him jump and the fans laugh. A wire got caught, and the charge went off by his leg, shattering the thigh bone. Another time, a bull knocked him into the chutes and rammed him over and over with its horns. Buck continued to work and found out a few days later he'd shattered a collarbone.

During the second section of bull riding, the final event of the evening, a bull named Friendly Frank tossed rider Mike Roan and then went for him. Buck, who no longer moves fast, made his way to the rider, helped him up and then stepped aside as the bull charged. Later, when another bull would not charge him, Buck yelled, "This is a union bull!" People laughed. They'd also laughed when he rode out into the arena on his Shetland pony, Domino. Buck and the horse pretended they were making camp in the arena and went to sleep under the same blanket, which the horse bit and pulled off Buck, over itself. "I can't stand a horse that pulls the cover," said Buck. Kids liked the act. The small boy with the young woman in Buck's car laughed a long time as he watched Buck and Domino.

"Sometimes," said Buck, "I worry more about people not laughing than I do about fighting bulls."

Frank McIlvain, Jr., came out of the barrel after the final event and said, "No, my daddy didn't push me into clowning at all. I just took to it, you know. I'm young, so I've got a real good start."

The announcer told everybody to drive carefully and come back again. "I enjoy this," said Buck. "I like the people, always have. I mean the cowboys, animals, everybody. But I don't know how much longer I'll be a clown. I guess until the promoters stop calling me. Twenty-four years is a long time, but I can't really say I'd change my life. I don't look back. A man has to look ahead and find out what's gonna happen, not back and see what happened."

The clown's paint came off Buck easily. He looked very tired, though I was not sure whether it was from age or doing what he had been doing for so long. I wondered at what point a man stopped playing a part and it began to play him.

The Winnebago was in the line of traffic leaving the grounds. Buck got into his car and talked softly to the young woman and boy who had waited for him. Frank McIlvain, Jr., stood by the gate, looking into the empty arena. He had not begun to take the paint off yet and stared blankly, as though watching himself go over the next horizon.

Chapter 5:
STOCK AND MAN

*I'll stick in the saddle and make him my own,
I'll ride him until he lies down with a groan,
Bring on your Strawberry Roan....
I steps up aboard him and raises the blind,
"Get outa the way boys, he's gonna unwind."
He sure is a broad walker, he heaves a big sigh,
He only lacks wings for to be on the fly.
He's the worst buckin' bronco I've seen on the range
Turn on a nickel and give you some change.
Oh, that Strawberry Roan; ohhhh, that
   Strawberry Roan;
That sunfishin' critter's worth leavin' alone.*

*There's nary a buster from Texas to Nome
Can ride that Strawberry Roan.*
      —"Strawberry Roan," origin unknown

A cowboy named Dick Griffin wrote an epitaph on a gravestone for the famous bucking bronc Midnight. It read:

*Under this sod lies a great bucking hoss
There never lived a cowboy he couldn't toss
His name was Midnight, his coat black as coal
If there is a hoss-heaven, please God, rest his soul.*

The rodeo was over ... anywhere, anytime. The morning after, they'd begun to load the rodeo stock into giant cattle trucks, which would take some back to the ranch to graze and others on down the road to another rodeo. Tommy Steiner, a stockman who runs the rodeo company that bears his name, reminded some of his men not to put two particular bulls together, because they might fight.

"They're just like people," he said. "They have different personalities, and some just don't get along. Put them together and they'll argue and fight."

The stock pens were emptying, and the chutes on the rodeo grounds were deserted; the only signs of recent activity were the footprints around the gates. The stage was being emptied and the props taken down; the players were leaving. Steiner was talking about rodeo's reputation for being inhumane to its animals. Grinning, he remembered an experience he'd had in Kansas City. He'd been quoted in the *Kansas City Star* regarding his policy of allowing anyone from various humane societies to come out and see firsthand how he treated his animals. A woman from one of the smaller humane groups took him up on his invitation. She hung around Steiner and his stock for a few days but became upset when he refused to actually let her get into the arena during the rodeo. He tried but had difficulty easing her feelings, so his every move was magnified.

During the saddle bronc event, Tommy was sitting on top of one of the chutes. The horse threw its rider and started back out the gate nearest him. As he started to climb down and get out of the way, the horse jerked its head, catching Tommy's left hand and hammering it into the gate. The blow split his palm and, as he later found out, broke his thumb in three places. His hand felt numb but, despite profuse bleeding, he shrugged it off until after the event ended, when friends talked him into going to the hospital.

"I want to see that horse," said the woman, charging into the chutes.

"Mam," said Bobby Steiner, "they took my dad to the hospital. He's hurt. The horse is fine."

"I want to see that horse," insisted the woman. "It appeared to me he hurt that horse when he hit it with his hand."

The horse, already loaded, was taken off the truck. A streak was barely visible on the horse's forehead, though the skin wasn't broken where it

Joe Alexander with an over-eager bronc.

had smashed Tommy's hand. The woman demanded medicine, which she dabbed on the horse. "Now, it's all right," she said.

"Yeah," said Bobby, "but my dad isn't."

"One time," Tommy continued, that morning as they loaded his stock, "we were in Louisville, Kentucky, and this humane group put out literature. It showed the picture of a horse with its tongue out. The tongue was cut clean across. The

Opposite top: Cowboys checking out a group of bulls in the stock pens at Cheyenne. Opposite bottom: *A long-horned bovine on his own in the arena.*

caption said it was a typical rodeo horse on which hacksaw blades were used as bits in its mouth and barbed wire for flank straps. That just teed the hell outa me."

An elderly lady in Memphis, Tennessee, had become upset over the use of a flank girth, the sheepskin-lined strap that is put around the flank of the animal. It's tightened as the animal leaves the chute and makes it kick in an attempt to shed the strap. The woman had seen a newspaper picture of a bucking horse and had phoned an animal inspector.

"I've just seen a picture of this rodeo horse with a strap around its testicles," she told the inspector. "Now, that's got to hurt."

"Yes, mam, if that's where the strap is, it *has* got to hurt," said the inspector, who went to see Tommy. Steiner showed him the horse in question and that the strap touched no part of its privates. Besides, the horse was a gelding. Informed of this, the woman said, "Well, it *would* have hurt."

"Yes, mam."

"Now, if you'll notice," Steiner continued, blankly watching one of his trucks leave, "those straps are heavily padded. They're not pulled real tight. If you pulled them too tight, the animal wouldn't buck. Well, just like you couldn't take a belt and make it real tight around an athlete's waist and expect him to perform.

"Listen, these animals are well cared for. Nobody's going to be cruel to them. Not me. Not the cowboys, who know the animals are also their livelihood. I've got a big investment in them, maybe half a million in stock and equipment. I'd be an idiot not to protect that kind of investment. If you're going to make it in this business, you've got to keep your stock well cared for and in good shape. Rodeo animals get better care than most any livestock around, better than show horses, and no drugs are used on them like with some race horses."

Horses and bulls buck, at the most, for eight seconds a performance. Steiner will send a particular animal out to buck an average of twice a week, using the animal in thirty to forty rodeos annually. So actual work time for the animals is four or five minutes a year. They're fed a high-protein diet, handled with special care as they're taken from show to show, and are allowed to graze in between. In 1976, a horse Steiner owned named Red Pepper, which had been to all National Finals through 1975, died of natural causes. The horse was thirty-five years old.

"Tell you what," Pete Gay had once told me, "When I'm reincarnated, I'd like to come back as a rodeo animal. You work eight seconds, then all you do is rest, eat, and screw."

Rodeo is only as strong as its stock.
—*Cotton Rosser, stockman*

They'd loaded and shipped out about eighty bulls, forty saddle broncs, forty barebacks, and maybe almost a hundred dogging steers and calves for roping. They were going, moving on down the road, and Tommy Steiner looked tired. His face seemed more lined than usual, but another rodeo was over and, in a few hours, he planned to drive home to Austin with his wife, Beverly, and his grandson, Shane. As we sat in the coffee shop of the Holiday Inn—any Holiday Inn, any town—he brightened as he spoke to friends and seemed to enjoy talking about rodeo and his business.

"There's been worst things happen than ladies from the Humane Society," he said. "I remember in Big Spring, 1948, we could have been shot. There was this bronc rider named Herb Frizell, who got mad as hell at a judge named Buck Jones. Buck was a big ol' tough boy and Herb was just a little guy. They'd been having trouble before, and when Herb got a bad score from Buck on his ride, he went berserk. He got his gun and started shooting at Buck. He got Buck, all right, but a lot of bullets were flying around. One killed a guy, name of Myers. He was a calf roper, just sittin' on the fence. We could have all been shot.

"Yeah, rodeo has changed. You don't see things like that happen anymore. The cowboys, as a group, ride better now and so the animals have got to be better, taken care of better with more modern food and methods."

If Tommy Steiner isn't the top man in his field, he's close. Each year cowboys vote the best stock to the National Finals. Over the years, Tommy has had more NFR stock than anybody. For a while he'd have had thirty-five, thirty-six head named to the Finals, but some other stockmen didn't think this was fair. One of them might have to haul a single animal all the way from Montana, hardly worth the effort. So stockmen agreed nobody could furnish more than fifteen head each year to the NFR. But the rule was bent a little in 1975. Tommy Steiner had sixteen animals, including bareback horse of the year Stormy Weather and Black Six, a bull that shared bull of the year honors with Tiger, owned by Mike Cervi.

"Oh, you've got to feel a little competitive," continued Tommy, beginning his fourth cup of coffee. "If I didn't think I had the best line of stock, I'd quit. Other guys feel they do, too. But I think of it this way: say I went to the people at the State Fair Rodeo in Dallas and tried to get that contract again. I wouldn't go there and say, 'You ought to use me because I have the *second* best stock in the country.'"

Tommy finds his stock in a number of ways and talks about certain animals as you would people. And in a way there is a correlation with pro sports. "You've got to keep a good lineup going, like a pro football team," explained Tommy. "You've got your veterans to depend on and you bring in a few rookies each year to move out or replace ones that are over the hill. It's a never ending deal."

Steiner also will scout, or have employees or friends scout, amateur rodeos. He might find a good bucker at one of the stock sales held around the country, but success is usually limited. Tommy and other stockmen aren't apt to put an animal that is bucking well up for sale. So, ordinarily, the stock sales serve as a kind of waiver system. The stock you find there is usually over the hill, just not tops. But, as in football, you might spot a certain characteristic about an animal you like and, with some adjustments in the way it's handled, it might perform for you.

"They used to have a good deal on this Indian Reservation in Dakota," said Tommy. "You could drive up there and they'd bring in three hundred to five hundred horses for you to try out. What they'd do was raise these horses for five years, then sell one for one hundred dollars. But somebody in the Indian management convinced them they'd be better off raising cows. Each year the cow would have a calf, which would bring one hundred dollars."

Some have tried breeding bucking horses, though Tommy says that's about like expecting the son of a major league pitcher to have a big league arm. "I know I haven't been successful breeding

them," he said. "Now, they say that in breeding some stallions, a percentage of their colts will turn into buckers. But another reason there's not a lot of breeding is that you can't use them until they're five, six years old."

Nobody really knows why an animal bucks. Certainly, it is not because it's a "wild" horse. Some horses are docile, even gentle, in the chutes. Yet once the gate opens they leap, kick wildly, and spin. When the rider is thrown or the buzzer sounds, once again they simmer down and are easily handled.

"You can't train a horse to buck, that's for sure," said Tommy. "If I figured out how to do that I'd save a fortune. What you have to do is try them out, just see if and how they'll buck.

"But, generally speaking, you look for bigger-sized horses for saddle bronc. Broncs are the most temperamental. Sometimes you get them in a strange place and they won't do anything. Bare-backs, well, you don't care if they're small. You try to spot a combination of good things in horses, like you would a good athlete. I mean, like an athlete, they've either got heart or they don't.

"No way to predict. Lots of times you get one who's never been broken, never touched by human hands, and he won't buck worth a darn.

"Now, if you see a bull which is a little nervous-acting or has some fight in him, then he's more apt to buck."

A good bull might bring $2,000 and a bronc $1,000, though Tommy says ordinarily he pays about $200 to $500 for bucking horses and anywhere from $750 to $1,000 for proven bucking bulls. As mentioned, horses usually won't perform consistently until they're six or seven years old. Bulls usually come around at about four.

"The market is getting higher," said Tommy. "I tell you one thing which has hurt, and that's because they're shipping horsemeat overseas. They're giving about thirty-two cents a pound for horsemeat which they send to Europe for human consumption."

If a horse is unsuitable for practical work or riding, and can't make it in rodeo and isn't shipped to Europe as meat, it's likely to end up as dog food in the United States. This is something those in the business don't like to talk about, but it's done on a wide scale. "It's sad but true," said Tommy.

Tommy has not only got stock in unusual ways at bargain prices; he's also been known to pay a great deal of money for an animal.

Stormy Weather, a dun gelding, was bought from a Cleburne, Texas, dairy farmer for $250. The farmer not only couldn't break the horse but also had trouble keeping it from jumping fences. "One of my pickup men heard about the horse and I bought him," said Tommy.

Tommy traded a Charolais for Black Six, a medium-size bull that has one droopy horn. "I was able to trade for him because he was being used with cows and wasn't producing many good

Stock pens at Cheyenne, empty until the next time.

The wild horse race at Cheyenne. Three-man teams battle the unbroken mustangs, to get the saddle on and ride across the finish line.

calves," said Tommy. "He was scrawny, but we fattened him up. You get a lot of stock like that. If they're like poor or weak looking and still have the heart to buck, you can get them in shape and they'll really cut loose."

The most Tommy ever paid for a saddle bronc was $4,500. The horse, named Bonanza, had impressed rodeo star Harry Tompkins. It belonged to an Indian in North Dakota, but Harry told Tommy the horse was something else. Tommy decided to buy it sight unseen. He phoned the guy and established a price of $500. But the Indian called back and said he'd have to get $1,000. Okay, said Tommy. Later he phoned the Indian to find out when he could pick up the horse and the Indian said he'd been thinking and needed $2,000 for the animal. Tommy agreed.

"Next day we were hooking up the trailer to go get him, and the Indian calls and says he's got to have three thousand dollars," said Tommy. "I even agreed to that. But I kinda got the drift of things and started hurrying those boys hooking up the trailer. But, sure enough, the phone rings again and the Indian says he wants five thousand. I said I'd give him forty-five hundred, and we agreed. After that I took the phone off the hook.

"When that horse arrived, I was sick. He looked awful. But we got him in shape and he was the most outstanding bronc I ever had. He went to the National Finals seven times and was voted horse of the year twice.

"But I tell you something: you build your reputation with good horse trading, but it's luck. You just don't tell anybody."

Steiner admitted he once went to Wyoming, bought 227 head of wild horses off a big ranch, and got only three bucking horses out of the entire bunch. He also wasn't too proud of the way a deal turned out he'd made for a registered Paint horse.

"The Paint looked good," he said. "But for some reason it wasn't bucking. I tried him out, and he did all right, so I gave the guy four hundred

dollars. The Paint started out well for us, but as the season progressed, he got worse and worse. At the beginning of the following year, I shipped him off to the ranch to rest, thinking that might help him.

"Well, one day my dad phoned me and said this feller had offered six hundred dollars for the Paint. I told him to take it. Even I can spot a profit of two hundred dollars. This feller who bought him started taking the horse to shows and fairs. And the thing was winning all kinds of prizes. He was named Grand Champion at a horse show in Houston. Next thing I hear the horse has been sold for five thousand dollars to Lamar Hunt. I'm sure you've seen that horse. He's the mascot for the Kansas City Chiefs, the horse that guy rides around the stadium when the Chiefs score a touchdown. They call him War Paint, though I might think of something else to call him now."

Tommy's favorite horse was Black Magic. He found him at a black rodeo on Juneteenth (the annual celebration of the Emancipation Proclamation). "The horse's original name was actually Juneteenth," said Tommy. "They'd buck him ten or twelve times a day at that annual rodeo. He was a little thing but just had tremendous heart. I got him for two hundred dollars, and he was a star.

"He died in Greensboro, North Carolina, of twisted intestines."

Wild horse racing. It's man against beast—and often the latter wins.

A horse will sometimes roll over in a field. When it does, its intestines can get twisted, and if it doesn't roll back over, a knot can form. "That's what happened to Black Magic," he said. "Boy, I miss that horse."

I asked him about his favorite bull. Actually, he doesn't go out and buy many bulls, because he raises them himself. But he once bought a bull named Jim, upon whose side the previous owner had branded in giant letters J-I-M.

"Jim was the greatest fighting bull in the country," said Tommy. "He bucked good, too. But turn that animal loose in the arena and he wiped out everything in sight.

"His back was broken while he was bucking at a rodeo in Pine Bluff, Arkansas. They put him on a sled and dragged him out of the arena. Nothing could be done, so Jim had to be killed, put out of his misery. They had to shoot him fourteen times in the head before he died. That was some bull."

"It's a good thing the lady from the Humane Society wasn't there," I said.

"I imagine," said Tommy, "if I'd broken my back, she'd have had me shot but not that bull."

Tommy Steiner rested in a chair by the window of his motel room. Beverly was sitting on the bed, and Shane, two and a half years old, roamed around the room. Steiner, a man of fifty, looked fifteen years younger with his hat on. But he took it off, showing baldness, and seemed to age on the spot. Without his hat, he just didn't look the same. It was as if he'd taken off his nose. Some cowboys are like that.

The Steiners were about to leave for home late that afternoon. Another page turned for the year. "One time," Tommy was saying, "we were at this rodeo in Arkansas. We were riding in for the grand entrance, all of us dressed up, holding flags and riding the pretty horses. Then, suddenly, all the horses started bucking, going crazy. We had some of the damnest wrecks you ever saw.

"Well, we found out later a bunch of kids were sitting in the front of the stands, shooting water guns full of a burning substance at the horses.

"But nobody was seriously injured, though I will say some of us lost our poise."

I have seen it written many times that a horse doesn't really try to hurt you but a bull does. If a horse injures a cowboy, it will not be deliberate, though a bull will try to hook, stomp, and hurt a cowboy any way it can.

"Not all bulls try to hurt you," said Tommy. "And I tell you some horses don't mind running over you. I was trying out one for bucking the other

Opposite: *The stock-pen maze at Calgary.* Below: *Part of the easy life of a rodeo animal is good eating and lots of rest.*

day. When the rider came off, the horse chased him all over the arena, trying to bite him. You think you know everything about animals and that's the time you get fooled." Again, I thought, like people.

"Shane," said Tommy, "come here. Right here. Tell this man about that ol' bull Number Sixty hooking you."

Shane, wide-eyed, cute, stays skinned up like most boys his age who are active. He had a skinned spot on his back, from a childhood fall, but was convinced he'd been hooked by Ol' No. 60. One day he'd been walking by the pen on the ranch, and No. 60 stirred and snorted at him. Shane jumped back, yelling the bull had hooked him.

He went to Tommy and told him, "He hookee me. He hookee me, Ol' Nummer Sixty."

"He shows everybody that scratch on his back and says he's been hooked," said Tommy, laughing.

Beverly phoned Bobby, who had taken a string of the Steiner stock to another rodeo, to find out how things had gone. Bobby, the world champion bull rider in 1973, had retired into the business with his father, much as Tommy once did with his dad, Buck Steiner.

I remembered something Bobby had told me. "If I'd stayed active as a bull rider much longer, with all that travel and constant competing, I'd have ended up on a funny farm."

Bobby's wife, Joleen, a barrel racer, now helps run the Austin ranch. Beverly handles much of the paper work, and another son of Tommy's, Bill, competes in rodeo and also works on the Steiners'

other ranch, where commercial cattle are raised.

"When Bobby and Joleen were going together, they were both ranked high in their events," said Tommy. "The year they got married, neither one was worth a flip."

He paused and added, "Bobby's doing a great job with our rodeo stock. He's actually going to more rodeos now than I am. He gets along well with the committees, knows stock well, and, of course, the cowboys knew him when he was one of them.

"Bill placed in his event here."

Shane, moving back and forth across the room, found his granddad's lap again. "Beverly and I have always traveled together," continued Tommy. "For a while we tried the military school bit for the kids after they started to school. They liked it, but we didn't. We missed them. So we just started taking tutors around with us. I been rodeoing and working in this business for thirty years now. If I'd have had to leave my wife and kids at home, I'd have done something else.

"But I didn't. They went with me, and we've all enjoyed this business. I think the thing I like most about it is the people you meet, the friends you make. I don't think I can go anywhere now that I don't bump into somebody I've met in rodeo."

Once Tommy and Beverly went to California to visit actor Dale Robertson and his wife. They decided to go to the races. As they were taking their seats an usher walked up to Tommy. "Hello, Tommy, how you doing? Remember, I talked to you at that rodeo in . . ."

He watched Shane. "Bobby's already had him on a steer," he said. "He does what I used to do with my boys. You put them on a steer and run along with them, holding 'em by the belt. That way you can just lift them off. But they think they're bucking like hell.

"Now Shane's real tickled already about rodeos. Shane, tell him about Ol' Number Sixty."

Shane, grinning, said, "That Ol' Nummer Sixty baad sonagun. He hookee me. Yes he did."

The Hill Country in Central Texas is a vast section of escarpment that stretches west and north of Austin and into the San Antonio area to the south. Many varieties of trees—cedar, live oak, Spanish oak, and cypress—cover soft, rolling hills that can suddenly become steep. In season, the state flower of Texas, the bluebonnet, carpets the ground with a blue tint. The Hill Country can be a contrasting section, with different landscapes just over the next rise. Small rivers—the Guadalupe, Llano, Blanco, and Pedernales—move quietly, but the huge Colorado River leaves a massive indentation as it moves through the area and the center of Austin, the state capital.

It is the country of J. Frank Dobie; an area that William Sydney Porter, known as O. Henry, used as early background material; it is LBJ country, where the late president came to relax, to escape. It is both a hard and soft area, one in which you might find dreamers, poets, or the Marlboro Man.

The Steiner Ranch where rodeo stock is kept—140 to 150 bulls and about 100 horses—is about a twenty-minute drive northwest from Austin, just below the Mansfield Dam, where the Colorado is trapped to form Lake Austin. About eight miles of the ranch is lakefront, and the Colorado, making a horseshoe twist, serves as one boundary of the 5,300-acre spread. The commercial ranch, 5,000 acres, is near Bastrop, southeast of Austin, and has about 1,300 head for commercial purposes.

Now the ranch on the Colorado is rustic, ignoring the modern in favor of tradition. The main house, built of stone, is 100 years old, and the pens and corrals look like something out of a Western movie. In fact, movie companies often use the ranch for scenes that, if not authentic, are at least shot in an authentic place. Tommy and Beverly Steiner actually live in Austin, almost equidistant from both ranches. When Tommy is home, he spends his days at the ranches.

People who know the Steiners say Tommy inherited his horse trading ability from his father, though that makes me think of the son of a major league pitcher growing up with a big league arm. Buck, now seventy-six, started the ranching and rodeo stock business a half dozen decades ago and still operates the Capitol Saddlery, a boot shop that is an Austin landmark.

"Being in rodeo, running stock, all came naturally to me," said Tommy. "It was what my dad was doing, what I'd grown up around, so I just came right into the business. I was always going with my dad to rodeos. Yeah, I do remember my granddad. But all I can picture in my mind is him sitting on the front porch in his rocking chair, smoking a pipe and taking it all in.

"There used to be these Wild West shows which came to Austin when I was a kid. They'd give you five bucks if you could ride one of their wild buffalo. That's how I got my first experience riding wild stock. My dad would take me to the Wild West Show and I'd ride those buffalos.

"I don't really know what I'd done if I hadn't gotten into rodeo. I was always interested in aviation but I imagine I'd just been a regular rancher."

Once he'd said his goal was to put on a rodeo someday in which nobody rode his bulls and horses. So I asked him how it felt to be the only guy at a rodeo pulling for the stock.

"I don't really get as much of a kick out of seeing somebody thrown off one of my animals as I do just seeing the animals perform well," he said. "I'm happy if I see a cowboy make a good ride on a good bucking animal.

"But the thing I don't like to see is a guy make a sorry ride on a good bucking animal. That makes me a little mad. 'Course, I also get mad when one of my animals doesn't do its job."

Tommy had driven for hours from the rodeo to his ranch and complained about the fifty-five-mile-per-hour speed limit, which has helped keep the highways safe but definitely deters cowboys trying to get on down the road.

"This is a tough business," he added. "You've got to like it. I've cut down on my rodeos now and Bobby will be making more and more for us.

"Yeah, to be successful in this business you've got to be part cowboy, part lawyer, part vet, and do a little politickin' on the side. But those things won't help you if you don't have any luck hoss tradin'."

He was quiet for a minute. I think his mind had wandered and he was thinking about Shane riding one of those steers.

In a Chicago rodeo, Tommy Steiner used a horse that had a big scar across its face. It had once been a deep cut and hair wouldn't grow around the wound. The animal had apparently run into a barbed wire fence as a colt, cutting its face. But that was long before Tommy bought the horse.

As the horse tried to shed its rider, a man in the stands began to yell. "Get that horse outa there, ya bums! Can't you see he's been injured! Look at his face! Get him outa there!" The crowd began to yell along with the man.

Rather than cause a big scene Tommy walked into the stands and, politely as he could, asked the man to please come down to the pens with him and examine the horse. He did. Tommy explained the horse had been eight years old when he'd bought it and the injury had apparently occurred when it was a colt. He showed him the scar was old, long healed over. The man thanked him for his trouble and, satisfied, walked back into the stands.

The crowd started cheering the man, yelling for him, and the man raised both arms in victory. He had showed them, become a hero. Tommy Steiner saw the man go back into the stands, heard the crowd cheering, and just shook his head slowly in disbelief. Ever so slowly.

Jim Shoulders

Casey Tibbs

Chapter 6:
DAKOTA KID AND AN OKIE

If wars can ever really be called romantic, then World War II, the last romantic war, had ended. The give-'em-hell years of Truman would close, Ike would be swept into the White House, and we would go through a new kind of war, that crazy Asian war. McCarthyism would diminish us all. Russia would launch Sputnik, which Secretary of State Charles Wilson would call "a neat scientific trick." Blacks, tiring of tokenism, would march, picket, sit-in. Rock 'n' roll boomed . . . Gary Cooper in High Noon *. . . Hemingway's poetic prose in* The Old Man and the Sea *. . . short skirts, long skirts. America liked itself and was booming. Along with it, sports boomed.*

It was a good time for sports, a golden time. There was the Yankee Dynasty, the graceful Joe DiMaggio and the baby-faced Mickey Mantle. Pete Rozelle was an ambitious sports PR man at the University of San Francisco. Pro football became a television habit, a part of Americana, when, on a Sunday afternoon in 1958, Baltimore—led by cast-off quarterback John Unitas—beat the New York Giants in sudden death.

Athletes were breakfast-cereal heroes. We puffed them up, admired them, wished we were them. And the biggest rodeo stars, formerly almost unknown nationally, were emerging. They were the Bill Lindermans, the Toots Mansfields, and the Harry Tompkinses. But the biggest and brightest were Casey Tibbs, a South Dakotan who was breeding wild horses for a living when he was ten, and Jim Shoulders, the man from Oklahoma, who might have been the best ever.

It was like no other time, and more than any, it was their time.

Jim Shoulders looked out the window, across the wing of the DC-3, and could barely see the Empire State Building, dark and gray against the oyster sky. There had been a movie named *King Kong* when he was a kid, in which the giant ape had stood on that building. He was sitting next to Casey Tibbs; they were en route to a rodeo in Omaha. The DC-3, a reliable but loose-jointed plane, rattled and shook as it hit turbulence, then rain, outside New York. Dishes crashed in the back of the plane, and a number of passengers were getting sick.

Casey, who always looked as if he were about to break into a smile, was eyeing an elderly lady directly across the aisle.

"They didn't have sick bags then but just regular ice cream cups with the lid on them," recalled Shoulders. "Well, I remember Casey just sittin' there watching this old lady, who was maybe fifty, sixty years old. Seemed like for an hour she had been holding that cup by her face, just about to thow up. A lot of people were sick, but I felt sorry for that old lady.

"Anyway, Casey started watching her, and I could see the wheels turning in his crazy head. So he picks up his cup and starts going 'Urrrggghhh' real loud, actin' like he's thowin' up. The old lady would look at him and then back into her cup.

"'Ohhh, my goodness, urghhh!' said Casey. The woman looked over at him again. But this time, Casey pulls the cup away from his mouth, looks into it, and then puts it up to his lips, like he's drinking it.

"That did it. She got sick all over the place. 'Why you onery sonuvabuck,' I said. And when we got off that flight, I wouldn't even sit by him anymore. 'I don't want anybody to know I even seen you, much less knowed you,' I told him.

"He was always doin' something like that. One time the plane was late when we landed in New York for the big rodeo in Madison Square Garden. You know how you'll get off and walk down the

Right: *Casey Tibbs today.* Below: *Tibbs in 1967, on Wood Burn.*

ramp and see somebody you know and run and hug them. Well, Casey didn't know a soul there and neither did I. But he saw all these people huggin' and kissin', so he picks out this woman and runs to her and starts huggin' her and telling her how much he's missed her. She like to of jumped out of her skin. I mean this guy with a big hat and boots runs up and starts huggin' her.

"But that's just Casey."

Casey was the best bronc rider to ever stick his foot in pointy-toed boots. Jim would sit in the middle and spur bulls everybody else said couldn't be ridden.
—Dave Stout, former roper, editor of Rodeo Sports News

Tibbs was the wild man, the clown jester, of rodeo. Used to be a guy named Bill McMacken wore white linen suits who we called "the Count," but Casey did it more. He was flamboyant and brought the cowboy out of the old humdrum image.

We traveled together and rodeoed hard. I think it must have been a year after the Korean War started before I knew it was going on.
—Harley May, steer wrestler

He was a slender, handsome young man with dark blond hair and a leprechaun's twinkle in his eye. He had a quick wit and a natural flair for being colorful. Lavender was his color: he wore fancy silk lavender shirts, lavender bandannas around his neck, lavender boots, and he drove a lavender Lincoln Continental with the big initials "CT" on the doors. He dated cowgirls, New York models, Hollywood starlets . . . Hollywood starlets and cowgirls and New York models. He had the physical (and mental?) makeup to handle an early morning party and then go out and ride a bucking bronc. He spent money almost as fast as he made it and was called the Babe Ruth of his time. Casey Tibbs didn't just pass through. Everybody knew he was there.

"I was plumb scared to go to bed, for fear I might miss something," he once said.

When it was pointed out to him that he might look a little "sissified" wearing his purple silk shirts, he said, "I'd love for 'em to think they was gettin' beat by a sissy."

They got beat. Casey won his first saddle bronc title at the age of nineteen, in 1949, and before he was through he won six bronc titles, one bareback championship, and All Around titles in 1951 and 1955. He participated in all five major events when he started, but eventually confined himself to bareback and saddle bronc, an event he revolutionized, beginning the style still used today.

Before and during the war years, bronc riders employed the style similar to the one riders used on the range to break wild horses. They sat upright in the saddle, putting pressure on the rein held near the swell. High-backed saddles, so different from the small Association saddle of today, made it difficult to dislodge a rider. Riding broncs was as much a physical battle as anything else.

Casey did it differently. He sat loose in the saddle holding the rein almost daintily out in front of him as he leaned back and raked the animal with his spurs. When the horse lunged forward, the force would throw him backward, and as the animal landed on all fours, the shock would pitch him forward again. The results put him in a wild rocking motion while, at the same time, he spurred in a wide, cadenced arc. For Casey, riding broncs was rhythm, coordination, and timing. And sometimes he thrilled the crowd even more. He wouldn't wait for the pickup man but would almost rocket out of the saddle at the buzzer, landing on his feet. Most of the time.

"When I make a good ride," he said, "I get the same kind of satisfaction a fellow gets who fights good or hits a baseball good. This is the most competitive sport in the world. You're competing against both man and animal."

Casey was flaky, cocky, and good. A picture on the cover of *Life* magazine seemed to capture him perfectly. It showed Casey, at five feet, eleven

Jim Shoulders at ease in Fort Worth, in 1967. The clown on the right is John Routh; on the left is D. J. Gaudin, the Kajun Kid.

inches, a slim 140-150 pounds, standing in the chutes, looking out over the arena. He was wearing a silk shirt and had his hands on his hips. He looked as if he owned it all. At that time, *Life* magazine sold for twenty cents.

Do not get the impression he wasn't physically tough. Shoulders told a story about Casey that took place in Nampa, Idaho, in 1952. As the buzzer sounded, the pickup man snubbed the bronc's rein on his saddlehorn just as Casey started to grab the man's shoulders and jump clear. At the same instant, the bronc bucked once again, sending Casey over its head. The animal he had been riding and both pickup horses ran over him. Rushed to the hospital, he couldn't move his legs. The doctors diagnosed a blood clot on his spine. They gave him a good chance to walk again, in two or three months, but cast doubts over his riding career.

"Nine days after the accident, Casey phoned this friend and told him to park his car just outside the hospital," said Shoulders. "The guy came and Casey grabbed his crutches and hooked 'em out of the hospital. When the nurses and all rushed to the window to look out, they saw Casey smashing his crutches and getting into the car. I believe it was about three weeks after that when he won the bronc ridin' at Rapid City, South Dakota, on a horse that had never been ridden."

In 1956, Casey was heeding the lure of show business and thinking about retiring for a career in television and movies. He'd had bit parts in movies and had acted as a stunt man and advisor. When he entered the first rodeo of that year, in Denver, he was bucked off and dragged, and suffering four broken ribs.

This hurt his pride. Two weeks later he wrapped his ribs tightly and entered the indoor rodeo in Fort Worth, drawing a horse named Peaceful, which had thrown him in Cheyenne the previous year. Rider and horse had excellent nights, and observers said it was one of the most classic rides they'd ever seen. Casey won day money and the average.

Toughness came naturally to him. His parents were homesteaders along the Cheyenne River in Stanley County, South Dakota, near Fort Pierre. When Casey, the last of six boys among the ten children born to the John Tibbses, came into the world on March 5, 1929, his parents told everybody a coyote had brought him. Raised around animals, Casey was breaking horses at five dollars each when he was ten. He entered his first professional rodeo at fourteen but continued to break horses and work around ranches for a living. It was 1947 before he was able to go into rodeo for an earnest living.

"He was working with the late Ken Roberts [a top rodeo hand and later a stock contractor] when he first come out of South Dakota," recalled Jim Shoulders. "Well, Ken had one of them bobtailed trucks with a combination livestock and grain bed on it. They went over to a rodeo in Peabody, Kansas, with a load of steers.

"They stopped in some town, might have been Wichita, to get gas. When Ken wasn't lookin', Casey pulled the dump [power gear] back. Ken got back

Opposite: Jim Shoulders, up on a big black bull, giving a lesson in how it's done. Above: Shoulders has won the All Around title five times.

Above: *Lyle Sankey showing perfect form.* Opposite: *Using a black rope doesn't make staying on a bucking bronc any easier.*

into the truck and put it in gear and started out. The dump started raisin' and Ken didn't know what was happening. He jumped out of the truck but left it in gear, and it went up and the back end fell down. Steers fell out the tailgate right in the middle of town and started going every which-a-way. Casey just sat there laughing."

Fort Pierre was and is proud of Casey. Colin Lofting, a former rodeo hand and writer, was traveling with Casey and two strangers over a bridge across the Missouri River into Pierre. They saw a sign that read "Site of World's Largest Earthen Dam and the Birthplace of Casey Tibbs." Eyeing the two strangers, Lofting remarked, "How long did it take you to build that bridge, Casey?"

Casey, straight-faced, said, "I had a helluva time. See, the city would only give me nails. I had to save for the lumber. And so's not to get caught, I'd build 'er at night, by headlights comin' over the bridge. Pop up and drive a nail, then hide."

In Strong, Kansas, Casey nearly caused a riot while helping round up horses. The small hotel in which he was staying had only one bathroom on each floor. Casey wanted to break-in a new saddle by soaking it. So he went into the bathroom, filled the tub, and dumped in his saddle. He wired the door shut with a coat hanger, crawled out the transom, and went out. When he got back, he noticed that people were lined up and down the hall, waiting for the bathroom. Casey, grinning, went to bed. The next morning, a scream woke him up. A maid, worrying that somebody might have drowned in the bathroom, had climbed up on a chair and peeked over the transom. Dye had come off the saddle and colored the water. She saw something floating in what appeared to be bloody water. She screamed, and Casey did a lot of explaining when he claimed his saddle.

"Sometimes Casey would work all day to play a joke," said Shoulders. "He *was* onery."

Harley May recalled the time Bill Linderman and Gene Pruett were invited to play golf at plush

Above *and* opposite: *Tibbs changed the style of saddle bronc riding, making it a matter of rhythm, coordination, and timing. On these two pages, two of his protégés try their luck.*

Broadmore Hotel in Colorado Springs. It was a very exclusive place and the cowboys showed up all decked out in their golf attire. Casey had heard about where they were playing and he beat them there. He snuck out to the first hole, before daylight, and relieved himself in the cup. You can imagine the reaction when one of the players reached into the cup for his ball.

I told Shoulders I was surprised somebody hadn't whipped Casey's tail. "Aw, he kept it movin'," said Jim. "Casey wasn't a fighter, though he never walked away, either. But he'd usually just laugh and con 'em out of it."

"Casey was ridin' high, literally," said Harley May. "He, Jack Buschbom, and Gerald Roberts got themselves this old army-surplus plane. It had two engines and was called the Bamboo Bomber. Pilots during the war had given it that name because, they said, once it caught on fire, it would burn up in thirty seconds, like bamboo."

Tibbs decided to announce his coming to one rodeo in style. He got his pilot to buzz low around the grounds and he dropped his calling card—in this case his saddle—right smack in the middle of the arena. Everybody was impressed, though Casey got a sick feeling when he found out the fall had broken his saddle.

"They were always running out of gas and having to land on the highway or in some wheat field," said May. "Just a wonder they weren't killed. They did finally crash-land in a field and totalled the plane, though they all walked away."

At a time when Casey was looking to Hollywood and elsewhere for other ventures, he signed with some high rollers who formed Casey Tibbs Enterprises. On a black, trick horse called Midnight (not the great bucking horse), Casey would perform at rodeos in which he was competing. Cowboys kidded him a lot and called him "Captain Midnight" or "Cap." At a rodeo in Lubbock, Texas, Casey was all dressed up and leading Midnight through its tricks when Jim Shoulders ran into the limelight and handed him a guitar.

He often took the trick horse to perform at children's hospitals. Casey has had a lifelong romance with children. A bachelor most of his life, he has spent a lot of time raising money for recreation areas and other benefits for kids. Lofting recalled watching Casey play with six nephews and a niece. Casey, wearing a false nose and glasses, sat for hours playing with the kids. Finally, the place was in shambles and he was wrestling with them all over the floor. "Uncle Casey will never grow up," said his niece.

"I got run over by this tractor working on a

post hole," recalled Cotton Rosser, former contestant and now a stockman in California. "There was no insurance for the cowboys then. I was in a wheelchair with two broken legs and had some bad financial problems. Well, Casey and some other guys got up this benefit match roping and riding for me. They raised five thousand dollars and paid my bills."

Casey didn't talk much about his charity work, though he always admitted he liked girls, drinking, and gambling. "I never claimed to be no angel," he once reflected. "But I never went around pushing little ducks in the mud, either. I never hurt anybody but myself. I did like to gamble. Once stayed at a crap table for three days and three nights. I've lost as much as eleven thousand dollars playing craps and poker in one week's time.

"You got to have a little gamble in you to rodeo, but I respect a fella like Jim Shoulders, who'll salt 'er away. I was too wild."

Tibbs left rodeo in 1964 for what he felt, and was led to believe, would be a starring career in Hollywood. He worked as a stunt man, double, and technical advisor, and was later to have the television series "Stoney Burke" patterned after his life. He would also later take another shot at the movies, this time as a producer director, but he still yearned for rodeo and made a comeback in 1967. He won firsts in nine of the first ten rodeos he entered, but his star faded.

"He was a little heavier when he came back, and I'm not sure things were quite the same with him," said May. "But Casey was a helluva guy and a helluva hand. Yeah, those were good times."

Above: *Tibbs usually landed on his feet, as this rider is about to do.*

I've woke up and I've thought and I've had tears come to my eyes about gettin' out of it, quittin' rodeo.
—Casey Tibbs, age twenty-five

Perhaps it was the last true roundup and trail drive. Casey Tibbs, entering his forties, and his hired wranglers were living, not acting out, an episode of the Old West by driving hundreds of wild mustangs from the Lower Brule Indian Reservation to new grazing land near Fort Pierre, some 120 miles away.

They had reached the banks of the Missouri when a storm hit. The rain, light at first, became harder. Then it hailed, and the wind, gaining momentum until it reached some sixty miles per hour, whipped the river into wall-like sheets, rising four or five feet. It was time to stop, tie down, wait. But when the wind had subsided a little, the cowboys watched as Casey, fearless, plunged on ahead, riding a big gray horse into the surging river. Tibbs, who could not swim, yelled back at the cowboys just before water swept over him and the big gray. He was motioning them away, but they thought he wanted them to come on.

The cowboys, reluctantly, drove the horses toward the river, but the animals' instinct knew better and the horses bolted, scattering along the crumbling banks and away from the raging water.

"We couldn't see Casey anymore," said a witness. "He'd been holding onto a rope tied to the saddle and the big gray was pulling him along. But then they both were gone. We knew he'd been drowned."

After what seemed like an hour, the big gray

appeared on the far bank. With Casey. Tibbs looked at the cowboys on the other side, then collapsed.

At 4:30 the next morning, he was up again for breakfast at the chuck wagon. This was his way of making a movie. He was a different man, a more serious one, and had decided to produce and direct what he felt was an authentic Western. He felt the Westerns made in Hollywood just weren't like the real thing, and when the government asked him to move his horses, which had been grazing on the Indian Reservation, he got the idea. He'd hire real wranglers and move the horses the way it used to be done. Whatever happened, as it happened, would be put on film.

"Aw, nothing much happened," he said later, the grin back on his face. "All we got in the film is a stampede in the middle of the night, stallions that nobody—including me—could stay on, a snowstorm that damn near froze us to death, and that tornado hitting when we were trying to drive them across the river."

The film, ninety minutes in color, was called *Born to Buck*, and it became an artistic and financial success. It won an award from Wrangler. But, in the end, things didn't work out for Casey as a producer or director. Perhaps a key to his problems may be found by what is said to have happened when he was introduced to a big money man, a Hollywood executive who could help him.

"I know you," Casey was quoted as saying, "you're the SOB who went around telling folks that I drink too much. I'm not a violent man, but if you ever talk about me again, I'm gonna stomp you from here to Tucson and back."

Casey still does bits for movies, but in Hollywood's big money league it was, perhaps, like crossing that raging river. But then again, Casey was always best at being himself.

In a way, Casey Tibbs, today, still has that look

186

Above: *Saddle bronc rider getting ready. As per the rules, that's an Association saddle.* Opposite: *Monty Henson making his way, in bicentennial boots.*

about him, though it isn't as whimsical, the twinkle isn't as bright. His face is more jowled as he goes into his late forties, but his rugged, good looks remain. Now he sports a mustache, which, I imagine, is not as much a sacrifice to the altar Now as to the past, the way it was. At times, his weight will go up to 180, then go down again—the plague of middle age.

He is called Western Equestrian Director of San Diego Country Estates, a development. It's a good job, though it saddens the authentic. Casey is a true cowboy, surrounded by modern plastics, prefabrications. In his job, he gives instruction in riding and puts on roping shows, rodeos, and trail drives for property owners and their guests. Sometimes he'll stage an old-timers' reunion, serve as grand marshall in a parade, attend a big rodeo, make public appearances.

Casey isn't a tragic or broken man, though some of his hopes have faded and his dreams paled. Everybody's do.

"Listen, he's still the same wild man," said Tommy Steiner. "My wife and I rode out one day with him to the finals in Oklahoma City. He revved that car up and was driving like crazy, going the wrong way down a one way street, just about anything you could think of. Scared us to death. Don't ever get in a car with him."

But everybody knew he was there.

Casey shore helped this business. They'd write stories about him and he'd get publicity for rodeo. Like Mahan does. If it wadn't for guys like Casey and Mahan gettin' publicity, there wouldn't have been as many tickets sold. Sure, Casey partied, but it was his money, wadn't it?

Now me, I tried to save what I could. I'm kinda like this friend of mine said back in fifty-two, the first time the cattle market went kaput. He never did win much money rodeoing, but he scuffled around, working the labor lists and doin' everything he could to make money. He took care of his money, put it away. By doin' without all those years he got him some cattle, bought this lil' ol' place. Then the cow market crashed and he lost it all.

So he told me, "I cussed Linderman, Tibbs, and those boys for thowing their money away when they was winnin' and havin' a good time. Now, I'm in as bad a shape or worst than they are, and I saved and never had a good time."

I got caught in the market crash myself. But I'm still workin' and tryin' to keep it goin'.

—Jim Shoulders

The Jim Shoulders spread is located southeast of Henryetta, Oklahoma, a small hamlet of some 7,000 people. It has an old rock house, several barns, corrals. His son, Marvin, married last year, and his son-in-law, Bobby McAfee, a National Finals clown, have parked their trailers on the spread and live there when they're not on the circuit. The ranch is rolling grasslands; Jim calls it "hoot owl country." Today, Jim Shoulders keeps stock, contracts about a dozen rodeos a year, has a hand in the Mesquite Rodeo Corporation—which leases the land for the Mesquite Rodeo—and stages various rodeo schools. Jim was the first, years ago, to have a riding school, which was attended by, among others, a guy named Phil Lyne. Now he also runs a school for clowns, for rodeo announcers, and whatever, though nobody has come up with a school to teach anybody how to become another Jim Shoulders.

Rodeoing involves a lot of leather.

The ranch is called the J Lazy S. J is for Jim, S is for his wife, the former Sharron Lee Heindselman, whom he married right out of high school. "Yeah," he said, "I been married all my life." And he has remarked, "I been stuck on her all these years, too. It's kinda like a friend of mine named John Carter said. 'I stayed married for so long because of the kids, but they got grown and left home and I come to find out I was stuck on my wife all the time.'"

Besides Marvin, a fine bull rider, the Shoulders have three daughters. "I been awfully lucky," said Jim. "All my kids turned out fine. I know some people have had a lot of problems. I ought to include Bobby [married to his daughter Jana] in that. I'll sure brag on him. He's like one of mine, too, because he was always around here when he was growing up."

Shoulders, forty-eight, has remained remarkably trim and is easily recognizable with his crooked smile. His only real concession to age seems to be his silver-white hair. Silver, like a fox. Asked why he wore a particular championship belt buckle, he said, "To hold my pants up."

He said that rodeo hasn't changed that much. Hasn't and has. "When I started during the war, it was pretty easy. There wasn't that many guys that rodeoed for hunnert percent of their income. Most of them had other jobs, except for about twenty or thirty of us.

"Then there was a tremendous boom after the war. Everybody was wanting to do something, to be entertained and, I guess, forget about the war. Sports boomed and more got into rodeo full-time. It got tougher and tougher.

"In those days, you entered a rodeo and stayed there. Nowadays, cowboys enter two or three at the same time. If they don't draw a good one they might turn out. What hurts is that a guy like Donnie Gay or a Larry Mahan are written up in the press. People go out to see them and maybe they're off somewhere else because of a bad draw. That ain't right. Everybody's tryin' to out-figure it.

"That'd be about like me going to a Dallas Cowboy game and Roger Staubach, figuring his team might lose, just didn't show up in order to save himself for the next week.

"But I ain't knocking their ability. When I started, you'd go to a rodeo and figure you had ten guys to beat, later twenty. No tellin' how many these guys today have got who could beat them. The bigger money today is attracting more top athletes.

"You hear more different things about these guys today because there are a few reporters who write about something besides blood and guts. Toots Mansfield did more pushups before breakfast than Larry Mahan or Shawn Davis, but nobody ever wrote about him. Only time they'd write about you was if you got drunk and showed your ass. There wasn't much exposure for the boys active in church work or family men.

"But I enjoyed my period. You have to enjoy rodeo if you do it for a livin'."

Jim Shoulders was on his second bareback at the Lewiston Roundup, and the horse, small and active, launched into the air and jerked, abruptly, as it hit the ground. Jim felt a sharp, firelike pain hit the shoulder of his riding arm, as if he'd been stuck with a knife. He hung onto the suitcaselike handle of his rigging, putting the pain out of his mind as he'd done so often. Pain wasn't important. The ride was. It's about over . . . anytime now . . . spur, rock. The buzzer sounded. Shoulders won day money.

But the horse had jerked his arm so fiercely his collarbone had been broken. Jim insisted that the doctors fit him in a metal collar, and he rode again the following day.

In March, 1959, at Houston, Jim was being jerked inside out by a 1,800-pound bull, but he wasn't about to be thrown. He was working with the animal, for points, and yet the bull was trying to get him off, on the ground so it could hook him.

On solid, spurring the shoulders.

When the animal kicked up its back feet, it felt Jim slide slightly forward and knew it was time. The bull shot back its head and hooked at him, smashing into his face. This made Jim Shoulders madder, more determined. He stuck it out for the ride. Later, doctors found seventeen fractures in his face, which required plastic surgery to repair.

During his career, Jim also suffered a broken nose, arm, elbow, ribs, a number of concussions, and had collarbones shattered a couple of times.

When I asked him at his ranch that day if he'd had any serious injuries, tongue-in-cheek, he said, seriously, "Oh, I skinned a finger one time."

Pressed, he added, "The only thing about injuries was how long they kept you out. Actually, my collarbone problems were the main thing. I broke it again when a bull fell on me. They put a pin in it and I went back out and got the pin bent. So they had to operate and pull it out. I was out six months. A year ago I broke the same one and was out three weeks."

Shoulders had the advantage of many successful athletes—a strong pain threshold. Some people just hurt more than others because they can't conquer pain with their mind, can't put it aside and concentrate on the job at hand. Jim always could.

He competed for thirteen years and won sixteen world titles, an accomplishment that might never be equalled. Five times, he was All Around champion, including four times in a row from 1956 to 1959. He won seven bull riding titles and four bareback titles.

"Jim was," said Dave Stout, "a guy who'd never bail out like you see some of them doing today. He stuck it out, no matter what, even if he failed to mark out."

Tough, determined, seemingly without nerves, Jim was almost nonchalant. Neal Gay remembered once when Jim stopped at his house on the way to the airport, where he would catch a flight to San Francisco for the final big rodeo of the year. Jim, who does like to talk, sat for a long time talking, and a little after 4:00 P.M., Neal asked him what time his flight was leaving.

"About four-forty-five," said Jim. "I was just thinkin' I might ought to get started."

They grabbed his gear, jumped in Neal's car, and rushed to the airport. They missed the scheduled take-off time. But the plane was late leaving so Jim got on. The money he won at San Francisco proved the difference in his winning the All Around.

Shoulders's secret was consistency. Others would almost match him in big purses but they lacked his consistency. In 1958, Jim entered forty-five rodeos and finished in the money forty-three times. He'd split a second here, win a fourth there. But he'd pad his total.

"You go out and really try to hook it up in every one of them," he said. "You try to win your day money every time that gate cracks and not be worryin' about the average. That's always been my policy."

In 1956, he got his hands on $43,381, a record that wasn't broken until Larry Mahan won $51,996 in 1967. He'd won $39,964 and $37,682 the two previous years.

Unlike Casey Tibbs, Shoulders didn't come into riding bucking animals naturally. The son of an auto body mechanic, his family lived on the outskirts of Tulsa, where the wildest animals raised were chickens. His elder brother, Marvin, for whom he named his son, rodeoed and got Jim interested in the sport. He took Jim to his first rodeo when he was thirteen. Scared to death, Jim scampered to safety when the bull tossed him on its first lunge. "Okay, get back on," said Marvin. "It's now or never for you." It was now. Jim got back on and rode the bull.

His first major rodeo title came in Madison Square Garden, in 1947. At the age of nineteen, he won two titles and $5,000. Even today, he says New York was his favorite rodeo.

"I used to always say that New York was the

cowboys' Christmas," he said. "Used to be such a big event. We got fifteen bulls and fifteen horses to ride. It wasn't a drawing contest. It was a ridin' contest. They'd have the rankest horses, just like in Oklahoma City now.

"When I started, nobody much was going to New York, up that way. I think most cowboys thought it was in Europe. But you could catch a plane up there and move around pretty easy to Boston, Chicago. Everybody soon started going to New York."

Jim Shoulders is the only rodeo cowboy in the Madison Square Garden Hall of Fame.

Shoulders the man was almost the opposite of Shoulders the rodeo star. He was and is a God-fearing family man who, when once asked why he rodeoed, said, "How else could a green ol' country boy with just a high school education get his hands on this much money?"

A few years ago he told a youth group, "You hear a lot about God is dead, but I know He's not. He's helped me too many times."

Jim Shoulders began to fade from among the top winners just after the sixties began. But he'd already bought his spread, begun stock contracting, and furnished the bulk of the money to start the Mesquite Rodeo. I asked him when he actually retired, and he snapped, "I *never* did say I quit. Casey retired. Mahan retired. All those guys talk about retiring and, 'fore you know it, they're back out there again. That's something I'll never do—say I retire.

"The only thing that happened to me was I stopped winning."

He rode in his last rodeo, in Houston, in 1971, placing third on a bareback. Then his career, already wound down, ended. But he didn't retire.

When I talked to him at his ranch, Jim Shoulders said, "You keep hearing people talking about how they look back and wouldn't change a thing. Not me. There's a lot I'd change. Maybe I wouldn't hit the ground in the same places."

There had been something I wanted to clear up in my mind about Jim Shoulders's career. I'd heard hints about something that had happened but apparently was hushed up. Some of his contemporaries had said he should have won the 1954 All Around but instead finished second to Buck Rutherford by $440 in the official standings of the RCA for that year.

"That's past," he said. When I asked him again, he explained, "Detroit was supposed to be the last rodeo of the year. Buck and this guy come up to me and asked me how much I'd won. I was over four hundred dollars ahead. I didn't think any more about it, knowing I'd won the All Around. Next thing I know, this guy is sending in some late results from Hugo, Oklahoma. It was six months late and the approval fee hadn't been paid when it was held. Well, they sent in the approval fee and the results half a year late. Buck had won some money but there was also something wrong with the results. It was too late to find the judges to correct those results. All of a sudden, they'd staged another quickie rodeo in Arizona, after Detroit. It also didn't get approved or sanctioned until after the year was over. He won some there, too."

"Did you get a lawyer, try to get it straightened out? That would have given you six All Around titles."

"No. I wouldn't hurt the rodeo business. It had been pretty good to me. I was never one to bellyache. I just felt like they'd have hell getting enough of those late rodeos approved or fixed to beat me out of it again." Shoulders won his four All Around titles in a row after that.

It did call attention to what could happen, and so steps were taken to avoid such controversies in the future. Surely, something like that couldn't happen again. Or could it?

When our conversation was over, I thought how much Jim Shoulders—and Casey Tibbs—missed rodeo. But it wasn't as much as rodeo missed them.

Chapter 7:
A MEETING OF CHAMPIONS

Somebody says they like this rodeo or that rodeo better. Heck, my favorite's always the National Finals at Oklahoma City. You got the best stock, the best cowboys.
—*Don Gay*

Everybody's up for the National Finals.
—*Jerome Robinson*

Well, I'm glad I went into football, even if I did just rodeo in my spare time. I guess the thing I regret most is that I didn't go to the National Finals. I'd like to have made that just onc't.
—*Walt Garrison*

When I found out I was going to the National Finals, I felt so good that I prayed if I had to be killed in a car wreck that it happen after *the National Finals, not before.*
—*Skipper Voss*

From the time the first gate opens to begin a new year, rodeo moves from a small truck-stop-like arena in West Texas to Canada, from New York to California; it transcends dry dust bowls, glamor extravaganzas in Calgary and Cheyenne, giant indoor events in Madison Square Garden, Fort Worth's Will Rogers Coliseum, Houston's Astrodome, and San Francisco's Cow Palace. It is the longest year, a seemingly endless road where you can't see around the next turn, over the next hill. There are girls, excitement, capsuled glamor, the satisfaction of the freedom that comes with movement, of living out your own dreams. Yet there is also the sameness of bad hot dogs, neon love, six-packs down the road, burned coffee, pills to stay awake and to ease the pain; of jumping out of bed and not knowing for a minute whether you're in Deadwood, South Dakota, or Odessa, Texas. But if the road is really taking you anywhere, it will lead to Oklahoma City and the National Finals Rodeo—the sport's Super Bowl, its showcase of talent, its summit.

After its beginning in 1959, the NFR was held for three years in Dallas and then three more in Los Angeles, before coming, in 1965, to Oklahoma City, where it has apparently found a home. Oklahoma City is a young, modern, and yet Western city with its multimillion-dollar National Cowboy Hall of Fame and Western Heritage Center. The NFR has turned a nice profit since coming to the Sooner State, and Oklahoma City, naturally, welcomes the some $3 million the event brings. In 1975, each of the ten shows, over a nine-day period, were sold out long before they were staged.

Only the best go to the National Finals Rodeo. The top fifteen winners in calf roping, team roping, steer wrestling, bareback, bronc and bull riding, and barrel racing qualify to compete in a gathering of the stars. Stock, chosen by the contestants, is the rankest, the best.

However, though championships have been settled in the past at the NFR, a new format was begun in 1976 that assures the added drama and excitement of knowing the All Around and individual-event World titles will be on the line in Oklahoma City. Formerly, monies won in the NFR were added to the winnings during the overall year, with cumulative totals comprising the final standings for the All Around and each event. Now, those leading individual events prior to the NFR will be designated "Professional Rodeo Cowboys Association Champions." But the top fifteen cowboys making the NFR—no matter how much money they've won getting there—compete for the more prestigious All Around Cowboy and World Champion individual titles. So, actually, the fifteenth-ranked cowboy coming into the Finals could be the champion if he won the most money in Oklahoma City. Some cowboys like the new setup. Some do not. But professional football has found a great deal of

Left: *NFR announcers Bob Tallman and Jay Harwood.*
Above: *The prize.*

Above: *Red Steagall singing "For Freckles Brown."* Opposite top: *Freckles at the annual tribute to him.* Opposite bottom: *Longhorn cattle turned loose in the arena to simulate a cattle drive.*

success and notoriety with its playoff system and Super Bowl. Baseball crowns as its champion the World Series winner, not the team that won the most games during the regular season. And now rodeo has a similar system to determine who'll win the top trophies in each event: the silver-inlaid, hand-stitched saddles and belt buckles the size of a man's hand. Still, winning means more than that. Winners in each category have the satisfaction of knowing that they were the very best in their event. And for the All Around winner, the World Champion Cowboy, there is the pride of being the best of the best.

However, the old format certainly had its dramatic years, years when cowboys came into the Finals with money winnings so close that the final standings might change. One of those years was 1975, a banner season in which 595 PRCA-sanctioned rodeos paid a record $6.1 million. A trio of very different men—Leo Camarillo, Tom Ferguson, and Larry Mahan—made their way to Oklahoma City to decide the All Around championship that year. They faced ten go-rounds that drew more than 90,000 people. Predictions continually changed during those nine days, and the championship was finally decided in the final hour of the final day; its ramifications sent the sport swirling into the biggest controversy in its history.

He'd become absorbed in his thoughts and daydreams and couldn't remember the last half hour nor the forty-odd miles he'd driven. It's often that way when you drive the highway a lot. You still react physically to the bumps, dips, turns, contours of the highway, and even the traffic, but none of these things registers mentally. Leo Camarillo had driven a lot. At times rodeo got lost in endless highway instead of it in rodeo. He pressed his aching back tight against the seat and stretched his arms against the steering wheel. His wife, Sharon, was asleep beside him. Gamby, their housebroken pet rabbit, stirred in the backseat. One rabbit's foot

was lucky; Leo wanted four. The clock on the Mercury's dashboard checked with his watch. Oklahoma City must be sixty or sixty-five miles away, and there were still two hours to make the 3:00 P.M. rehearsal for some kind of banquet or other. He wasn't sure. Maybe it was an awards banquet, preceding the rodeo, which was to begin the following day, Saturday.

Highway I-35 sliced, almost straight, through soft rolling plains of red dirt, salted by cottonwoods. To think, Oklahoma had once been Indian Territory. A billboard caught his attention. It told motorists that the National Finals Rodeo was about to begin and showed a picture of a smiling cowboy. Figures, thought Leo, believing the picture must be Tom Ferguson or Larry Mahan. Hey, he thought, let's get it on.

A diesel truck, sending black smoke into the sky and trailing it in its wake, approached from a nearby hill, heading south to Texas, probably Dallas, and points beyond. Leo took his CB microphone, switched on the radio, and said, "Hey, good buddy, how's a northbound look over your shoulder? You got a copy. This is a tired roper goin' to O-City." A voice, barely audible in static, came over the radio, "Well, this Big Daddy movin' on down. I think them smokeys must be havin' coffee. You got a clear shot, 'far's I know, next twenty miles." Putting the speaker back to his mouth, Leo said, "Appreciate it. That's ten-four, good buddy."

Leo pressed the accelerator, felt his car surge, and glanced in the rearview mirror at his horse, Stick, in the trailer. He'd checked the hitch, which was tight, secure. Ol' Super Stick, he thought. You

and me. He'd gone over the situation in his mind many times, as he'd often do the following week, checking the figures, reevaluating. This could be the time for him. He could be rushing to the apex of his career as a rodeo cowboy, the goal of his life, a dream he'd had since he was old enough to know what it was all about, a dream his father had had before Leo was born. His chance had come. It was there. Somebody had called it the brass ring you either grabbed or didn't. By God, he'd grab it.

A team roper had never won the All Around title, but Leo was leading and just might do it, might be the first. He liked to think about the scene, being awarded the gold buckle, called Champion of the World. That was a damn sight better than being in one of those small shacks on a rich man's spread, where he'd grown up, ignored by the outside world, facing adult realities while still wrestling with childhood. His official winnings were $49,481, with an all-time high of $26,504 in his specialty, team roping. But, though he'd won money in calf roping and steer wrestling, he'd made the Finals in only one event, whereas Ferguson had qualified in calf roping and steer wrestling and Mahan in saddle bronc and bareback riding. He led Ferguson, the defending champion, by $3,266 and Mahan, the six-time All Around titlist, by $3,597. But nobody gave him much of a chance. In team roping Leo had to split his winnings with partner H. P. Evetts. So the most he could make by winning a go-round was $469.49. If he won the average, he'd get about $1,000. But Mahan and Ferguson could earn $892.82 by winning a go-round in either of their events and almost $2,000 by taking the average. Leo figured if he got hot he would win about $5,000 in the nine go-rounds, but his rivals could each make as much as $10,000. Could but wouldn't. Leo wouldn't settle for second best this time. He remembered telling a reporter, "You can't go to Levi Strauss for a possible endorsement and say, 'Hey, I'm the second greatest cowboy in the world'—though I guess you could go to Avis."

He'd finished second the previous year after tearing cartilage and ligaments in his left knee and missing ten weeks following surgery. The knee still bothered him. Actually, he'd figured to take it easy most of the year and allow his knee to become sound. But after he got hot early there was no choice but to go for it, all of it. "I'll do it and we'll see who's a cowboy," said Leo, becoming excited and talking out loud. Sharon stirred, adjusted her head on the pillow softly wedged between the door and seat. The trailer hitch clicked as Leo drove through a dip in the highway, and he looked in the mirror and said, "Easy, Stick. Easy." Leo laughed to himself when he remembered how he'd gotten Stick.

Leo had been demonstrating his art during a team roping school in South Dakota when he'd first seen Stick, the horse his sponsors had provided for him to ride. Later, Leo said, "I knew he was mine the first time I got on him. He just had the right feel, the right reaction to me." Leo bought the horse for $2,500, though he took a great deal of kidding from cowboys. They said he'd bought a "dink," a "stick," as in stick-horse of the five-and-dime variety. The name stuck. He used the horse in a few go-rounds at the 1971 National Finals and did well. Then he used Stick exclusively at the 1972 NFR and won team roping. That was when he changed the horse's name to "Super Stick." Describing Super Stick, Leo said, "He doesn't have exceptional breeding nor does he have exceptional looks. And he doesn't do anything really outstanding except win. He's an athlete, a winner."

To Leo, horses are something more than animals. "When you're raised on a ranch like I was, you learn that horses have personalities and are temperamental, just like people," he said. "Sometimes you have to be tough with them, sometimes kind, and reward them for what they do, just like you do with kids. I respect them. They respect me. I think of myself as their coach, working them out, rewarding them when they do well. I spend time

Clockwise from opposite top left: *Freckles Brown in Phoenix in 1943, leaving Five Minutes to Midnight; Brown at the 1967 National Finals, aboard Tornado, the bull "that had never been rode"; Brown today.*

Right: *A. J. Swaim.*
Opposite: *Clown Bobby McAfee moving in as Jerome Robinson gets hooked.*

202

every day with my horses, and you get very close to them that way."

Signs beside the highway. More signs, plants of progress. A sign told Leo that Oklahoma City was fifty-one miles away. Another read, "Paul's Valley, Population 7,000." Unconsciously, he looked up at the rearview mirror. What he saw didn't seem real but rather like something he might see on a screen, a television set. For an instant he had a detached feeling, then snapped into reality. The trailer had come loose and was getting smaller and smaller as it wobbled back down the highway, like a crazed, living object being shaken and propelled by some unseen force. "Hey," cried Leo. "Hey! Sharon, the trailer come undone!" He braked the car, trying not to look in the mirror but looking just the same. The trailer, with Stick, tumbled, somersaulted three, four, five times, before coming to a dead stop in the narrow drainage ditch.

"You can't imagine how emotionally involved you are with an animal until you see something like that happening," Leo said later. "I knew Stick was dead. Nothing could survive a wreck like that, the way the trailer was tumbling. I thought about what was happening to him, when I'd first seen him, so many things. I could fill a book with the things

which went through my mind in that minute or so of the accident."

Leo was out of the car seconds after it screeched to a stop, running toward the trailer, what was left of it. The trailer had stopped off the road, fortunately, but was lying on its side, the top and back mangled. Stick's leg was hanging over the divider. Leo thought the leg was broken. The horse was moving, breathing. Leo held its leg, then put it back inside the trailer so it wouldn't be twisted more. Then he began jerking, yanking with all his strength at the top and door, trying to make an opening. "It's all right, Stick, boy. It's all right." Stick was huddled into a ball at one side. It's over, Leo thought. All over. Stick was dying and would have to be put out of his misery. Hopes were gone. Hopes for the All Around title, lifetime hopes and dreams—all were shattered. The highway has no compassion.

Leo pried the door back. Stick moved, then,

Above and opposite, top to bottom: *It looked like Sandy Kirby was dead. Bull No. 40 knocked him unconscious and rolled over on him. Clowns Bobby McAfee (polka dot shirt) and Wick Peth (striped shirt) did their job—it was McAfee that finally got Kirby's hand free. The next night, Kirby rode two bulls and won the bareback go-round.*

pushing with its front legs, backed out of the trailer. The horse shook as it stood up, then walked away from the wreckage and started nibbling grass. Leo watched in mild shock, disbelieving. "I'll be damned," he said, wanting to both laugh and cry. "I'll be damned!" Then Leo started laughing as Sharon got there. "He's okay, Sharon. I think he's okay. Damn, look at him. Old Stick bounces all over the highway, upside down, every which a-way, and now he's out there eatin' grass."

Leo felt he'd seen a miracle. "I'm meant to win," he thought. "It's my destiny. And hell, even if I don't, I've already won because this horse is alive." He never did figure out why the pin in the trailer had broken.

"Ladies and gentlemen, we'd like to welcome you to rodeo's finest hour, the National Finals," the announcer began, as a capacity crowd of almost 9,000 fans settled into their seats in plush, snug Jim

Two ways of dealing with bulls at the National Finals. Opposite: *Donnie Gay demonstrating how to ride.* Below: *Clown Bobby McAfee showing the fine points of bull standing.*

Norick Arena at the State Fair grounds on the west side of Oklahoma City. Outside, a norther, riding the crest of twenty-five-mile-per-hour winds, had swept into the area on the final Sunday of the National Finals, the final day of Rodeo, '75. "It's been a most exciting week for us all, a week in which we've seen near tragedy and the elation and excitement that can come only from competing at the top—and winning. We have spoken to rodeo crowds here the past few days about the self-discipline our nation needs in the bicentennial era. This self-discipline, this courage, has been exemplified by these contestants. If you saw Sandy Kirby, knocked out and with a 2,000-pound Brahma bull rolling over him, come back and place in two go-rounds, you saw true American self-discipline."

Cowboys in the riding events say Sandy Kirby is the toughest man to get on the ground. A former child trick-rider, from Woodstown, New Jersey, he competes in all three riding events and could well become an All Around Champion. But it wasn't only a matter of riding bull No. 40, a crossbred animal from the Beutler & Son string. On that Wednesday night, before the bull ever got out of the chute, it reared up on the fence, striking Sandy in the head. "I started seeing double and then don't remember anything," Sandy said later. "I guess I was just knocked cold." As the gate swung open, the bull

Denny Flynn bull riding in Lufkin, Texas, in 1976.

stumbled, then fell into Sandy, who had slid down its side with his hand still tightly wrapped in the bull rope. The bull then rolled over on Sandy, who did not hear the screams of the crowd. Clowns Wick Peth and Bobby McAfee were on the bull, getting the animal to its feet. No. 40 then kicked and began to spin to the left, waving and jerking the unconscious Kirby as though he were a mannequin. Peth, a fine athlete, got there first, but as he was loosening the rope, the bull kicked him away. McAfee, who is the son-in-law of Jim Shoulders, literally leaped on top of the animal, finally jerking Sandy's hand loose. Sandy collapsed on the ground as the bull was lured away and out the gate.

For nearly two minutes, Sandy didn't move. Then he regained consciousness and was helped up and out of the arena to a waiting ambulance, while the crowd gave him a standing ovation. He never heard it.

Sandy talked, walked, was checked by doctors, but later said he had no idea of what happened during those two hours. He suffered a concussion, strained neck and back muscles, and other bruises, but, amazingly, he had no broken bones. "I just put what happened out of my mind," he said. "If a guy thought about things like that, he couldn't survive out here." The following night, he stayed on two bulls, one of which had thrown all riders in the NFR and thirty others during the year, and also won the bareback go-round.

"... And you'd be surprised," the announcer continued, "if you'd been in the Salt Palace in Salt Lake City in mid-July, when Denny Flynn was gored by a Brahma bull, the horn missing his heart by a quarter of an inch, and his own intestines, if you will, pouring out. If you'd talked to the people who took him to the hospital and stayed with him and then saw this man in sixty days come back and ride again and come to National Finals Rodeo and be leading in bull riding going into this afternoon's final go-round, you'd know what the professional rodeo athlete is all about...."

Denny Flynn, twenty-four, from a small Arkansas town outside Fayetteville named Springdale, had been riding bulls professionally for less than two years and wasn't about to miss his chance at making the NFR as long as he could stand up. But he almost never stood up again after that day in Salt Lake City.

I suppose it takes eight of the longest seconds in the world to ride a bull. But when the buzzer finally sounds, and you've stayed on for that allotted time, there are few greater highs, because you've conquered fear, fate, the unknown, and successfully met the challenge of explosion and power generated by a very mean animal that weighs up to 2,000 pounds. You have met the animal.

That July at the Salt Palace, Denny Flynn met the challenge and heard the buzzer, which slices through all the sounds and the smells of fear and courage. The bull, oblivious to buzzers, was still thrashing. Denny reached down to loosen the rope, which held his hand tightly to the bull's back, right at the shoulders. As his hold slackened and he was about to get off on the fence, the animal leaped, stabbing the air with its horns. Denny went up, ever so briefly, but the bull hooked him as he came down.

Often, when you're slugged, hit hard, shot, or stabbed, you're stunned and don't feel the pain immediately. It is not uncommon for a bull rider to be hit by a horn. This is part of the danger, as both Sandy Kirby and Denny Flynn know, and you just hope the blunt edge doesn't break a rib or your skull.

"You get grazed or hit by the horn all the time, usually in a glancing way," said Denny. "But this felt a little different when it happened. I reached down and felt something in my shirt. Something was coming out of a hole in my shirt. It wasn't blood."

He got up and ran to the fence, his mind and adrenaline racing madly. As he climbed up, he saw his friend, Randy Magers. "I been ripped!" he

yelled—or heard himself yell, as though he were inside a play, watching himself.

"I just thought the bull hit him with the horn," recalled Magers. "Then I saw the hole in his shirt. I helped him down off the fence and then pulled back his shirt. I like to fainted. Something was coming out, protruding."

The bull's horn had shot up under Denny's rib cage, splitting his liver and stopping only a few inches from his heart. When the horn was jerked back out, as quickly as it had gone in, some of his intestines came with it.

Denny Flynn, his face grayish white, thought he was dying. "I was scared, I guess about in shock, but I thought it was over. My mind was racing back on my life, different things I wished I'd done." Attendants from the ambulance wanted him to lie down. But whenever he did, the fluid would move into his lungs and he couldn't breathe. "I kept getting up," recalled Denny. "When I stood up I could breathe. I never lost consciousness. I was afraid to close my eyes because I thought I'd die."

"I kept him talking all the time," said Magers. "I was afraid if he stopped talking, he'd pass out and die. I thought he was a goner."

Talking: "Hey, I feel like I'm bleeding inside. Hey."

"It don't look too bad, Denny. Just relax. We'll be at the hospital soon. Just relax."

"Bad. It looks bad."

"No, it don't, Denny. No, it don't. It'll be all right. Just relax as much as you can. We're about there."

They got him to the hospital and rushed him

Team ropers at work. Above: Heeler Jerold Camarillo working with Bucky Bradford. Opposite: Heeler J. D. Yates, 15 years old, roping with header, his father, Dick.

into surgery. Before they put him to sleep, the doctor told him he would be fine and Denny believed him. "That's the first time I thought I'd make it," he said.

Less than three months later, Denny Flynn won second money on a bull. We talked as he stood near the chutes one night at the NFR, and it all came back to him. It'll never leave him completely. "The doctor told me to be prepared for a long stay in the hospital," he said. "We figured three, four weeks. But I was out of intensive care in three days, and in three more I was out of the hospital. They let me go home. 'Course, the tubes were still in me and I felt a little shaky.

"Soon as I was able to move around pretty good and could get out the tubes I went out and got on this ol' muley bull I had. It made me feel a little uneasy, but I pretty well knew what that bull would do. I was back on the rodeo circuit at Madison Square Garden in October. I placed, and then I won me that second in Memphis."

The bull he rode in Memphis had long horns. "Yeah," he continued. "I saw that bull and almost turned out. But, you know, you got to do it sooner or later. I was scared to death when I got on, but then I forgot what had happened before."

Magers watched Denny Flynn ride a bull at the NFR and shook his head in amazement, disbelief. "That took a lot of courage, to get back on bulls after a thing like that," he said. "But when something like that happens, you got to do it at the soonest. But I dunno. I've seen cowboys get hurt on bulls a lot of times, but that's the worst I ever saw where the guy lived.

"But, look at him, he's riding damn good here."

Denny Flynn was fifteenth in bull riding, the last spot in which he could make the Finals. By the Finals, Don Gay had already clinched his second straight bull riding championship, but Denny didn't care. "Well, I'm just happy to make it," he said. "You qualify and there's no way you miss it. No way."

Gay, Sandy Kirby, and Denny Flynn were the only ones to stay on as many as nine bulls during the ten go-rounds at the NFR. Some five months after being seriously gored by a bull, Denny Flynn was to win the average at the NFR, finishing one

point ahead of Gay. The NFR that year was happy, sad, exciting, and there were many amazing performances. But perhaps the most amazing thing was that Denny Flynn was there.

Outside Jim Norick Arena, the chilled wind was playing havoc with late arrivals. A man and woman got out of a pickup in the parking lot and walked, huddled and arm-in-arm, toward the entrance. Suddenly, the wind got under the man's Western hat, lifting it from his head and sending it tumbling along the ground.

"Dammit," said the man, leaving the woman in order to chase his hat. Running in his cowboy boots, he looked like an ostrich. The hat would bound along, then stop, teasingly, only to start moving again just as the man was about to pick it up. Then it stopped suddenly, but the man couldn't slow down in time and stepped squarely on the crown of his hat, mashing it flat. "Dammit!" he yelled. "Oh, dammit! Dammit, dammit, dammit!" The woman, walking toward him, said, "Bill, now Bill." The man glared at her, forced the hat back on, down to his eyes, and charged toward the entrance. The woman, ignored, followed a few yards behind.

Inside, the announcer was saying, ". . . and you have seen the twists and turns of luck, or fate, if you will . . ."

The week had been frustrating for Larry Mahan, who stood in the dressing room under the stands, talking to friends, on Wednesday, before the fifth go-round. "I've had a bunch of sorry-ass horses, but I got a good bareback the other night. And then, for some stupid reason, I missed him out of the chute, which screwed me in the average. But I've still got a shot at the average in saddle bronc. Tom and Leo are having their problems, too. They're starting to crush. If they can't handle the pressure, I can."

Two men and a boy came into the room and started talking to Mahan. They were from Los Angeles. Mahan introduced them to me and said, smiling wryly, "These gentlemen are working with me on a record album. I was talking to Jerry Jeff Walker the other day, but didn't tell him I'm about to put on my singing spurs."

"You can't sing," I told him.

"Can't sing! What do you mean—hmmmmm!"

Mahan visited with the Californians and then said, seriously, "I just wish I'd gone to about ten or fifteen more rodeos. I'd be ahead now if I had."

He had a chance but had lost ground. "Hell, yes, I can still catch them," he said. "Leo's out of the average and Tom isn't doing too well."

"Hey, Larry," yelled a cowboy from across the room, "I hear *Six Pack Annie* is playing here. You goin' to see it?"

"You seen it?" Larry asked me.

"I don't go to the kind of theaters that show it," I told him, grinning.

"Yeah," he said, "somebody told me they saw you at *Deep Throat*, wearing a trench coat and carrying a paper sack. Boy, I've gone from one end to the other. From R-rated *Six Pack Annie* to the G-rated movie with Roy Rogers." When I left, he said, "Remember, I'm not out of it yet, with a little luck."

That night, Mahan, riding High Dive, brought the crowd to its feet, scoring an 81 and winning the go-round in saddle bronc, for an $892.82 payoff.

But he didn't have a little luck. On Saturday, he still had an outside chance, but his horse stumbled coming out of the chute, dipping its head. Mahan fell over the horse's head, landing on his arm. The blow dislocated his elbow and finished his chances, which, considering what happened on the final day, were better than any of us had imagined. "Not sure what happened," he said later. "The horse just jerked me over its head. I had both knees up high, and he dived and I hit." Mahan had won $1,450.82. For him, the rodeo was over, but he was far from through for the week. Still in pain, his arm in a cast, he did the color broadcasting for ABC on Sunday, when it was doing a segment for "Wide

World of Sports." Larry Mahan had landed on his feet again.

"There's been something for everybody here," the announcer continued. "Certainly, we've seen the youth of our country served as a fifteen-year-old named J. D. Yates worked the team roping with his father to capture all our hearts...."

J. D., beginning high school in Pueblo, Colorado, had waited poised, as his dad, the header, roped the steer. Then J. D. was right on the animal's tail, lassoing its heels. Their time was 6.6, good enough to win the fourth go-round. That was the same night Leo Camarillo missed the heels of his steer, hurting his chances in the average. But as Leo—a heavyset man of five feet, eight inches, with large almond eyes and a Roman nose—watched the kid that week, he could relate to what he saw. He could remember.

Leo's earliest memories of childhood are of when a calf, stiff and scared, was born; when his younger brother, Jerold, was stung by a bee; and of roping. Always roping. "I must have been about four," he recalled. "My father would give Jerold and me these little ropes and set up soda-pop bottles for us to rope. He was pleased when we'd do well, and, naturally, we liked to please him.

"Later, my father built us a dummy out of railroad ties to rope. He put legs on it and a head and horns. My father was very crafty. We roped the dummy every day. He would not say, 'Do you want to rope today, my sons?' We just roped. It was a way of life. My father was a very tough man, very tough. He was determined we would succeed and that he could live a life he treasured through us."

Leo's father, Ralph Camarillo, was a ranch hand in California. He worked hard, but ends never seemed to meet, and there was little frill in their lives, no extras. In Leo's early childhood, they lived in California's Santa Ynez Valley, but they later migrated to the Oakdale area, where his father found ranch work. His father had a yearning for rodeo—its wildness, unpredictability, and excitement served as an escape from the endless boredom of work that got him nowhere. He would often leave to rodeo for the weekend; sometimes he'd be gone for weeks at a time, but lack of money always brought him back to the life that had been laid out for him.

"My father was a pretty good hand," said Leo. "In California, there was an organization called the Cowboys Athletic Association. He was the All Around Champion, winning calf roping and steer wrestling. There is no telling how good he might have been, because the man was always burdened by putting bread on the table.

"I love my mother very much. She worked her tail off all her life for us. I remember little about her when I was a kid, except seeing her work. But, as far as rodeo was concerned, she hurt my father. When he'd come home a winner, she'd say, 'I knew you must win because I prayed for you.' When he'd lose, she would tell him, 'It was not God's will that you go, Ralph, and I knew you must lose this time.'

"He couldn't handle that kind of pressure. Economic pressures. Religious pressures. That's why he turned to Jerold and me, trying to put himself in us. We would live for him. He would live the life he longed for through us.

"But, God, he worked our ass off."

Leo remembered working from 4:00 A.M. until 10:00 P.M. He baled hay, worked cattle, wrangled horses, and, in his early teens, hauled hay and mended fences. "My father became a kind of foreman on this ranch," he said. "He would pay a normal hand fifteen dollars a day. He had to pay us nothing, so he could save money that way. We worked, did chores twice a day. But he always found time for us to practice roping. By the time we'd get to bed, we'd be too tired to dream of the things ordinary children might think about. I never thought of going off in big ships, of being a soldier. I thought only of being a champion roper."

His father often ran roping jackpots, in a small

Below: *Leo Camarillo at the National Finals.* Bottom: *Camarillo and H. P. Evetts rushing out of the barrier.* Right: *Evetts throwing a long one as Camarillo closes in.*

arena at the ranch on which he was working. Leo and Jerold helped. "I was about eight," said Leo. "Jerold and I would push in the cattle, take off the ropes, work the chutes. And we roped every day after the regular competition was over."

When Leo was nine and Jerold was seven, Ralph Camarillo bought his sons two small ponies and took them around to various area rodeos where they would give roping exhibitions. The two small, brown Americans, of Indian-Mexican descent, became a popular attraction, though, unlike other kids, they never seemed to laugh or even smile much at all. "I lived in fear," continued Leo. "We both did. I had to be the header because Jerold was too small. As I look back, that was fortunate for me because I did my work, roped the calf's head, and was through quickly. Jerold, my poor brother, he'd be trying to rope the animal's hind legs and my father would be yelling at him to hurry. '*Andalé, muchacho, andalé!*' Jerold would be following the animal around the arena with my father after him, whipping his horse, whipping Jerold, yelling. We'd both have tears rolling down our cheeks while we tried to do what my father asked of us. We had to do it. We had to do it right, because there was no such word as 'can't' in my father's vocabulary."

One day, when Leo was ten or eleven, he burned his fingers on a rope when a steer pulled away and jerked the rope through his hands. Although his fingers were bleeding badly, his father said, "Rope another one." "My fingers," said Leo. "I can't do it right now." His father jumped off the fence from which he was watching and charged at the boy, yelling, "I have told you, my son, we do not use the word can't! There is no such word! Now do it again! Now do it right!" Leo did it again, and again, until he had done it correctly.

Leo was afraid of his father, and yet it was not this fear alone that made him want to please him. He said he would never forget a traumatic time when he was sixteen, nor the bittersweet feeling it left. His father had always emphasized to his boys

that they had the responsibility to do their work, their chores, even when he was gone. Ralph Camarillo was called away by the death of a relative, but left a telephone number where his family could reach him in case of emergency, such as a fire in the barn or the house.

"I had just gotten my driver's license," said Leo. "So we got a phone call from a man at a nearby ranch who wanted my father to haul some horses to Bay Meadows, the racetrack. I had not heard of Bay Meadows at that time. Our entire world consisted of a one-hundred-mile radius from our home, and anything outside that area was outlaw country."

"It's up by Salinas," the man told Leo.

"I've been to Salinas but have not heard of this Bay Meadows," said Leo. "How far past is it?"

"Just a little way. We'll pay your father five hundred dollars to deliver the horses."

Leo said his mind raced wildly. "My father won't be back for a few more days," he said. "But I'll try to reach him, and perhaps my brother and I can deliver the horses. I will phone you back."

"We need to know," said the man. "It has to be done in the morning."

Leo could not reach his father by phone. "I didn't know what to do," he recalled. "We had no money. To us, five hundred dollars was like thousands of dollars." Leo paused in telling the story, the memory sinking in. "Decisions! Decisions!" he said. "All my fuckin' life I have to make decisions for everybody!" He phoned the man and told him he would take the horses.

"We picked up the horses before dawn because I wanted to make sure we got there in daylight and had enough time to drive back and do our chores. We needed to be back about five that night. I thought how proud my father might be, having the unexpected money.

"Jerold and I were very scared. We had some valuable horses in the truck. I watched one side mirror, and Jerold kept his eye on the other. He

215

acted as my lookout man. We knew the road to Salinas and got there okay. But when I asked how far to Bay Meadows, I was told it was seventy more miles. This frightened me. We had to drive through strange terrain. I was responsible for the horses, my father's truck, I honestly didn't know if something would jump from the side of the road and try to rob us.

"But we got there safely and quickly unloaded the horses. They asked if we would stay for a while, but I said, 'No, we must get back home as quickly as we can.' We stopped for nothing going back. All I thought about was that I'd made my father some money and now I must get back and do the chores. He would be happy. I could see that. He would be proud of me, he would see that I had made such a fine decision.

"Well, sonuvabitch! He was there when we got home, mad as hell. He was yelling that we didn't do the chores. I tried to tell him that I had had to make the decision, that I'd tried to phone him and we'd do the chores now. He wouldn't listen. There was no talking. He yelled, beat the shit out of us.

"I think that is still one of the biggest letdowns of my life. I remember it and still get the empty feeling inside. I had taken the responsibility, made money for him, and then got in trouble. Me, I didn't get a fuckin' thing out of it! But he had the bad temper."

But shortly after Leo finished telling the story, his anger passed. "My father taught us well," he added. "He never overmatched us when we were young. You know, the way the Mexican family structure is set up, the father makes the way for his children. And they, in turn, make their parents' lives easier. We have tried to do that.

"And, though I have felt he was unfair at times, I love my father very much. I love and respect him more than anybody in the world."

The crowd had given J. D. Yates a standing ovation. For a moment, just a fleeting moment, Leo Camarillo saw himself.

Prior to the rodeo each day, they would introduce the cowboys, who'd come riding out into the arena, smiling, some of them waving their hats in acknowledgment of the applause. Tom Ferguson would ride out, mostly unsmiling, looking neither right nor left. He would appear deep in thought and looked out of place, not because he was a champion, but because he wore his old college letter jacket.

Watching him from the press-box area, two rodeo officials—a man and woman—were talking. "Tom's not too easy to get to know," said the man. "I think he feels the world owes him something. He seems all business, doesn't take a lot of time to meet people. Leo's more outgoing. It might be better for the sport, as far as public relations is concerned, if Leo won the All Around."

The woman, who had a lot of opinions, agreed. When we'd talked earlier, and I mentioned I was using Skipper Voss as my key rodeo clown in this book, she said, "Him! He's nothing. Ask anybody. You best find you somebody more important than Skipper Voss. Nobody thinks he's the best."

"Most bull riders do."

"Nobody does," she added. She didn't care that much for Tom Ferguson either.

"I can't decide about Tom," said the bareback rider waiting in the chutes. "I mean, I don't know if he's conceited, stuck-up, or just plain shy."

"If you figure it out, let me know," said the bull rider. "He don't socialize much."

"There's not much communication between those in the riding events and timed events," said Tom Ferguson. "There's a lot of jealousy in rodeo. I'm just me. I don't try to be somebody else. I'm not a forward person, a flamboyant-type guy. I want to get as much out of rodeo as I can, while I can, so I just look at it like a guy would a business."

Tom Ferguson, twenty-seven, and four years younger than Leo Camarillo, had done well in his business, rodeo. At his age and with his ability in calf roping and steer wrestling, he seems the man

Opposite top: *Tom Ferguson, one hand on his saddle and one hand around the steer, about to do a little wrestling.* Opposite bottom: *Camarillo throwing for the heels—Evetts has already secured the head.*

most likely to break Larry Mahan's record for winning All Around titles, though he will not approach Mahan's status as a public relations man, an ambassador of goodwill for his sport. But then again, nobody will.

Tom looks like a collegiate defensive back. He's a solid five feet, eleven inches, 175 pounds, much smaller than the men in his events. But all this means is that he has tremendous balance, quickness, and general athletic ability. There is a cleancut, country-boy look about him. On occasion he appears almost boyish and shy, but he misses this mark a little because, in a way, his smile seems to be an afterthought. At other times he seems aloof or perhaps preoccupied. Tom reminds me of someone who has just achieved stardom, notoriety, and looks up to see the limelight in his face. It is a little blinding. He knows he must do something but isn't sure exactly what. Tom wants to be champion but would rather be on down the road, making money, than stopping to talk, visit. Tom Ferguson is not one to stop and smell the flowers.

Claude Groves knows him. Early the following year, Claude and I were having a beer in the lobby of Will Rogers Arena, where the Fort Worth Fat Stock Show was being held. Claude wasn't competing but had caught a ride to Fort Worth anyway, and said he was going to get back on the circuit just as soon as he got money to get on down the road. A prominent saddle bronc rider walked past us, and Claude yelled at him. The guy either didn't hear Claude or ignored him, noting, perhaps, that Claude was sagging a little at the seams with beer. "Boy, I tell you what," said Claude, "me and that kid used to go on down the road together. Shee-it. Now, he's embarrassed to know me."

Tom Ferguson, walking through the lobby, had seen us and stopped. I had written a column in the *Dallas Morning News* in which I'd called Tom somewhat withdrawn and businesslike and Leo Camarillo more outgoing (though he didn't used to be) and generally more popular with his contemporar-

ies. Tom said he hadn't read the column but someone had mentioned it to him. "Who told you that?" he said, not abrasive but quietly. "It's not true. You talk to the cowboys and you'll find out it's not true."

"Tommy!" said Claude, putting his arm around Ferguson, who was not drinking beer. "Listen, Bob, this ol' boy is the same as he always was. He's good people. Tommy and I used to get on down the road some together. See, he ain't like that feller just passed me by. Tommy still talks to me. We're still friends. You got that wrong. Tommy's more popular, you-goddamn-right."

I remembered how I hated Gallup polls and felt mine could be wrong, that maybe I had miscalculated with my pop psychology. But Leo always seemed to be there, whereas Tom just wasn't seen that much out of the arena—he was on down the road.

Tom and his brother, Larry, a top rodeo hand in his own right, grew up in a rodeo family, though there was more freedom of childhood than, say, under the iron hand over Leo Camarillo's youth. They had access to all the horses and stock they needed, to learn, to practice. Tom's parents, Ira and

Above *and* opposite: *Steer wrestling: pure muscle against pounds of force.*

Maxine Ferguson, remember when he wasn't big enough for the smallest of calves, so he would grab a small rope and try to lasso the family cat. His enthusiasm to ride grew much faster than his body, so he had to shinny up a rope tied to a saddle horn in order to mount a horse.

He attended Cal Poly—the Notre Dame of rodeo—was runner-up in both collegiate steer wrestling and calf roping one year, and won the championship the following year. While he was in college, Tom also competed in PRCA events and was runner-up to the All Around title in 1973.

"I was paying my way through college and also making a lot of extra money," he said. "I had so much momentum going I decided to quit school and go full time."

He not only won the All Around title in 1974 but set a record by winning $66,929 in official

money (over $20,000 more in bonuses, most of which came from Winston). He finished $32,000 ahead of runner-up Leo Camarillo. But Leo had the lead coming into the NFR of 1975, and Tom seemed to be luckless through the first eight go-rounds. He had split a third and fourth twice and tied for still another fourth in calf roping. However, he had been leading in the average, which would be worth $1,941.88, going into the fifth go-round on Wednesday night. Tom came out of the box so quickly it appeared he might well be on his way to winning day money. He shot the rope quickly around the calf's neck and jumped off his horse. But before he got to the animal, his rope snapped, sounding like a giant firecracker going off. By the time he had his second loop out and had tied the animal his time had soared to 36.5, dropping him to tenth in the average.

In steer wrestling he was just .3 out of second in the average as he started into the sixth go-round. Tom caught his steer quickly, but somehow the animal squirmed and got away. He had to remount and chase down the animal again. He didn't have him officially thrown until 43.2 had elapsed, sending him crashing to the bottom in average. But his best was yet to come, and the All Around race would tighten with Leo Camarillo, whom he didn't particularly like.

Tom Ferguson nearly always seems to be in a hurry. But I stopped him once, when he didn't seem to be rushing anywhere in particular, and asked him how he felt about Leo. "No, I don't like him," he said. He went on to tell me he thought Leo had once faked an injury because he had a bad draw and then recovered all at once when he had a good draw. But when most cowboys say something negative about someone, they'll usually either preface it or add a postscript. "Oh, I'm not knocking Leo," added Ferguson. "We used to be friends. But I don't see he's more popular."

One of the other few times I'd seen him completely relaxed, wasting time, was during the State Fair Rodeo in Dallas. That particular night's show had ended, and the cowboys were leaving the arena. Mahan was walking with three or four people along the fence toward the exit. He had said something funny, and they were all laughing. They passed Tom Ferguson, sitting on the fence, looking down at the ground. He was alone.

"I was raised around cowboys, real cowboys," Leo Camarillo was saying, as we sat in the coffee shop at Holiday Inn West, where most of the NFR cowboys were staying. "I was actually a cowboy on a ranch. When I say I'm a cowboy, I mean it in the literal sense of the word. I appreciate what Larry Mahan has done for rodeo. We get along fine but don't have a lot in common. When he says he's a cowboy, well, he's a cowboy in the limelight, a Rhinestone Cowboy.

"Sometimes it pisses me off that I did these things [roping and rounding up cattle] on a ranch for a living and then a guy like Tom Ferguson comes along and wins the world title. Sure, he's a tremendous athlete, but *cowboy*? Hell, I could take him out on a ranch and he couldn't round up cattle to brand.

"Tom's all right. I used to take him down the road when he was an amateur. Now he treats me like dirt, just ignores me. I used to talk rodeo with him, try to help him out. One time we were in Phoenix, tying calves the night before the rodeo started. It's something you don't have to do but it's just an unwritten understanding that everybody helps a little. Slack started at seven the next morning and, no, I wasn't going all out. I was just out there doing my part but wasn't about to wear myself out. So this kid, Tom Ferguson, comes up to me and says, 'You're not doing a good job. That's not the way to do it.' I just looked at him and said, 'Hell, I know I'm not perfect, son. But I was making a living doing this while you were out messing around somewhere.' "

We were sipping our fifth cup of black coffee in

Jeff Copenhaver, champion calf roper, pulling in the slack.

Below: *Melvin Coleman, his ride finished, waiting for the pickup men.* Bottom: *Pete Gay, acting as judge, walking over to bareback rider T. J. Walter.* Opposite: *Rusty Riddle, on Moon Rocket, chasing the number one spot. He lost out to Joe Alexander.*

early afternoon. Leo seemed rested. He'd taken his wife, Sharon, out to dinner the night before, visited with Butch Kirby, Sandy's brother, and then come back to the motel. A friend of mine, Ed Knocke, who covers rodeo for the *Dallas News*, Dave Knight, of Winston, and I had gone to a late, late party held by Justin in a suite at the Holiday Inn. Country and Western singer Red Steagall, who was entertaining during the rodeo, showed up with some of his group and picked and sang until about 5:00 A.M. One I liked to hear him sing was called "I Gave Up 'Good Mornin', Daddy,' and 'I Love You, Darlin',' for *This*." About 4:00 A.M., Knocke and I had attempted a duet, dedicated to Steagall's girl friend. I think she liked our singing before we ever started. In retrospect, I believe our only problem was we were singing different songs. Knight, much more discreet, was doing background for us, going "Waa-waa-waaah!"

"You should have been there," I told Leo.

"I don't drink or party much," he continued. "You can't be a world champion and a hell-raiser at the same time. It takes too much concentration on the job to be out drinking every night."

He has that in common with Tom Ferguson—but little else. Leo can't understand Ferguson, nor his attitude toward him, anymore than Ferguson can understand Leo, though there is total lack of subtlety in both. It is difficult to gauge the complete effect of growing up a poor Mexican-Indian. There is always the underlying prejudice nearby—real, hinted, implied. You are of the minority, different, this way or that. Be black and have rhythm; be brown and be happy, have a tortilla, and go to sleep under a tree. People often typecast races for the most ridiculous reasons.

"I do have this defensive attitude of the Mexican-Americans, though I've gotten over a lot of it," admitted Leo. "I guess you grow up and look for things, for prejudices. But after a while, you get used to them. Like if I told you: this horse is lame. I keep telling you that and pretty soon you have looked at the horse so much you start imagining it is lame.

"In the PRCA you run into a lot of jealousy. Some people see something that bothers you and they peck at it, rub you raw. But I'm not so uptight. I've mellowed a lot."

A battle is going on inside Leo. Deep down there is an old bitterness, but now he is also happy, which gives him a better perspective on his past.

We were laughing about the effects of growing up without much money. I told him it took me years after I'd graduated from college before I could buy anything but cheap shoes. I might be wearing a $25 shirt, but inevitably I'd go into a shoe store and purchase a pair of $10 shoes. Leo, laughing, said, "Like buying a car. I might go out and pay six thousand dollars for a car. But I'll be in a store and see a thirty-five dollar jacket I like. I question myself over and over. Do I really need that jacket? Is it necessary?

"Even when I started getting endorsements, I had this deal with Tony Lama. Free boots. I got free boots. I could pick out a two-hundred-dollar pair if I wanted. But not me. I'd go in and get the cheapest.

"Now, my wife's just the opposite. Values never enter her mind. She'll say, 'Hey, get what you want.' Then I'll tell her, 'Listen, I grew up broke. Hey, I ate beans. Maybe the money will run out.'"

"I still can't eat chicken on Sunday," I added.

"Rodeo's been good to me," he said. "If I hadn't gotten into rodeo, I'd have been a hand on some ranch, financially living from day to day. I can thank my father for that, though at times it was difficult. But he also had our best interest in mind, physically. For instance, he wouldn't let us bulldog. I wanted to bulldog more than anything in the world. But a relative of his had once been badly hurt while my father was helping him bulldog. It's odd, but last year that's how I tore up my knee, bulldogging. I hadn't planned to bulldog much this year, but I was forced to because of going for the All Around title.

"But my father, he was something. He had my brother and I competing in all the junior rodeos.

Top: *Larry Mahan making a go at his favorite event.* Opposite left: *Mike Marvel stretching out.* Opposite right: *Joe Alexander, bareback champion, losing his hat again.*

We won everything they had to offer. We took all the amateur events and used to follow the pro champions around and beat them. In the big jackpots and calcuttas [in which fans pick competitors and bet on them] I was selling higher than the pros. Even today, I make maybe ten thousand dollars a year in jackpot rodeos.

"One time my cousin Reg came down and joined Jerold and me. We all went to a jackpot rodeo and won just enough to enter another one. We pooled our money, less than forty dollars, and went all out. We won eleven hundred dollars apiece. Hey, Bob, that was like winning a million to us. We thought there would never be another poor day."

He remembered joining the PRCA and the mixed emotions of his rookie year, 1968. "I was the top money winner among all rookies and Jerold was second," he said. "So neither of us was rookie of the year [Bowie Wesley won]. Again, I think it must have been politics. But that just made me more determined.

"I like guys who are real determined, even though they might have handicaps. Look at Nate Archibald. He's small, but he's the top scorer. I'm a big football fan and admire Billy Kilmer. He doesn't have all the ability, but he's a winner. And Fran Tarkenton. Look how small he is and the way he hangs in there."

"Whenever there's a Monday night football game," Sharon had told me, "we stop. We shut down. Leo has to watch the NFL games."

Leo sees a correlation between his event and football. During the National Finals, he frequently

paralleled his situation to a game. "I'm not going to sit back here," he said. "I'm going to come out throwing bombs. I'll win or go out winging."

Bill Smith, who sat nearby in the coffee shop, could relate. Bill—called Cody Bill because he's from Cody, Wyoming—won saddle bronc titles in 1969, 1971, and 1973. He's one of the most avid and knowledgeable Dallas Cowboys fans I've ever met. He first became interested in the team because of his friendship with Walt Garrison and now takes everything the team does, or doesn't do, to heart. As aids to keeping abreast of the team, he subscribes to both Dallas newspapers and also the club's weekly newsletter. We had Leo, a Washington Redskins and Los Angeles Rams fan, outnumbered.

Opposite top: *Jack Ward.* Opposite bottom left: *Mahan between go-rounds.* Opposite bottom right: *Australian Jim "Digger" Dix—the first person from outside North America to qualify for the NFR—lying down for a bareback ride.* Above: *John Forbes hung up.*

"What about them Cowboys!" Bill would say over and over, when we ran into one another. He's one of the nicer guys I met on the rodeo circuit and seems about as informed about pro football as he is about his own sport. At a moment's notice, and often without provocation, he would launch into a discussion about the pluses and minuses of a certain player or of Tom Landry's Flex Defense. Whenever he could find a willing accomplice, he'd play catch with a football outside the motel.

Cody Bill wasn't having a particularly good Finals and I asked him on Friday night if he was a little nervous about his bronc on Saturday afternoon. "No," he said, thoughtfully, "actually, I'm more nervous about the Cowboys playing the Redskins on Saturday afternoon."

H. P. Evetts was perfect for Leo's plans to "come out throwing bombs." Evetts, a tall, thin man with a handlebar mustache, favors bolting out of the box with his rope winging, and he throws the longest lasso in the business. Most headers don't like to try to control steers on long ropes, preferring to work in close even if it entails chasing the animal halfway across the arena. Evetts wastes no time at all. Once he threw his rope so quickly he accidentally looped part of the gate as he charged out of the box. "I throw long and quickly because that's where the money is," he said in one of his longer conversations. Like Leo, he was bred for rodeo by his dad, who was a roper. And he's a former team roping champion, which speaks well for his theory, his style.

"H. P. doesn't talk much," said Leo. "Sometimes a sentence is a conversation for him. I asked him to rope with me in the Finals, to help me win the All Around and he said he would. That's a lot to ask of another guy. There's so much pressure, so much at stake. But he said he'd do his best. I guess we make a pretty flamboyant, wild-looking team out there."

Leo is somewhat unorthodox himself. Ordi-

Top: *Monty Henson, winner of the saddle bronc competition, finishing a ride.* Above: *Scotty Platts bareback riding at his third NFR.*

narily, heelers throw a rope that skims the ground under the steer, standing up just in front of the animal's legs. Leo's loop seldom touches the ground but appears just to hang in midair as the steer steps into the loop. Ironically, Leo had teamed with Evetts in 1974, helping H. P. win the team roping title. He had also teamed with his brother and Billy Wilson to win the average at four National Finals and the world title in his event twice.

As Leo pointed out, timing between the ropers —the header and the heeler—is as important as timing for a quarterback and wide receiver. The header, first out of the box, must rope the steer around either both horns or the neck, then turn it to the left as the heeler moves in, roping the animal's hind legs. When the horses are facing each other, with ropes taut, time is recorded.

"First of all, you've got to know your horse," said Leo. "Secondly, you want to take full advantage of the livestock you're roping. You try and get a reading on the steer's character, what he's likely to do. Being raised on a ranch, I think I have an advantage. I can spot these things. For a heeler like me, it's like watching a wide receiver [header and steer] pass in front of you. You better hit quick or you lose. You blank the crowd and everything else out of your mind. If a steer breaks this way or that way I got to find my position and get there to make my shot. You don't hear the crowd while you're competing. If you do, you're screwed up because you're not concentrating."

Around team roping circles the event is often referred to as "the Camarillo Benefit." Stockman Tommy Steiner had told me, "Listen, those Camarillos are just in another world."

"Sometimes," Leo continued, "I can't even explain what happens. You have to have some natural ability and work hard. I know I have a lot of confidence in my ability. You won't believe this, but I've had the rope actually slip out of my hand, dropping part of the loop and getting it all screwed up, and then go ahead and feed it and open my hand at the same time and the damn thing would hit the target and I'd win one thousand dollars."

Going for broke, Leo usually either won or didn't place at the NFR. Often his luck seemed to be running much as was Ferguson's. In the first go-round, H. P. missed the head of the steer. Leo rode on up and lassoed the steer's head while Evetts dropped back and threw a second loop at the animal's feet. But he caught only one foot, causing a five-second penalty and upping their time to 36.8. In the fourth go-round, Leo missed the heels and had to use his second loop. In the sixth go-round, Leo caught only one foot and had to take another five-second penalty. Otherwise, they'd have had a time of 7.4. In the seventh go-round, H. P. missed and had to use a second loop, and Leo was off mark in the eighth go-round, catching only one foot.

But they split a first on the second go-round, took the third go-round in 6.4, and, at the halfway mark, stood a good chance to win the average. H. P. came out of the box on Wednesday night, his rope zinging over the steer's head like a fishing reel. Leo was right behind him but felt Stick cutting across too much; he had to hold Stick back slightly so he'd be in the right spot when H. P. turned the steer. When he arrived at what he felt to be the proper place his rope was already shooting out, hanging an instant under the steer's hind legs. He had the steer. H. P. turned to face him and they drew the rope tight. Their time was 6.7, another first, and Leo looked up into the stands at his wife, Sharon, and gave her the Number One sign. Number One. The Number One Cowboy.

Sharon, the former Sharon Meffan, smiled and waved back. She had been both excited and tense as Leo came out of the box but started cheering wildly as he got the steer. They had been married a little over a year, and before Leo made his way into the stands to sit with her, she was saying, "I didn't even like Leo when I first met him. He seemed so sold on himself. But, obviously, I changed my feelings. At first he'd just phone me up at the last minute and ask me out. I told him he'd have to do more planning in advance. I think he thought I was like one of those girls who are so impressed with a big rodeo star that they'll jump at the chance to go out with him. But I'd been around that type before."

Sharon, slim, with sandy hair, pale eyes, and high cheekbones, almost made the NFR in barrel racing. She attended Cal Poly on a rodeo scholarship and upon leaving school became a stewardess for Western Airlines. The job bored her. She decided to go on the rodeo circuit full-time.

"One time I was at this rodeo," said Leo. "You know how you'll be looking or glancing around and something or somebody will catch your eye. I saw her and just stared for a minute, like time stopped. But then I just shrugged and let it pass.

"Anyway, I was married at the time."

Leo's marriage busted up after seven years, becoming, as some marriages do, a pointless relationship, mired, going nowhere. "It was like I was out there trying my ass off to win and then I'd come home and there'd be no love," he said. "Nothing. I'd just sign checks for bills and be gone again. I withdrew almost completely into myself. When the marriage ended, I lost everything—except for my ability."

The first time he dated Sharon, they had an argument. Leo was very defensive about most everything concerning himself, and Sharon would have no part of that. Finally, he just said, "I don't need you in my life." But he did.

Sharon's background was the antithesis of Leo's. Her father was a very successful aeronautical engineer. But her grandfather was interested in horses and got her started in rodeo. However, her parents didn't particularly care for her getting serious about a rodeo cowboy, whom they felt was just a vagabond with a hat. Sharon and Leo defied her parents and eloped, going to Las Vegas on a honeymoon.

Barrel racing at the NFR. Top: Diane Sleeter making a turn. Above: Connie Combs coming around.

"My parents are happy about us now," said Sharon, "because we're happy." Sharon still competes, too, so they travel the circuit together as much as possible and also compete as a team in jackpot roping.

"It's tough to be married to a rodeo cowboy," said Leo. "But somebody in the business herself can understand. When you win, it's great. But it gets tough when you try and cope with losing.

"Someday I'd like to have a successful business going and just rodeo as a hobby. If I could win this All Around, we'd move a lot closer to that goal."

Sharon smiled. Neither knew that Wednesday night of the fifth go-round would be the last money Leo would win in the National Finals Rodeo.

We stood by a blower in the stock barn, adjacent to the rodeo arena but not nearly as warm. Cowboys would stop, put their hands behind them, and then nudge in as close to the blower as they could, warming their backsides. Often, I suppose, being cold is a state of mind. At times you feel cold when the weather isn't that bad. When I was a kid and in doubt if I was actually cold or not, I'd always judge this on whether or not I could see my breath. I blew air out of my mouth, and if it was white, I knew I was cold. The air was white around us in the barn. Leo had stopped by the rodeo office to find out which steer he'd drawn. Then he'd looked in on Stick. People would come to the blower, warm up, and leave, being replaced by other early arrivals. But we stayed there for three-fourths of an hour.

"H. P.," said Leo, "is one of the best partners I ever had. He feels real bad about missing some this week. But, hell, I missed some, too." He stared over at a horse acting up, and the two cowboys holding it, but he didn't really see them. Evetts had missed on Friday night, the seventh go-round. On the Saturday afternoon go-round, Leo missed with his first loop and then took a five-second penalty for roping only one of the animal's feet. But on Saturday night, the next-to-last go-round, everything seemed to come crashing down on them. They were flagged out with an illegal catch and forced to take a no-time. This ruined their chances for the average. If anything, Leo had been counting heavily on making money in the average.

"Well, it's done now, it's over," said Leo. "Things don't look good for me. At least, we have to go win this go-round. Tom Ferguson came through Saturday night. I got to give him credit. He cowboyed up. He gambled and won."

It had all been just right for Ferguson. In one of the rodeo's highlights, he sent the crowd to its feet by breaking just right from the box and throwing his steer in 3.5, the best ever in eleven years of National Finals Rodeos. This won him an $892.82 first place, moving him within $1,048 of Camarillo. Ferguson also finished just .5 behind the fourth-place finisher—the last spot that paid—in calf roping; otherwise, he would have been $223.21 closer. But going into the final performance Tom was seventh in steer wrestling and fourth in calf roping average. If he had only a fair day, and maintained these positions, he would stand to win $1,272 in average money. And this didn't count money he might make for placing in Sunday's go-rounds. The most Leo possibly could win was $469.49 for first place in the go-round.

"Nope, it doesn't look good," Leo said, rubbing his hands together to generate heat. "I guess you might say I'm leading by a field goal in the two-minute period. But my opponent has the ball in my end of the field and is driving."

Ralph Camarillo came and talked to Leo, just before he left to go to the pens. He's a gray, stocky man, a quiet man, and I felt I might be seeing a strong resemblance to what Leo would look like in twenty-five or thirty years. He wished his son luck and left. His moment, the moment of his life, also seemed to be diminishing before his eyes.

When Leo and I got to the pens, Tom Ferguson was already sitting on the fence, staring at the steers. "How's it look?" Leo asked him. Ferguson glanced up at Leo, nodded, and continued to watch the stock. Then he got down off the fence and walked off. "I wouldn't have even spoken to him," said Leo, "but he was concentrating too good. I wanted to break his concentration, psych him a little.

"You know, when I got into pro rodeo, the thing I had going, besides ability, was that I could beat people with my head. I was tough mentally. I guess it came from my background. I know I've been controversial over the years. I used to be a pretty bitter guy. But, anyway, I'd beat guys psychologically. I'd get sarcastic. I might encourage a man even if I knew he couldn't beat me.

"Sometimes a man might come up to me and I could tell he wanted me to say something nice.

Maybe he'd just been givin' a good time. But I'd say, 'Shit, you can't expect to win anything. You're not that good a roper.' I might be joking, but it was in a serious way. The guy would walk off with one thing on his mind, beating that asshole Camarillo. But when he got mad, that helped me.

"I really had a bloodthirsty attitude. That hurt me in some of the jackpot rodeos. They banned me in some places."

Leo found the steer he'd drawn and watched him. "If I see something unusual about him I'll tell my partner," he said. "This one looks average to me. But, look over there, you see that one?" The steer moved to the outside of the pen. "He ain't too mean because he doesn't look mean. But notice that other one, kind of wide-eyed looking. Twitchy, nervous. He's dangerous. He'll walk into fire.

"You can look at a true Mexican steer and know he's going to be pretty honest [run straight, be consistent]. But if he's got a little Brahma in him, he can be trouble. Spastic. He might try to outrun you.

"I can usually tell about my steer. But I don't want him lying down in the pen. If I see him do that I'll stand him up. I don't want him resting."

Leo reflected for a couple of minutes. Finally, he said, "I like to come back here to the pens early and sit and watch. Sometimes it's very relaxing."

But there was no more time for relaxing.

"And this afternoon," the announcer continued, "you'll see the world title decided in bareback between Joe Alexander and Rusty Riddle. Never before in the history of National Finals has the All Around title, the most coveted title in our sport today, been decided in the final performance. But this afternoon, Leo Camarillo and Tom Ferguson will decide that very same title. The self-discipline these men have is something we sorely need today and, once again, as we're talking about our country's bicentennial, great self-discipline just didn't happen because of rodeo. We believe it happened because one hundred years ago the West was settled by men and horses and cattle involved in a lifestyle which required a great deal of self-discipline. We feel our society today would be better off if some of this same self-discipline was more widely perpetuated. . . . But now, travel with us, if you will, back to one of the most exciting pages in American history, to the day when the longhorn cattle came down the Chisholm Trail. . . . "

Longhorn cattle were turned loose in the arena, simulating an old cattle drive. Then a rider came tearing across the arena on a bucking horse, fanning his hat, as Red Steagall sang "Little Joe the Wrangler." The crowd cheered history, I suppose, more than those acting it out. Freckles Brown, now fifty-four, waited by the chutes—the wings, if you will. Before each rodeo performance, there was a tribute to Freckles, because on Friday, December 1, 1967, at the National Finals, he rode Tornado, a bull that had never been ridden.

Freckles Brown was forty-six years of age when he conquered Tornado in Oklahoma City. It was one of those performances in sport that seems to stop time and leave a permanent indentation on those who see it. Freckles made better rides, more spectacular rides, but the fact that it happened at the National Finals, when he was competing among the best, before rodeo's aficionados against an animal that had built a reputation of invincibility, made it forever special.

Freckles, a small, easy-going and modest man, said, "Yeah, one year in San Francisco I rode a bull called Eight-Ball. He had the reputation of being among the rankest of the rank. I got an eighty-three. That was the highest mark of the year, almost unheard of back then. People talked about that ride for almost a year. Then they forgot it.

"Not that Tornado deal. I'm not sure myself what it is about that ride. It's snowballed, I know that. I think, mostly, it was because I was so derned old when I rode him."

For each performance, Steagall, who once had

Barrel racing is the fastest NFR event and the only event for women.

an unsuccessful try at being a bull rider, sat, on a two-by-four that went along the top of the fence near the chute, and sang. He likes cowboys, likes to sing about them, be around them. "They're special people," he said. "It's a fraternity. They're rugged, yet very gentle. The thing I like best about these people is their honesty. I guess you'd say their inability to hide their feelings. You never have to wonder about where you stand in rodeo."

But mostly, he likes Freckles Brown. He'd met Freckles for the first time the year before and was completely taken by him. "I knew I was going to write a song about Freckles Brown right after I met him," said Steagall. "Freckles is the most loved man I've ever known. Anyone who's ever met him idolizes him." Steagall jotted down his song about Freckles Brown on a flight from Dallas to Nashville. He called it "For Freckles Brown" and sang it before each performance, as a bull, representing Tornado, ran into the spotlight of the arena along with the cowboy, Freckles Brown.

Well, the year was sixty-seven, National Finals Rodeo,
December One's Friday night that all bull riders know;
There's cowboy heroes made and born at rodeos like this,
'Cause the cowboys are the toughest, the stock's the best there is.
Then Chuck announced that in chute two's the cowboy we all know,
He's a young man now of forty-six and he's made a mighty draw;
His bull is from Jim Shoulders' string, Tornado's how he's known;
Yes, Freckles Brown had drawed a bull no one has ever rode.

CHORUS:
And tonight bull ridin' hist'ry's made, a cowboy gained a crown;
His bull was called Tornado and the cowboy, Freckles Brown.

He lowered himself on dark red hide, he pulled his bull rope tight,
He wrapped her twice and jerked her hard, made sure he pulled her right.
Then two big old shiny horns looked Freckles in the eye,
With a snort and a nod the chute gate swung as Freckles yelled, "Let's ride!"
Two thousand pounds of boilin' hell was turnin' wrong side out
And showin' four feet to the Lord and givin' Freckles hell;
Eight thousand fans were on their feet and he couldn't hear a lick,
'Cause the only sound he listened for was the buzzer and then he quit.

It seemed the world exploded as Freckles hit the ground,
And he swung his hat around his head and he shouted with the crowd;
A cowboy hero born that day and Freckles totes the load;
Two hundred times that bull had bucked, the first time he'd been rode.
Now while we're giving credit where we know the credit's due,
Yes, Freckles is a hero, but Tornado gets some, too;
'Cause without the bull to show him off a cowboy's no call
And the only time he'll ever win's get lucky when he draws.

So if bulls have got a heaven, and somehow we're sure they do,
Let's hope Tornado's up there and the Lord has let him through;
Hope his pasture is the greenest and his stock tank's never dry,

And I hope there ain't a single spur to gouge his ugly hide;
And I hope them cowboys up there keep him fat and treat him kind,
And I hope he lives forever on bunch grass, belly high;
And tonight bull ridin' hist'ry's made, a cowboy gained a crown;
His bull was called Tornado and the cowboy, Freckles Brown.

Freckles, taking his hat off, walked back to the chutes as the crowd gave him a standing ovation. "Oh, yew bet, I could still ride," he said. "But I hurt my neck at Tulsa last year and I've got arthritis in it and I don't think I could take a real bad fall. My neck's just not very flexible anymore. So, I'm not gonna get on any more bulls."

The lights, dimmed, were turned up again. The final day of Rodeo '75, began.

The suddenness with which it was over completely belied the circumstances. For 364 days, Joe Alexander and Rusty Riddle had battled for the bareback title. Joe was going for a fifth straight title, unmatched in the history of the event. But Rusty, the perennial second-place finisher, had a chance this time. He'd trimmed Joe's $1,078 lead coming into the NFR to $520, though Alexander led him in the average. For Rusty to win, he needed to take the go-round and Alexander must slip, perhaps be thrown. The draw seemed to have settled the situation. Alexander drew Little Dan, a highly rated horse he'd ridden five times for four firsts and a second. Rusty had Sorrell Storm, which had been placed on only four of twenty-four times that year.

"I knew I had him when I saw the draw, as long as I could mark my horse out," said Alexander. "My only worry was missing him out of chutes."

Rusty did about all he could, but marked 68, putting him out of the go-round money. Joe, like a true champion, didn't play it safe. Though he knew all he had to do was stay on the horse, he came out recklessly, spurring wildly, and scored an 80. He was the champion and Rusty was left to ponder, perhaps, the luck of the draw. In a total time of 16 seconds, the championship had been settled.

Steer wrestling was the second event, and Tom Ferguson prepared to make his drive at Leo's lead, which had dwindled to $1,048. They paid the top six places in average. Tom was seventh, but it would be difficult for him to make sixth, the spot held by his brother Larry, who was a total of 16.8 seconds ahead of him going into the final go-round. But, competing before Tom, Larry missed his steer as it set up, then ducked, and he had to chase it down before finally taking a 37.7 time. Only because Larry missed did Tom have an opening to move into the payday for average. He took it, throwing his steer in 4.9 and claiming sixth, a $334.81 payoff. He'd cut Leo's lead to $714.

"Larry had a bad steer," said Frank Shepperson, who won the world title in the event. "Two guys, Darrel Sewell and Casper Schaefer, had missed him earlier. But, no, I wouldn't put it past him to help his brother out. If it was my brother going for the world title, I think it'd be hard not to help him."

Camarillo knew he had to do something, because all Ferguson had to do was maintain his average in calf roping to take the title. Tom stood fourth, which would pay $1,272. Even if he dropped to fifth, he'd win $937 and still beat him—unless Leo won the go-round.

Leo, as is his nature, didn't show tension as he waited for his turn in the next event, team roping. But he felt it. The crowd felt it. So did Tom Ferguson. "Let's go for broke," Leo said to Evetts. H. P. got a good jump out of the box and roped the steer before it got midway through the arena. He turned the animal as Leo moved in and quickly tossed his loop. He missed the steer's heels and the rope lay on the ground, no longer alive, just lying there. Leo knew it was over, all over, but he quickly threw

The 1975 NFR World Title winners (left to right): Jimmie Gibbs, barrel racing; Donnie Gay, bull riding; Jeff Copenhaver, calf roping; Monty Henson, saddle bronc; Frank Shepperson, steer wrestling; Joe Alexander, bareback; and Leo Camarillo, team roping.

another loop, snaring both the steer's hindlegs. Leo then stared blankly at an official. His head slightly bowed, he rode from the arena. In the stands, Sharon watched him, then looked down at the ground.

"His chances," she said, "just dropped to a thousand to one."

"I don't even remember looking at the official," said Leo, speaking very softly. "I—I just missed that first time and, you know, wanted to get it right even if it meant nothing. Just get it down right.

"I blew it. No excuses. Just blew it." Leo dismounted, put Stick in a stall, and then made his way slowly back toward the arena and out along the walls to watch the remainder of the rodeo with the other cowboys. His walk was leaden, as though a weight had suddenly been added to his shoulders.

Larry Mahan, in the arena nearby, was explaining the situation for the viewers of "Wide World of Sports." A cast covered his arm, from the wrist to the top of the biceps. They'd put his elbow back in place, but surgery was needed to remove bone chips and secure it more tightly.

"I can't decide whether to stay on here and let them do it or go back to Dallas," he said.

"Why don't you let Pat Evans [the Dallas Cowboys' team physician] do it?" I said. "You'd be back in Dallas, at Baylor Hospital, where they keep a room open for you. We could all have a wake in your room—chanting, drinking, dancing."

"I've got to send you a shirt," he said. "You need another hat. You look like Tom Mix. By the way, I've lost Dr. Evans's phone number. Do you have it?"

I gave him the phone number. He put his hand on the cast and said, "I wished to hell this was off. It'd be great to be in the middle of this thing today." Then he walked off, back to ABC.

Leo, in the middle, stood silently at the fence as Tom C. Miller scored an 80 and won the saddle bronc go-round and average for the National Finals. Monty Henson had long before cinched the saddle bronc title for the year. Monty had come to the NFR almost $7,000 ahead of runner-up Sammie Groves, Claude's brother, and just under $10,000 ahead of Miller. When the NFR had ended, Henson was still $8,000 ahead of Miller and yet, under the new rules, Tom C. Miller would have been World Saddle Bronc Champion. This was one of the drawbacks the cowboys had been talking about.

Sammie Groves stood by the chutes after the event, and I asked him what Claude was doing. "Who knows?" he said. "I haven't heard anything from him. You know, it's a shame he don't get more serious. Listen, I don't say this because he's my brother, but ask anybody, if you don't believe me. I mean Claude can ride with any of these boys here in the Finals. He sure can."

The moment of truth, calf roping, was the next event. A 15.8 wouldn't come close to placing in the go-round, usually won in times such as 10 to 11. A 15.8, a below average effort, was all Tom Ferguson needed to take fourth in the average and win enough money to pass Leo Camarillo and take the All Around championship again.

"I wasn't nervous," Ferguson said later. "I just wanted to be careful and make sure I didn't break the barrier. Sure, I thought I'd had it. To do the time I needed would be, to me, about as difficult as putting on my boots."

Leo, still standing by the fence, wore a mask with a grin on it. "I feel like a football coach on the last play of the game," he said. "I'm ahead by a field goal but the other team is on my one-yard line and has one play left."

Tom didn't break the barrier but had good timing as he came out of the box and roped the calf. But his rope, jerking against the full forward impetus of the calf, flipped the animal into the air and over backward. Ferguson was on the calf in seconds and it appeared certain he'd be around 10 to 12 seconds at the most. But the calf seemed limp. Tom tried to get it to stand up so he could throw it down

and tie it, but the animal didn't respond. A calf must be on its feet before it can legally be thrown. Finally, he stepped back and pulled the calf's tail and still couldn't get it up.

"I believe the thing's broke its hip," somebody said from the rail.

Ferguson, disgusted, literally pulled the 300-pound calf to its feet, then threw it down to the ground and tied three legs. But 24.3 had elapsed. "Everybody thought it had dislocated its hip," said Tom. "But it hadn't. The calf was just stunned, knocked out. There wasn't much I could do."

Everybody calculated in their heads. Nobody was sure if Ferguson had enough. Surely, he did. Jerold Camarillo, who had checked the winnings, came along the fence and found Leo, still dejected.

"Hey, that drops him to sixth in the average, Leo," said Jerold. "Hey, you won!"

Leo grabbed Jerold by the shoulders. "Won! Are you sure? Are you sure!"

"Hey, I'm sure."

"Yippeeee! Talk about fumbling in the end zone!"

For minutes there was almost silence around the arena. Suddenly, a black hat sailed out, landing not fifteen feet from where Tom Ferguson had experienced the most frustrating time of his career. It was Leo's hat. "God," he said, "is a team roping fan." Neither Ferguson nor Leo had done that well in the NFR. You might say Ferguson lost and Leo didn't. But Leo had won the All Around title by a mere $112, in the closest race in history.

Other events unfolded, a kaleidoscope around what had already happened. In the final event, bull riding, Randy Magers, who hadn't had a good Finals, found the courage and magic he needed to produce a helluva ride on Oscar, a bull that had been ridden just five of 177 times. Magers knew he had it and began spurring and fanning his hat before the buzzer. He got an 85, as the crowd cheered wildly.

Leo talked to the media, answered the same

questions over and over, and smiled and wondered if it had really happened, if it was real. Sharon was there, his father was there. He tasted what he had become, saw what he had become, as well-wishers crowded closer to get a closer look, to touch.

Leo Camarillo was swept up in what he had become.

A month after the finals in Oklahoma City, Leo Camarillo had competed in the big rodeo in Denver and had attended a champion's banquet—as the All Around champion of 1975. Shortly thereafter, he was taking Sharon and her parents to dinner and stopped to phone California, where he was competing in a rodeo. When the call went through and Leo identified himself, a voice at the other end told him the PRCA in Denver had been trying to reach him, apparently not knowing he was still in that city.

"Well, they want to talk to you. There's been an error in the All Around totals."

"What are you talking about?"

"There's definitely an error. Looks like you didn't win."

Later Leo recalled the conversation and said, "Just like that. Some voice says it's all not true. I froze inside. It was like having a bad dream. You wake up, scared or feeling awful, but find out the bad dream wasn't real. This was real."

The final totals after Oklahoma City had been audited. But Tom Ferguson went by the PRCA office and found a mistake in Leo's totals. "There was a mistake, and it looks to me like I won the most money," said Tom. Leo, in turn, had an audit conducted and said Tom's totals were not correct.

Officials, naturally red-faced, met and met again. They talked to both Leo and Tom and an agreement was finally reached. The PRCA announcement read, in part:

Concluding a two-month investigation, the Board of Directors of the PRCA has declared that both Leo Camarillo and Tom Ferguson are the World Champion All Around Cowboys for 1975. After three special meetings of the Board of Directors, two reaudits of the final championship standings, and weeks of fact-finding, it was the conclusion of the Board that due to apparent auditing errors in PRCA records, the previously released final point totals for both Camarillo and Ferguson were incorrect.... Therefore, in order to be as fair as possible to both cowboys, and to permit each to benefit from his championship year, the Board has declared both Camarillo and Ferguson to be the 1975 World Champion All Around Cowboys.

Leo Camarillo used his championship winnings, plus his Winston bonus money, to buy 152 acres of land in California's rolling foothills near Clements. The area is bordered on the west by land upon which gold was once discovered and on the east by rich wine vineyards. When I last saw them, Leo and Sharon planned to build a home on the highest point of the property, where they could look out over their land and see that sometimes dreams come true.

Leo started a business, selling rodeo products. He endorsed other commercial products. But he felt a great letdown and became very despondent over sharing a title that he felt he had won. So he didn't attend many rodeos for a while. Tom Ferguson, a driving, relentless man, never slowed down.

But finally, Leo Camarillo picked up his gear and got on down the road.

EXPLANATION OF EVENTS

Courtesy of Professional Rodeo Cowboys Association

Saddle Bronc Riding

The identity of the first man to tangle with a bucking horse is hidden in history, but saddle bronc riding is the cornerstone of all rodeo competition. Experience and know-how are paramount in this event where the rules are strictly in favor of the animal.

Equipment

Saddles are uniform in design. They must comply with measurements set forth by the Professional Rodeo Cowboys Association. One rein is used, usually of braided Manila, some 6 feet long and an inch and a half thick. It is fastened to the halter of the bucking horse. Spurs are short-shanked, with dull rowels. Chaps are of light leather, snugged tight around the thigh.

Rules

A rider is disqualified for:
1. Failing to keep spurs over the animal's shoulder points when its feet hit the ground on the first jump out of the chute (called "starting" the horse).
2. Touching animal or equipment with free hand during the ride.
3. Losing a stirrup.
4. Bucking off before official end of the ride.

How They Ride

Leaving the chute, the rider tries at once to find "timing" with the bronc's action. His spurred feet should fall into rhythmic stride, going to the animal's shoulders as it kicks high behind, moving back toward the saddle's cantle as the bronc jumps.

Some common causes of buck-offs are too long a rein, which lets rider back up on the cantle and then get thrown forward; too short a rein, which pulls him over the horse's head; a spurred foot catching momentarily in the animal's shoulder, which levers him off on the side the spur hangs up.

Bareback Riding

This is the youngest of rodeo's three standard riding contests. Developed in the arena, it has no actual tie-in with workaday ranch duties. Since becoming a requirement at all Association-approved rodeos some twenty years ago, bareback bronc riding is now one of the game's most popular events.

Equipment

Instead of saddles, a double-thick leather pad, called a rigging, is cinched on the bronc's back. No stirrups or rein are used. Slightly off-center at the top of the rigging is a leather handhold. Bareback riders like the one handhold as snug-fitting as possible, for good grip. Spurs and a glove are the only other riding gear needed, but chaps often are worn, similar to those used in saddle bronc riding.

Rules

Same rules of disqualifications as used in saddle bronc riding, with exception of rule 3 (losing a stirrup).

How They Ride

The higher and wilder a bareback rider spurs, the better his marking by the judges. Feet forward at all times—in contrast to saddle bronc riding style—the rider clings close against the rigging handhold and tries to keep his legs flailing in time with the bronc's jumps. A strong hand and fine sense of balance are needed to keep from being jerked back away from the handhold, a situation that generally leads to a buck-off.

Bull Riding

Serious injury occurs more often in this event than in any other in rodeo. Capable of savage, sustained bucking, crossbred Brahmas were first introduced into the arena about 1921. Fast and powerful, most of them weigh over 1,500 pounds. The loose-hided animals add injury to insult by trying to gore or trample a fallen rider. They are dangerous as well in the chute, where their leaning weight can easily break a rider's legs.

Equipment

Woven with a single handhold, a flat-braided length of Manila rope about an inch and a quarter in width is used noose-fashion around the bull, set just behind the animal's shoulders. A weighted bell also is attached to the rope, which allows it to fall free when the ride is completed. Tightly strapped spurs and a riding glove complete the necessary gear. Chaps are sometimes worn.

Rules

More leniency is shown than in saddle and bareback bronc riding. A bull rider is not required to spur his mount but may receive additional credit from the judges if he does so; if the rider is in the air but still holding some part of his rope when the official end of the ride is signaled, he rates a qualifying mark.

Disqualification comes from hitting the ground before the eight-second ride is completed; failing to have a bell attached to the rope; or touching the mount with the free hand at any time during the ride.

How They Ride

Some cowboys claim a Brahma bull can buck anybody off, anytime it turns on full power. One thing is certain: the snuffy slack-hided animals devise more spine-rattling action in the arena than any other breed of bovine. Staying in the middle of one calls for balance and a strong riding arm.

If possible, the rider stays seated close up on his rope handhold, legs held slightly forward clutching the bull's rib cage. If the rider slips back off the rope, thus straightening his riding arm, the bull's power will jerk his hand loose, usually on the next jump.

Spinning bulls are considered more hazardous to ride than those that buck straightaway. There is more danger of being trampled or butted if a rider falls to the inside of the whirling animal.

Since the bulls fight a man on horseback just as eagerly as a man on foot—unlike saddle and bareback broncs—no pickup men are used. Instead, a rider dismounts on his own, depending on the bullbaiting clown to keep the animal's attention while he gets out of range.

Calf Roping

A coordinated effort of horse and rider against time, calf roping has been honed to such high competitive polish that only tenths of a second divide the winners.

Since every phase of a roper's actions is planned to coincide with his mount, any disruption of the pattern costs him precious seconds. A solid, true-working horse is valuable property. Today such an animal commands a four-figure price tag.

Equipment

Lariat ropes, generally about 25 feet long and three-eighths of an inch thick, are tied at one end to the saddle horn, the other end forming the catch loop. If the roper misses the first throw, he may use a second rope coiled ready on the saddle. He is allowed only two throws. If he misses with both, he must retire with no time.

A slimmer 6-foot length of rope, usually tucked in the roper's belt, is used to tie the calf. Horse gear, such as the saddle and bridle, are the roper's own selection.

Rules

The event calls for two or more timekeepers, a field flag judge, and a scoreline flag judge. The length of score (headstart) given the calf depends on the arena's size. The roper remains behind a barrier until the calf crosses the scoreline. Breaking through the barrier adds 10 seconds to the roper's time.

Crossbred Brahma calves must weigh at least 200 and not more than 300 pounds, and native calves such as Hereford and Angus must not weigh more than 350 pounds. After the catch, the roper must throw the calf by hand, cross any three legs for the tie, then signal for time by raising his hands. Field judge then passes on the tie.

Things to Watch

Long tedious hours of practice and schooling go into this action. More than the roper, watch the horse, rating the speed of the calf, stopping on cue, then backing fast to keep the rope taut as the roper runs to his quarry. How well the horse carries out these hard-taught maneuvers is the difference between wins and losses. Calf-roping mounts may be any bloodlines, but because of their natural, early speed, quarter horses are used more than any other. The most important requisite, though, is heart.

Steer Wrestling

Developed in the rodeo arena, steer wrestling, like bareback bronc riding, was never a part of ranch work. Its origin in the early 1930s is laid at the door of a cowboy, Bill Pickett, who worked in a Wild West show.

With time taken between flags, steer wrestling is a series of practiced moves beginning when a contestant, aided by another mounted cowboy called "the hazer," leaps from a running horse to the steer's horns, bringing the animal to a halt and then wrestling it to the ground.

Equipment

Other than a steer wrestling mount and the hazer, whose duty is to keep the steer running as straight as possible, no equipment is needed. The hazer is paid an eighth of what the steer wrestler may win. Many cowboys own a team—both steer wrestling mount and hazing horse—and by serving as a hazer for others, get a fourth for their use.

Rules

Officials are two or more timekeepers, a field judge, and a scoreline judge. Contestant waits, with hazer posted on opposite side of the release gate, until the steer crosses the designated scoreline. Breaking barrier adds 10-second penalty. Steer must be on its feet before being wrestled down. Running falls do not count. Steer is to be flat on its side, all four legs extended, before official time is given.

Things to Watch

The spot where a steer wrestler's feet hit the ground after taking hold of the steer is a key to further action. A good steer wrestling horse sweeps on by, leaving the cowboy's legs extended at a 45-degree angle to the steer's path. Bringing the animal around in an arc, at the top of the swing, the steer wrestler reaches for the right horn tip, using his left hand as additional leverage under the steer's jaw. Off-balance momentum plus upturned head cause the steer literally to throw himself.

Team Roping

Catching cattle by the horns and hind feet has been a simple way to doctor injuries or brand since early range days. Rodeo's version is a speeded-up contest against time. Highly popular in California, Arizona, and Nevada rodeos, with bankers, doctors, and dentists among ardent competitors, team roping is not one of the sport's standard events.

Team roping calls for a man on a horse known as a header, who chases the steer and throws his loop around the horns, turning the animal back to where the heeler can get in position to throw a loop around the steer's heels. Both men must dally, or wrap the ropes around their saddle horns after making their catches, and time is called when both horses turn to face each other, with the steer in the middle and ropes taut.

Equipment

Team roping requires fast-handling mounts. Saddles and bridles are the ropers' own choice. Ropes, some 28 feet long, are used. Dally roping saddles usually have a higher horn to facilitate turns with the catch rope.

Rules

Two or more timekeepers, a field judge, and a scoreline flag judge are used. Steer is given designated start with both ropers behind a barrier. Breaking the barrier is an automatic 10-second penalty. Heel roper is assessed a 5-second fine if he catches only one hind foot; a 5-second fine is assessed if a front foot is caught along with the head. A total of three throws is allowed. Ropers must face their horses toward steer with ropes taut for official time.

Things to Watch

Head ropers place their roped quarry in position most advantageous for the heeler's throw. Snaring hind feet on a jumping, twisting steer must be timed to precision. Dally ropers run the ever-present danger of losing fingers in the slipping turns of the rope around the saddle horn.

Steer Roping

Tying down the big steers single-handed against time—calling for more precise skill perhaps than any other roping contest—is one of rodeo's original events. But only about a dozen rodeos today still have steer roping.

Cheyenne Frontier Days and the Pendleton Round-Up are two of the major rodeos left where the event's top hands gather each season.

A mounted roper snares the running steer's horns, laying the rope's slack over the steer's right hip. Then, as he angles his mount to the left while the rope tightens, the steer is spun to the ground. While his mount leans into the rope, keeping the steer prone, roper runs back on foot to group and tie any three legs.

Equipment

Lariat ropes are twisted nylon, about 28 feet long

and virtually unbreakable. Tie string is longer and heavier than that used in calf roping. Saddle, briddle, etc., are roper's own choice.

Rules

Two or more timekeepers, field and scoreline flag judges are the officials. Steer is given designated headstart while roper waits behind barrier. Breaking the barrier is a 10-second penalty. Steer must remain tied until approved by field flag judge. Only clean catch of steer's horns is allowed. Two throws are permitted.

Things to Watch

Steer horses are specially trained. They must be fast, and strong enough to withstand the steer's weight on the end of the rope. An important part of their training is to stop pulling at once, on command. The horses learn this through practice runs, made with a heavy log used to simulate a steer's weight.

Wild Horse Race

An added event, Association approved but with no championship award. Teams of three cowboys, on foot, try to saddle unbroken mustangs in the arena. One team member then tries to ride animal across given scoreline.

Wild Cow Milking

Another added event with no Association title award. Against time, two cowboys attempt to get at least one drop of milk from the cow into a small-neck bottle, then deliver it across designated line.

Steer Decorating

A Canadian variation of steer wrestling. Contestant jumps from his running horse on the steer, placing an elastic band on the animal's horn instead of wrestling the steer to the ground. The event is not seen at rodeos in the United States.

GLOSSARY

Added money The purse put up by a rodeo committee in a particular town or city. Total prize money constitutes that purse plus money put up by contestants as entry fees.

Arena director A person who supervises all jobs and details connected with the actual rodeo arena.

Association saddle A saddle built to PRCA specifications and designed to be used in bronc riding.

Average Winner of the average is the person who, after the entire rodeo, has the highest cumulative score in the riding events or the lowest total time in the timed events. Prize money is paid for each go-round and *also* for the average.

Barrier A designated rope stretched across the front of a box that a steer wrestler or roper's horse starts when the flag is dropped. Steers or calves are given a predetermined start.

Breaking the barrier Riding through the designated barrier rope before it is released results in a 10-second penalty.

Closed event An event at an approved rodeo that is not open to all members in good standing in the PRCA. In order for an approved rodeo to have a local closed event, it must have the same event for all members of the PRCA.

Contract acts Any act, such as trick riding, that the rodeo committee has under contract to perform at a certain event.

Dally When rider wraps rope around the saddle horn after successfully roping a calf or steer.

Day money Prize money paid to the winner of each go-round in an event.

Dink A horse that is poorly trained or inadequate for roping or steer wrestling.

Dusted Thrown into the dirt by a horse or bull.

Entry fee Money paid by a contestant to the rodeo secretary prior to entering an event. Contestants pay separate entry fees for each event in which they compete.

Fishing A term used in roping for a near miss that turns into a legal catch, usually by accident.

Flank strap A sheepskin-lined strap with a self-holding buckle passed around a bull or horse. As the chute gate is opened, the strap is pulled tight. The theory is that the animal bucks higher and harder trying to rid itself of the strap.

Go-round When each contestant in an event has competed on one head of stock. The number of go-rounds varies, depending on the size of the rodeo and the number of entries.

Hazer A cowboy who rides on the opposite side of a steer in order to keep it from bolting away from the steer wrestler's horse.

Header The first man out in team roping who ropes the steer by the head or horns. A header carries two loops and is allowed to use the second if he misses with the first.

Heeler Second man in a team roping duo, who tries to rope one or both hind feet of the steer after his partner has roped the head. A heeler is also allowed two ropes.

Hobble Tying hind feet of a steer, already roped, just below the hocks with a short rope.

Honda Eye in one end of the rope through which is passed the other end in order to form a loop.

Hooker A bull that attempts to use its horns to rid itself of a rider.

Jackpot An event without a purse put up by the rodeo. Conducted ordinarily by contestants, with winners splitting all or part of entry fees.

Lick Downward action used by bronc rider with spurs on shoulders of his mount.

No time Signaled by a flag fieldman when a contestant has not caught or thrown his animal properly.

One-header Single go-round in a rodeo.

Pickup man Mounted rider who helps a bronc rider off his horse after buzzer sounds. Pickup man then removes flank strap and leads horse out of the arena.

Pigging string The short piece of rope used by a roper to tie a roped calf or steer.

PRCA Professional Rodeo Cowboys Association. Name changed from Rodeo Cowboys Association in 1975. Originally called Cowboys Turtle Association from 1936 to 1945. Governing body for rodeo.

Pulling leather When a bronc rider holds onto the horn or any part of the saddle. If done before buzzer, he's disqualified.

Rank An animal that's tough, hard to handle, and bucks well. One upon which a rider can get a high score.

Re-ride Awarded a rider when his first ride is unsatisfactory for any of several reasons, usually having to do with the animal.

Rowel Circular, pointed part of spur that protrudes behind heel of boot. Has starlike shape.

Spinner Bull that comes out of chutes and spins in close circles, in one direction or the other.

Well The area inside a spinning bull.

RODEO RECORDS

Most All Around Championships . . . . .Larry Mahan, 6
Most World Championships . . . . .Jim Shoulders, 16
Most Total Money Won . . . . .Larry Mahan,
$493,698 (through 1975)
Most Money Won One Year . . . . .Tom Ferguson,
$66,929 (1974)
Most Money Won One Rodeo . . . . .Edd Workman,
$9,305 (Houston, Texas, 1976)
Most Money Won In One Event In One Year . . . . .Joe Alexander,
$41,184 in BB, 1975
Most Bareback Bronc Championships . . . . .Joe Alexander, 5
Most Calf Roping Championships . . . . .Dean Oliver, 8
Most Saddle Bronc Championships . . . . .Casey Tibbs, 6
Most Steer Wrestling Championships . . . . .Homer Pettigrew, 6
Most Bull Riding Championships . . . . .Jim Shoulders, 7
Most Team Roping Championships . . . . .Jim Rodriguez, Jr., 4
Most Steer Roping Championships . . . . .Everett Shaw, 6
Youngest World Champion . . . . .Jim Rodriguez, Jr.,
at age 18, TR 1959
Oldest World Champion . . . . .Ike Rude, at age 59, SR 1953
Highest Scored Ride . . . . .John Quintana, in BR (96 pts.), 1974

No official times are kept in timed events because of varying "score" lengths.

STATISTICS

CHAMPIONSHIP COWBOYS 1929-1944

(From 1929 through 1944, rodeo's champions were named by the Rodeo Association of America.)

All Around Cowboy

Earl Thode, Belvidere, S.D.	1929
Clay Carr, Visalia, Calif.	1930
John Schneider, Livermore, Calif.	1931
Donald Nesbit, Snowflake, Ariz.	1932
Clay Carr, Visalia, Calif.	1933
Leonard Ward, Talent, Ore.	1934
Everett Bowman, Hillside, Ariz.	1935
John Bowman, Oakdale, Calif.	1936
Everett Bowman, Hillside, Ariz.	1937
Burel Mulkey, Salmon, Ida.	1938
Paul Carney, Galeton, Colo.	1939
Fritz Truan, Long Beach, Calif.	1940
Homer Pettigrew, Grady, N.M.	1941
Gerald Roberts, Strong City, Kans.	1942
Louis Brooks, Pittsburg, Okla.	1943
Louis Brooks, Pittsburg, Okla.	1944

Saddle Bronc Riding

Earl Thode, Belvidere, S.D.	1929
Clay Carr, Visalia, Calif.	1930
Earl Thode, Belvidere, S.D.	1931
Pete Knight, Crossfield, Alta.	1932
Pete Knight, Crossfield, Alta.	1933
Leonard Ward, Talent, Ore.	1934
Pete Knight, Crossfield, Alta.	1935
Pete Knight, Crossfield, Alta.	1936
Burel Mulkey, Salmon, Ida.	1937
Burel Mulkey, Salmon, Ida.	1938
Fritz Truan, Long Beach, Calif.	1939
Fritz Truan, Long Beach, Calif.	1940
Doff Aber, Wolf, Wyo.	1941
Doff Aber, Wolf, Wyo.	1942
Louis Brooks, Pittsburg, Okla.	1943
Louis Brooks, Pittsburg, Okla.	1944

Bareback Riding

(No Bareback champions named by the R.A.A. until 1932.)

Smokey Snyder, Bellflower, Calif.	1932
Nate Waldrum, Strathmore, Alta.	1933
Leonard Ward, Talent, Ore.	1934
Frank Schneider, Caliente, Calif.	1935
Smokey Snyder, Bellflower, Calif.	1936
Paul Carney, Galeton, Colo.	1937
Pete Grubb, Salmon, Ida.	1938
Paul Carney, Galeton, Colo.	1939
Carl Dossey, Phoenix, Ariz.	1940
George Mills, Montrose, Colo.	1941
Louis Brooks, Pittsburg, Okla.	1942
Bill Linderman, Red Lodge, Mont.	1943
Louis Brooks, Pittsburg, Okla.	1944

Bull Riding

John Schneider, Livermore, Calif.	1929
John Schneider, Livermore, Calif.	1930
Smokey Snyder, Bellflower, Calif.	1931
John Schneider, Livermore, Calif.	1932
Smokey Snyder, Bellflower, Calif. (tie)	
Frank Schneider, Caliente, Calif.	1933
Frank Schneider, Caliente, Calif.	1934
Smokey Snyder, Bellflower, Calif.	1935
Smokey Snyder, Bellflower, Calif.	1936
Smokey Snyder, Bellflower, Calif.	1937
Kid Fletcher, Hugo, Colo.	1938
Dick Griffith, Ft. Worth, Tex.	1939
Dick Griffith, Ft. Worth, Tex.	1940
Dick Griffith, Ft. Worth, Tex.	1941
Dick Griffith, Ft. Worth, Tex.	1942
Ken Roberts, Strong City, Kans.	1943
Ken Roberts, Strong City, Kans.	1944

Calf Roping

Everett Bowman, Hillside, Ariz.	1929
Jake McClure, Lovington, N.M.	1930
Herb Meyers, Okmulgee, Okla.	1931
Richard Merchant, Kirkland, Ariz.	1932
Bill McFarlane, Red Bluff, Calif.	1933
Irby Mundy, Shamrock, Tex.	1934
Everett Bowman, Hillside, Ariz.	1935
Clyde Burk, Comanche, Okla.	1936
Everett Bowman, Hillside, Ariz.	1937
Clyde Burk, Comanche, Okla.	1938
Toots Mansfield, Bandera, Tex.	1939
Toots Mansfield, Bandera, Tex.	1940
Toots Mansfield, Bandera, Tex.	1941
Clyde Burk, Comanche, Okla.	1942
Toots Mansfield, Bandera, Tex.	1943
Clyde Burk, Comanche, Okla.	1944

Steer Wrestling

Gene Ross, Sayre, Okla.	1929
Everett Bowman, Hillside, Ariz.	1930
Gene Ross, Sayre, Okla.	1931
Hugh Bennett, Ft. Thomas, Ariz.	1932
Everett Bowman, Hillside, Ariz.	1933
Shorty Ricker, Ranger, Tex.	1934
Everett Bowman, Hillside, Ariz.	1935
Jack Kerschner, Miles City, Mont.	1936
Gene Ross, Sayre, Okla.	1937
Everett Bowman, Hillside, Ariz.	1938
Harry Hart, Pocatello, Ida.	1939
Homer Pettigrew, Grady, N.M.	1940
Hub Whiteman, Clarksville, Tex.	1941
Homer Pettigrew, Grady, N.M.	1942
Homer Pettigrew, Grady, N.M.	1943
Homer Pettigrew, Grady, N.M.	1944

Team Roping

Charles Maggini, San Jose, Calif.	1929
Norman Cowan, Gresham, Ore.	1930
Arthur Belcat, Buckeye, Ariz.	1931
Ace Gardner, Coolidge, Ariz.	1932
Roy Adams, Tucson, Ariz.	1933
Andy Jauregui, Newhall, Calif.	1934
Lawrence Conley, Prescott, Ariz.	1935
John Rhodes, Sombrero Butte, Ariz.	1936
Asbury Schell, Camp Verde, Ariz.	1937
John Rhodes, Sombrero Butte, Ariz.	1938
Asbury Schell, Camp Verde, Ariz.	1939
Pete Grubb, Salmon, Ida.	1940
Jim Hudson, Wilcox, Ariz.	1941
Verne Castro, Livermore, Calif.	1942
Vic Castro, Livermore, Calif. (tie)	
Mark Hull, Stockton, Calif.	1943
Leonard Block, Denair, Calif. (tie)	
Murphy Chaney, Shandon, Calif.	1944

Steer Roping

Charles Magginni, San Jose, Calif.	1929
Clay Carr, Visalia, Calif.	1930
Andy Jauregui, Newhall, Calif.	1931
George Weir, Okmulgee, Okla.	1932
John Bowman, Oakdale, Calif.	1933
John McIntire, Kiowa, Okla.	1934
Richard Merchant, Kirkland, Ariz.	1935
John Bowman, Oakdale, Calif.	1936
Everett Bowman, Hillside, Ariz.	1937
Hugh Bennett, Ft. Thomas, Ariz.	1938
Dick Truitt, Stonewall, Okla.	1939
Clay Carr, Visalia, Calif.	1940
Ike Rude, Buffalo, Okla.	1941
King Merritt, Federal, Wyo.	1942
Tom Rhodes, Sombrero Butte, Ariz.	1943
Tom Rhodes, Sombrero Butte, Ariz.	1944

FINAL CHAMPIONSHIP STANDINGS 1945-1976

STANDINGS—1945

(No Rodeo Cowboys Association All Around award in 1945 or 1946)

Saddle Bronc Riding

Bill Linderman, Red Lodge, Mont.	$7,104
Ken Roberts, Strong City, Kans.	5,660
Bud Linderman, Red Lodge, Mont.	5,244
George Yardley, Ft. Worth, Tex.	5,240
Bill McMacken, Trail City, S.D.	4,854

Bareback Riding

Bud Linderman, Red Lodge, Mont.	8,313
Bill Linderman, Red Lodge, Mont.	6,919
Gerald Roberts, Strong City, Kans.	4,983
Hank Mills, Pueblo, Colo.	4,340
Paul Gould, Sweetwater, Tex.	3,898

Bull Riding

Ken Roberts, Strong City, Kans.	9,332
Dick Griffith, Scottsdale, Ariz.	5,792
G. K. Lewallen, Blackwell, Tex.	5,709
Todd Whatley, Hugo, Okla.	5,466
Gerald Roberts, Strong City, Kans.	5,397

Steer Wrestling

Homer Pettigrew, Grady, N.M.	6,630
George Yardley, Ft. Worth, Tex.	4,844
Royce Sewalt, King, Tex.	4,683
Buck Sorrels, Tucson, Ariz.	4,532
Dave Campbell, Las Vegas, Nev.	4,213

Calf Roping

Toots Mansfield, Bandera, Tex.	14,180
Homer Pettigrew, Grady, N.M.	8,450
Royce Sewalt, King, Tex.	6,291
Jess Goodspeed, Wetumka, Okla.	5,730
Tony Salinas, Encinal, Tex.	5,300

Team Roping

Ernest Gill, Madera, Calif.	1,122
Toots Mansfield, Bandera, Tex.	993
Tom Rhodes, Sombrero Butte, Ariz.	970
Sonny Edwards, Big Springs, Tex.	925
Joe Bassett, Globe, Ariz.	900

Steer Roping

Everett Shaw, Stonewall, Okla.	2,573
Buck Goodspeed, Wetumka, Okla.	1,137
Toots Mansfield, Bandera, Tex.	1,071
Carl Arnold, Buckeye, Ariz.	1,032
John Bowman, Oakdale, Calif.	845

STANDINGS—1946

Saddle Bronc Riding

Jerry Ambler, Glenwood, Wash.	10,657
Bill McMacken, Trail City, S.D.	6,027
Jackie Cooper, Newhall, Calif.	5,831
Paul Gould, Sweetwater, Tex.	5,476
Tom Knight, Cody, Wyo.	5,437

Bareback Riding

Bud Spealman, Ft. Worth, Tex.	6,689

Bud Linderman, Red Lodge, Mont. 6,129
Paul Bond, Carlsbad, N.M. 6,085
Sonny Tureman, John Day, Ore. 5,650
Wag Blesing, Bell, Calif. 5,520

Bull Riding

Pee Wee Morris, Custer, S.D. 7,147
Wag Blesing, Bell, Calif. 6,279
Ken Roberts, Strong City, Kans. 6,009
Glenn Tyler, Modesto, Calif. 5,282
G. K. Lewallen, Blackwell, Tex. 4,598

Steer Wrestling

Dave Campbell, Las Vegas, Nev. 10,472
Steve Heacock, Billings, Mont. 6,945
Dub Phillips, San Angelo, Tex. 6,579
Wilbur Plaugher, Prather, Calif. 6,257
Hank Mills, Pueblo, Colo. 5,307

Calf Roping

Royce Sewalt, King, Tex. 12,807
Toots Mansfield, Bandera, Tex. 11,272
Jess Goodspeed, Wetumka, Okla. 9,538
Lanham Riley, Ft. Worth, Tex. 8,468
Dee Burk, Comanche, Okla. 8,287

Team Roping

Chuck Sheppard, Phoenix, Ariz. 3,368
Jim Hudson, Dos Cabezas, Ariz. 3,157
Joe Bassett, Globe, Ariz. 3,028
Jim Brister, Lordsburg, N.M. 2,995
Manerd Gayler, Tucson, Ariz. 2,887

Steer Roping

Everett Shaw, Stonewall, Okla. 3,836
Buck Goodspeed, Wetumka, Okla. 2,588
Cotton Lee, Roswell, N.M. 2,561
Jiggs Burk, Comanche, Okla. 2,340
Dick Truitt, Stonewall, Okla. 2,111

STANDINGS—1947

The 1947 All Around Champion, Todd Whatley, was named by the Rodeo Cowboys Association after the season ended at the request of a national trophy donor. Records on the runnersup for that year for the big title were not preserved.

Saddle Bronc Riding

Carl Olson, Calgary, Alta. 8,765
Bill Linderman, Red Lodge, Mont. 8,250
Jerry Amber, Glenwood, Wash. 7,822
Buster Ivory, Hayward, Calif. 6,929
Casey Tibbs, Ft. Pierre, S.D. 6,565

Bareback Riding

Larry Finley, Phoenix, Ariz. 7,415
Bud Linderman, Red Lodge, Mont. 7,393
Bill Linderman, Red Lodge, Mont. 6,918
Sonny Tureman, John Day, Ore. 6,445
Wallace Brooks, Mertzon, Tex. 5,565

Bull Riding

Wag Blesing, Bell, Calif. 8,156
Todd Whatley, Hugo, Okla. 7,643
Ken Roberts, Strong City, Kans. 5,705
Gerald Roberts, Strong City, Kans. 5,281
Glen Tyler, Modesto, Calif. 5,176

Calf Roping

Troy Fort, Lovington, N.M. 18,482
Toots Mansfield, Bandera, Tex. 15,565
Zeno Farris, Las Cruces, N.M. 11,733
Buck Sorrels, Tucson, Ariz. 8,767
Jess Goodspeed, Wetumka, Okla. 8,626

Steer Wrestling

Todd Whatley, Hugo, Okla. 10,999
Homer Pettigrew, Grady, N.M. 8,958
Howard McCrory, Deadwood, S.D. 7,091
Ken Boen, Ft. Smith, Ark. 7,026
Charley Colbert, Wilson, Okla. 7,013

Team Roping

Jim Brister, Lordsburg, N.M. 3,546
John Rhodes, Sombrero Butte, Ariz. 3,251
Joe Bassett, Globe, Ariz. 2,410
Asbury Schell, Camp Verde, Ariz. 2,397
Jim Hudson, Dos Cabezas, Ariz. 1,995

Steer Roping

Ike Rude, Buffalo, Okla. 4,389
Carl Arnold, Buckeye, Ariz. 3,800
Buck Goodspeed, Wetumka, Okla. 3,702
Jim Snively, Pawhuska, Okla. 2,966
Buddy Neal, Van Horn, Tex. 2,202

STANDINGS—1948

All Around Cowboy

Gerald Roberts, Strong City, Kans. 21,766
Toots Mansfield, Bandera, Tex. 21,369
Todd Whatley, Hugo, Okla. 20,017
Gene Rambo, Shandon, Calif. 19,553
Harry Tompkins, Dublin, Tex. 17,296
Bill Linderman, Red Lodge, Mont. 16,878
Homer Pettigrew, Grady, N.M. 15,979
Chuck Sheppard, Phoenix, Ariz. 15,694
Buck Sorrels, Tucson, Ariz. 14,970
Vern Castro, Richmond, Calif. 14,642

Saddle Bronc Riding

Gene Pruett, Tieton, Wash. 11,221
Carl Olson, Cardston, Alta. 7,715
Casey Tibbs, Ft. Pierre, S.D. 7,633
Bart Clennon, Sturgis, S.D. 6,736
Gerald Roberts, Strong City, Kans. 6,627

Bareback Riding

Sonny Tureman, John Day, Ore. 9,813
Jack Buschbom, Cassville, Wis. 8,901
Bud Linderman, Red Lodge, Mont. 6,103
Harry Tompkins, Dublin, Tex. 5,982
Wallace Brooks, Mertzon, Tex. 5,919

Bull Riding

Harry Tompkins, Dublin, Tex. 11,313
Gerald Roberts, Strong City, Kans. 10,654
Sonny Lavender, Holiday, Tex. 8,417
Todd Whatley, Hugo, Okla. 8,397
Jim Shoulders, Henryetta, Okla. 6,212

Calf Roping

Toots Mansfield, Bandera, Tex. 17,812
Zeno Farris, Las Cruces, N.M. 12,260
Dee Burk, Comanche, Okla. 10,855
Jess Goodspeed, Wetumka, Okla. 10,352
Troy Fort, Lovington, N.M. 8,664

Steer Wrestling

Homer Pettigrew, Grady, N.M. 9,906
Dub Phillips, San Angelo, Tex. 9,411
Ken Boen, Ft. Smith, Ark. 9,347
Barney Willis, White Salmon, Wn. 8,546
Todd Whatley, Hugo, Okla. 7,523

Team Roping

Joe Glenn, Douglas, Ariz. 3,881
Marion Vincent, Porterville, Calif. 3,676
John Rhodes, Sombrero Butte, Ariz. 3,474
Clay Carr, Visalia, Calif. 3,397
Willie Clay, Visalia, Calif. 2,935

Steer Roping

Everett Shaw, Stonewall, Okla. 3,894
Ike Rude, Buffalo, Okla. 2,785
Toots Mansfield, Bandera, Tex. 2,633
Buck Goodspeed, Wetumka, Okla. 2,454
Carl Arnold, Buckeye, Ariz. 2,328

STANDINGS—1949

All Around Cowboy

Jim Shoulders, Henryetta, Okla. 21,495
Bill Linderman, Red Lodge, Mont. 20,680
Gene Rambo, Shandon, Calif. 19,494
Harry Tompkins, Dublin, Tex. 18,875
Homer Pettigrew, Grady, N.M. 18,553
Gerald Roberts, Strong City, Kans. 17,286
Vern Castro, Richmond, Calif. 16,896
Bud Linderman, Red Lodge, Mont. 16,550
Todd Whatley, Hugo, Okla. 16,337
Casey Tibbs, Ft. Pierre, S.D. 15,882

Saddle Bronc Riding

Casey Tibbs, Ft. Pierre, S.D. 12,867
Bill Linderman, Red Lodge, Mont. 10,471
Ross Dollarhide, Lakeview, Ore. 9,110
Bill Ward, Angels Camp, Calif. 8,229
Bud Linderman, Red Lodge, Mont. 7,631

Bareback Riding

Jack Buschbom, Cassville, Wis. 9,240
Jim Shoulders, Henryetta, Okla. 8,635
Duncan Brown, Clovis, Calif. 6,318
Ike Thomason, Sweetwater, Tex. 5,419
Harry Tompkins, Dublin, Tex. 5,336

Bull Riding

Henry Tompkins, Dublin, Tex. 13,290
Jim Shoulders, Henryetta, Okla. 12,860
Gerald Roberts, Strong City, Kans. 8,449
Todd Whatley, Hugo, Okla. 6,813
Buck Rutherford, Lenapah, Okla. 5,500

Calf Roping

Troy Fort, Lovington, N.M. 14,145
Homer Pettigrew, Grady, N.M. 11,496
J. D. Holleyman, Corona, N.M. 10,425
Toots Mansfield, Bandera, Tex. 9,928
Jess Goodspeed, Wetumka, Okla. 9,247

Steer Wrestling

Bill McGuire, Ft. Worth, Tex. 8,058
Homer Pettigrew, Grady, N.M. 6,957
Charlie Colbert, Wilson, Okla. 6,850
Todd Whatley, Hugo, Okla. 6,796
Jack Favor, Arlington, Tex. 6,637

Team Roping

Ed Yanez, Newhall, Calif. 6,050
Vern Castro, Richmond, Calif. 4,509
Clay Carr, Visalia, Calif. 4,480
Andy Jauregui, Newhall, Calif. 4,093
Olan Sims, Madera, Calif. 3,863

Steer Roping

Shoat Webster, Lenapah, Okla. 2,813
Everett Shaw, Stonewall, Okla. 2,111
Jack Skipworth, Roswell, N.M. 1,573
John Scott, Whittier, Calif. 1,278
Clark McIntire, Kiowa, Okla. 1,222

STANDINGS—1950

All Around Cowboy

Bill Linderman, Red Lodge, Mont. 30,715
Jim Shoulders, Henryetta, Okla. 27,583
Harry Tompkins, Dublin, Tex. 25,891
Gene Rambo, Shandon, Calif. 24,161
Casey Tibbs, Ft. Pierre, S.D. 19,958
Gerald Roberts, Strong City, Kans. 17,089
Buck Rutherford, Lenapah, Okla. 17,043
Vern Castro, Richmond, Calif. 16,557
Bud Linderman, Red Lodge, Mont. 16,457
Homer Pettigrew, Grady, N.M. 15,653

Saddle Bronc Riding

Bill Linderman, Red Lodge, Mont. 12,485
Casey Tibbs, Ft. Pierre, S.D. 12,308
Bill Ward, Angels Camp, Calif. 8,341
Ross Dollarhide, Lakeview, Ore. 7,636
Bud Linderman, Red Lodge, Mont. 7,404

Bareback Riding

Jim Shoulders, Henryetta, Okla. 11,988

247

Jack Buschbom, Cassville, Wis. ... 8,683
Buck Rutherford, Lenapah, Okla. ... 8,194
Wallace Brooks, Mertzon, Tex. ... 8,059
Casey Tibbs, Ft. Pierre, S.D. ... 7,042

Bull Riding
Harry Tompkins, Dublin, Tex. ... 19,213
Jim Shoulders, Henryetta, Okla. ... 15,595
Gerald Roberts, Strong City, Kans. ... 8,978
Dave Mason, Los Gatos, Calif. ... 6,237
Bob Maynard, Hollywood, Calif. ... 5,632

Calf Roping
Toots Mansfield, Bandera, Tex. ... 12,721
Don McLaughlin, Ft. Worth, Tex. ... 11,201
Dan Taylor, Dublin, Tex. ... 10,762
Gene Rambo, Shandon, Calif. ... 9,897
Ray Wharton, Bandera, Tex. ... 9,828

Steer Wrestling
Bill Linderman, Red Lodge, Mont. ... 11,946
Homer Pettigrew, Grady, N.M. ... 9,608
Dub Phillips, San Angelo, Tex. ... 9,541
James Bynum, Forreston, Tex. ... 5,368
Bill Hancock, Roswell, N.M. ... 5,157

Team Roping
Buck Sorrels, Tucson, Ariz. ... 4,636
Clay Carr, Visalia, Calif. ... 4,506
Vern Castro, Richmond, Calif. ... 3,668
Olan Sims, Madera, Calif. ... 3,065
John Rhodes, Sombrero Butte, Ariz. ... 2,890

Steer Roping
Shoat Webster, Lenapah, Okla. ... 3,226
Everett Shaw, Stonewall, Okla. ... 1,706
John Scott, Whittier, Calif. ... 1,409
Jack Skipworth, Roswell, N.M. ... 1,200
Shorty Valdez, Bakersfield, Calif. ... 1,170

STANDINGS—1951

All Around Cowboy
Casey Tibbs, Ft. Pierre, S.D. ... 29,104
Jim Shoulders, Henryetta, Okla. ... 27,244
Bill Linderman, Red Lodge, Mont. ... 23,666
Buck Rutherford, Lenapah, Okla. ... 19,923
Harry Tompkins, Dublin, Tex. ... 16,321
Del Haverty, Benson, Ariz. ... 15,402
Bud Linderman, Red Lodge, Mont. ... 14,825
Gerald Roberts, Strong City, Kans. ... 14,245
Vern Castro, Richmond, Calif. ... 12,827
Troy Fort, Lovington, N.M. ... 12,409

Saddle Bronc Riding
Casey Tibbs, Ft. Pierre, S.D. ... 15,594
Deb Copenhaver, Post Falls, Ida. ... 11,338
Gene Pruett, Tieton, Wash. ... 9,039
Bill Linderman, Red Lodge, Mont. ... 8,818
Buster Ivory, Hayward, Calif. ... 7,880

Bareback Riding
Casey Tibbs, Ft. Pierre, S.D. ... 13,244
Jim Shoulders, Henryetta, Okla. ... 10,465
Sonny Tureman, John Day, Ore. ... 7,444
Jack Buschbom, Cassville, Wis. ... 6,915
Del Haverty, Benson, Ariz. ... 6,488

Bull Riding
Jim Shoulders, Henryetta, Okla. ... 16,779
Harry Tompkins, Dublin, Tex. ... 10,920
Buck Rutherford, Lenapah, Okla. ... 10,614
Gerald Roberts, Strong City, Kans. ... 8,673
Bob Chartier, Imperial, Nebr. ... 6,123

Calf Roping
Don McLaughlin, Ft. Worth, Tex. ... 12,822
Troy Fort, Lovington, N.M. ... 12,241
Lanham Riley, Ft. Worth, Tex. ... 10,359
Dan Taylor, Dublin, Tex. ... 9,085
Doyle Riley, Ft. Worth, Tex. ... 9,008

Steer Wrestling
Dub Phillips, San Angelo, Tex. ... 10,957
James Bynum, Forreston, Tex. ... 6,971
Dan Poore, Imperial, Calif. ... 6,957
Jack Favor, Arlington, Tex. ... 6,590
Bill Linderman, Red Lodge, Mont. ... 6,395

Team Roping
Olan Sims, Madera, Calif. ... 3,546
Clay Carr, Visalia, Calif. ... 3,106
Tom Rhodes, Sombrero Butte, Ariz. ... 2,866
Vern Castro, Richmond, Calif. ... 2,845
Everett Muzio, Modesto, Calif. ... 2,526

Steer Roping
Everett Shaw, Stonewall, Okla. ... 4,020
Shoat Webster, Lenapah, Okla. ... 2,926
J. D. Holleyman, Corona, N.M. ... 2,126
Buddy Neal, Van Horn, Tex. ... 1,917
Toots Mansfield, Bandera, Tex. ... 1,915

STANDINGS—1952

All Around Cowboy
Harry Tompkins, Dublin, Tex. ... 30,934
Bucky Rutherford, Lenapah, Okla. ... 29,364
Bill Linderman, Red Lodge, Mont. ... 28,135
Jim Shoulders, Henryetta, Okla. ... 22,875
Harley May, Oakdale, Calif. ... 22,663
Del Haverty, Benson, Ariz. ... 21,600
Todd Whatley, Hugo, Okla. ... 20,837
Casey Tibbs, Ft. Pierre, S.D. ... 20,242
Gordon Davis, Templeton, Calif. ... 18,735
Elliot Calhoun, Las Cruces, N.M. ... 18,730

Saddle Bronc Riding
Casey Tibbs, Ft. Pierre, S.D. ... 14,631
Bill Linderman, Red Lodge, Mont. ... 13,389
Deb Copenhaver, Post Falls, Ida. ... 12,157
Buster Ivory, Hayward, Calif. ... 10,721
Gene Pruett, Tieton, Wash. ... 9,011

Bareback Riding
Harry Tompkins, Dublin, Tex. ... 14,152
Jack Buschbom, Cassville, Wis. ... 10,243
Billy Weeks, Abilene, Tex. ... 9,757
Jim Shoulders, Henryetta, Okla. ... 8,591
Buck Abbott, Apple Valley, Calif. ... 8,515

Bull Riding
Harry Tompkins, Dublin, Tex. ... 16,783
Jim Shoulders, Henryetta, Okla. ... 14,103
Elliot Calhoun, Las Cruces, N.M. ... 9,251
Bob Maynard, Hollywood, Calif. ... 8,869
Todd Whatley, Hugo, Okla. ... 8,038

Calf Roping
Don McLaughlin, Ft. Worth, Tex. ... 18,294
Jess Goodspeed, Wetumka, Okla. ... 14,980
B. J. Pierce, Clovis, N.M. ... 11,310
Gordon Davis, Templeton, Calif. ... 10,654
Doyle Riley, Ft. Worth, Tex. ... 9,835

Steer Wrestling
Harley May, Oakdale, Calif. ... 15,381
Todd Whatley, Hugo, Okla. ... 9,175
Jack Fowler, Arlington, Tex. ... 8,230
Bill Linderman, Red Lodge, Mont. ... 8,074
Buck Rutherford, Lenapah, Okla. ... 6,935

Team Roping
Asbury Schell, Camp Verde, Ariz. ... 5,311
Joe Bassett, Globe, Ariz. ... 5,039
Vic Castro, Richmond, Calif. ... 4,892
Buck Sorrels, Tucson, Ariz. ... 3,855
Chuck Sheppard, Phoenix, Ariz. ... 2,929

Steer Roping
Buddy Neal, Van Horn, Calif. ... 3,712
Jim Snively, Pawhuska, Okla. ... 2,896
Shoat Webster, Lenapah, Okla. ... 2,361

Ike Rude, Buaffalo, Okla. ... 1,340
Tell McMillan, Ada, Okla. ... 1,041

STANDINGS—1953

All Around Cowboy
Bill Linderman, Red Lodge, Mont. ... 33,674
Casey Tibbs, Ft. Pierre, S.D. ... 31,208
Ross Dollarhide, Lakeview, Ore. ... 28,035
Harry Tompkins, Dublin, Tex. ... 22,599
Eddy Akridge, Midland, Tex. ... 20,786
Del Haverty, Benson, Ariz. ... 20,570
Jack Buschbom, Cassville, Wis. ... 18,915
Todd Whatley, Hugo, Okla. ... 18,870
Don McLaughlin, Ft. Worth, Tex. ... 17,088
Gerald Roberts, Strong City, Kans. ... 15,646

Saddle Bronc Riding
Casey Tibbs, Ft. Pierre, S.D. ... 22,496
Deb Copenhaver, Post Falls, Ida. ... 20,221
Bill Linderman, Red Lodge, Mont. ... 14,913
J. D. McKenna, Sheridan, Wyo. ... 9,223
Bill Ward, Angels Camp, Calif. ... 9,126

Bareback Riding
Eddy Akridge, Midland, Tex. ... 17,302
Harry Tompkins, Dublin, Tex. ... 12,163
Jack Buschbom, Cassville, Tex. ... 12,131
Sonny Tureman, John Day, Ore. ... 10,865
Del Haverty, Benson, Ariz. ... 8,407

Bull Riding
Todd Whatley, Hugo, Okla. ... 13,146
Billy Hand, Loxahatchee, Fla. ... 11,124
Harry Tompkins, Dublin, Tex. ... 10,436
Dick Pascoe, Woody, Calif. ... 10,111
Gerald Roberts, Strong City, Kans. ... 9,343

Calf Roping
Don McLaughlin, Ft. Worth, Tex. ... 15,902
Jim Bob Altizer, Del Rio, Tex. ... 12,918
B. J. Pierce, Clovis, N.M. ... 11,678
J. D. Holleyman, Corona, N.M. ... 10,772
Buddy Groff, Bandera, Tex. ... 10,635

Steer Wrestling
Ross Dollarhide, Lakeview, Ore. ... 14,224
Bill Linderman, Red Lodge, Mont. ... 11,966
Willard Combs, Checotah, Okla. ... 7,488
Harley May, Oakdale, Calif. ... 7,246
Homer Pettigrew, Grady, N.M. ... 6,592

Team Roping
Ben Johnson, Hollywood, Calif. ... 5,858
Ed Lanez, Newhall, Calif. ... 5,163
John Rhodes, Sombrero Butte, Ariz. ... 5,104
Fred Darnell, Rodeo, N.M. ... 5,006
Vern Castro, Richmond, Calif. ... 4,616

Steer Roping
Ike Rude, Buffalo, Wyo. ... 3,336
Shoat Webster, Lenapah, Okla. ... 2,772
Everett Shaw, Stonewall, Okla. ... 2,713
Clark McEntire, Kiowa, Okla. ... 2,049
John Pogue, Miami, Okla. ... 1,778

STANDINGS—1954

All Around Cowboy
Buck Rutherford, Lenapah, Okla. ... 40,404
Jim Shoulders, Henryetta, Okla. ... 39,964
Casey Tibbs, Ft. Pierre, S.D. ... 36,553
Don McLaughlin, Ft. Worth, Tex. ... 25,923
Bill Linderman, Red Lodge, Mont. ... 23,834
Harry Tompkins, Dublin, Tex. ... 23,661
J. D. McKenna, Sheridan, Wyo. ... 23,078
Guy Weeks, Abilene, Tex. ... 22,215
Todd Whatley, Hugo, Okla. ... 20,197
Jack Buschbom, Cassville, Wis. ... 20,147

Saddle Bronc Riding
Casey Tibbs, Ft. Pierre, S.D. ... 23,052

Deb Copenhaver, Post Falls, Ida. 20,386
J. D. McKenna, Sheridan, Wyo. 13,835
Bill Ward, Angels Camp, Calif. 11,826
Guy Weeks, Abilene, Tex. 11,407

Bareback Riding
Eddy Akridge, Midland, Tex. 14,983
Buck Rutherford, Lenapah, Okla. 14,976
Jack Buschbom, Cassville, Wis. 14,798
Ike Thomason, Sweetwater, Tex. 12,727
Jim Shoulders, Henryetta, Okla. 11,264

Bull Riding
Jim Shoulders, Henryetta, Okla. 28,700
Billy Hand, Loxahatchee, Fla. 15,185
Buck Rutherford, Lenapah, Okla. 14,138
Todd Whatley, Hugo, Okla. 13,260
Harry Tompkins, Dublin, Tex. 11,705

Calf Roping
Don McLaughlin, Ft. Worth, Tex. 23,048
Buddy Groff, Bandera, Tex. 11,366
Dean Oliver, Boise, Ida. 11,158
Jim Bob Altizer, Del Rio, Tex. 10,666
Doyle Riley, Ft. Worth, Tex. 10,439

Steer Wrestling
James Bynum, Forreston, Tex. 12,578
Joe Madden, Lusk, Wyo. 10,168
Harley May, Oakdale, Calif. 9,630
J. D. McKenna, Sheridan, Wyo. 9,243
Ross Dollarhide, Lakeview, Ore. 8,536

Team Roping
Eddie Schell, Camp Verde, Ariz. 6,547
Dale Smith, Chandler, Ariz. 6,197
Olan Simms, Madera, Calif. 5,668
Fred Darnell, Rodeo, N.M. 5,258
Bob G. Jones, Merced, Calif. 4,973

Steer Roping
Shoat Webster, Lenapah, Okla. 4,189
Clark McEntire, Kiowa, Okla. 3,582
Jim Snively, Pawhuska, Okla. 2,694
Ike Rude, Buffalo, Okla. 1,935
Everett Shaw, Stonewall, Okla. 1,640

STANDINGS—1955

All Around Cowboy
Casey Tibbs, Ft. Pierre, S.D. 42,065
Jim Shoulders, Henryetta, Okla. 37,682
Eddy Akridge, Midland, Tex. 23,098
Harry Tompkins, Dublin, Tex. 23,060
Alvin Nelson, Sentinel Butte, N.D. 21,212
Guy Weeks, Abilene, Tex. 20,761
Dean Oliver, Boise, Ida. 20,090
Jack Buschbom, Cassville, Wis. 20,080
Bill Linderman, Red Lodge, Mont. 19,487
J. D. McKenna, Sheridan, Wyo. 19,178

Saddle Bronc Riding
Deb Copenhaver, Post Falls, Ida. 24,121
Casey Tibbs, Ft. Pierre, S.D. 23,947
J. D. McKenna, Sheridan, Wyo. 15,925
Bill Ward, Angels Camp, Calif. 11,791
Guy Weeks, Abilene, Tex. 11,476

Bareback Riding
Eddy Akridge, Midland, Tex. 18,213
Jim Shoulders, Henryetta, Okla. 14,069
Casey Tibbs, Ft. Pierre, S.D. 13,981
Jack Buschbom, Cassville, Wis. 13,534
Alvin Nelson, Sentinel Butte, N.D. 11,689

Bull Riding
Jim Shoulders, Henryetta, Okla. 23,073
Duane Howard, Minnewaukan, N.D. 13,448
Harry Tompkins, Dublin, Tex. 12,496
Billy Hand, Loxahatchee, Fla. 11,604
Gerald Roberts, Strong City, Kans. 9,368

Calf Roping
Dean Oliver, Boise, Ida. 19,963
Lanham Riley, Ft. Worth, Tex. 13,230
Toots Mansfield, Bandera, Tex. 13,033
Ray Wharton, Bandera, Tex. 10,274
B. J. Pierce, Clovis, N.M. 9,602

Steer Wrestling
Benny Combs, Checotah, Okla. 13,742
Willard Combs, Checotah, Okla. 13,055
Harley May, Oakdale, Calif. 10,780
Wilbur Plaugher, Prather, Calif. 9,678
Ross Dollarhide, Lakeview, Ore. 8,778

Team Roping
Vern Castro, Richmond, Calif. 6,227
Bob G. Jones, Merced, Calif. 5,442
Frank Ferreira, Fresno, Calif. 5,325
Fred Darnell, Rodeo, N.M. 4,804
Joe Glenn, Benson, Ariz. 4,112

Steer Roping
Shoat Webster, Lenapah, Okla. 5,163
Everett Shaw, Stonewall, Okla. 3,972
Clark McEntire, Kiowa, Okla. 2,157
Troy Fort, Lovington, N.M. 1,853
Carl Saywer, Torrington, Wyo. 1,310

STANDINGS—1956

All Around Cowboy
Jim Shoulders, Henryetta, Okla. 43,381
Harley May, Oakdale, Calif. 31,180
Guy Weeks, Abilene, Tex. 27,802
Eddy Akridge, Midland, Tex. 23,185
Bill Linderman, Red Lodge, Mont. 22,158
Harry Tompkins, Dublin, Tex. 21,523
Duane Howard, Minnewaukan, N.D. 20,395
Jack Buschbom, Cassville, Wis. 20,111
Alvin Nelson, Sentinel Butte, N.D. 18,677
Buddy Groff, Bandera, Tex. 16,963

Saddle Bronc Riding
Deb Copenhaver, Post Falls, Ida. 21,134
George Menkenmaier, Burns, Ore. 14,402
Alvin Nelson, Sentinel Butte, N.D. 11,979
Guy Weeks, Abilene, Tex. 10,982
Jackie Wright, Dayville, Ore. 10,300

Bareback Riding
Jim Shoulders, Henryetta, Okla. 23,376
Eddy Akridge, Midland, Tex. 16,330
Jack Buschbom, Cassville, Wis. 16,022
John Hawkins, Twain Harte, Calif. 12,854
Gene Kramer, Sutherland, Nebr. 8,584

Bull Riding
Jim Shoulders, Henryetta, Okla. 20,005
Harry Tompkins, Dublin, Tex. 13,401
Duane Howard, Minnewaukan, N.D. 10,455
Bob Wegner, Ponca City, Okla. 8,883
Billy Hand, Loxahatchee, Fla. 8,772

Calf Roping
Ray Wharton, Bandera, Tex. 21,311
Buddy Groff, Bandera, Tex. 16,551
Glen Franklin, House, N.M. 15,436
Jim Bob Altizer, Del Rio, Tex. 13,227
Guy Weeks, Abilene, Tex. 12,671

Steer Wrestling
Harley May, Oakdale, Calif. 19,253
Wayne Dunafon, Westmoreland, Kans. 16,167
Benny Combs, Checotah, Okla. 13,312
Willard Combs, Checotah, Okla. 12,448
John Jones, San Luis Obispo, Calif. 10,234

Team Roping
Dale Smith, Chandler, Ariz. 6,820
John Rhodes, Sombrero Butte, Ariz. 5,966
Bob Jones, Merced, Calif. 5,133

John Clem, Chandler, Ariz. 4,419
Harold Mattos, Newman, Calif. 4,369

Steer Roping
Jim Snively, Pawhuska, Okla. 3,855
Everett Shaw, Stonewall, Okla. 3,365
Don McLaughlin, Ft. Worth, Tex. 2,615
John Dalton, Federal, Wyo. 2,501
Sonny Davis, Kenna, N.M. 2,379

STANDINGS—1957

All Around Cowboy
Jim Shoulders, Henryetta, Okla. 33,299
Duane Howard, Minnewaukan, N.D. 29,994
Dale Smith, Chandler, Ariz. 24,209
Alvin Nelson, Sentinel Butte, N.D. 23,746
Guy Weeks, Abilene, Tex. 23,118
Don McLaughlin, Ft. Worth, Tex. 22,028
Harry Tompkins, Dublin, Tex. 21,528
Buck Rutherford, Lenapah, Okla. 20,533
Bill Linderman, Red Lodge, Mont. 20,181
Glen Franklin, House, N.M. 18,121

Saddle Bronc Riding
Alvin Nelson, Sentinel Butte, N.D. 21,813
Marty Wood, Bowness, Alta. 17,565
Enoch Walker, Cody, Wyo. 12,202
Guy Weeks, Abilene, Tex. 12,069
Duane Howard, Minnewaukan, N.D. 9,490

Bareback Riding
Jim Shoulders, Henryetta, Okla. 15,197
John Hawkins, Twain Harte, Calif. 15,179
Harry Tompkins, Dublin, Tex. 11,330
Jack Buschbom, Cassville, Wis. 9,625
Buck Rutherford, Lenapah, Okla. 9,572

Bull Riding
Jim Shoulders, Henryetta, Okla. 17,816
Duane Howard, Minnewaukan, N.D. 15,454
Harry Tompkins, Dublin, Tex. 10,198
Eddie Quaid, Oklahoma City, Okla. 9,028
Joel Sublette, Tucson, Ariz. 8,899

Calf Roping
Don McLaughlin, Ft. Worth, Tex. 19,575
Glen Franklin, House, N.M. 17,707
Dale Smith, Chandler, Ariz. 17,508
Ray Wharton, Bandera, Tex. 12,709
Herschel Romine, Big Spring, Tex. 11,668

Steer Wrestling
Willard Combs, Checotah, Okla. 16,112
Serman Sullins, Oakdale, Calif. 12,753
Wilbur Plaugher, Prather, Calif. 12,689
Bill Linderman, Red Lodge, Mont. 11,895
Benny Combs, Checotah, Okla. 10,303

Team Roping
Dale Smith, Chandler, Ariz. 6,521
Bob Jones, Merced, Calif. 4,136
Frank Ferreira, Fresno, Calif. 4,061
Gene Rambo, Shandon, Calif. 3,342
Eddie Schell, Camp Verde, Ariz. 3,308

Steer Roping
Clark McEntire, Kiowa, Okla. 5,184
Sonny Davis, Kenna, N.M. 5,067
Everett Shaw, Stonewall, Okla. 4,055
Shoat Webster, Lenapah, Okla. 2,970
Don McLaughlin, Ft. Worth, Tex. 2,390

STANDINGS—1958

All Around Cowboy
Jim Shoulders, Henryetta, Okla. 32,212
Guy Weeks, Abilene, Tex. 26,810
Benny Reynolds, Melrose, Mont. 26,450
Harry Tompkins, Dublin, Tex. 23,953
Jack Buschbom, Cassville, Wis. 20,293
Harley May, Oakdale, Calif. 18,770

249

Tom Nesmith, Bethel, Okla. 17,574
Bob Wegner, Ponca City, Okla. 16,560
Duane Howard, Minnewaukan, N.D. 15,704
Don McLaughlin, Ft. Worth, Tex. 14,687

Saddle Bronc Riding

Marty Wood, Bowness, Atla. 18,771
Enoch Walker, Cody, Wyo. 13,454
George Menkenmaier, Burns, Ore. 12,337
Deb Copenhaver, Post Falls, Ida. 11,470
Tom Tescher, Sentinel Butte, Ariz. 10,818

Bareback Riding

Jim Shoulders, Henryetta, Okla. 17,121
John Hawkins, Twain Harte, Calif. 15,724
Jack Buschbom, Cassville, Wis. 14,153
Harry Tompkins, Dublin, Tex. 12,210
Benny Reynolds, Melrose, Mont. 10,357

Bull Riding

Jim Shoulders, Henryetta, Okla. 16,092
Bob Wegner, Ponca City, Okla. 15,249
Harry Tompkins, Dublin, Tex. 11,743
Billy Hand, Loxahatchee, Fla. 10,153
Eddie Quaid, Oklahoma City, Okla. 9,666

Calf Roping

Dean Oliver, Boise, Ida. 23,269
Glen Franklin, House, N.M. 16,071
Don McLaughlin, Ft. Worth, Tex. 13,857
Tom Nesmith, Bethel, Okla. 11,523
Guy Weeks, Abilene, Tex. 10,791

Steer Wrestling

James Bynum, Forreston, Tex. 14,280
Wilbur Plaugher, Prather, Calif. 13,860
Willard Combs, Checotah, Okla. 12,365
Don Feddersen, Sidney, Nebr. 9,874
John Hatley, Uvalde, Tex. 8,933

Team Roping

Ted Ashworth, Phoenix, Ariz. 5,363
Dale Smith, Chandler, Ariz. 5,350
John Bowman, Oakdale, Calif. 5,175
Gene Rambo, Shandon, Calif. 4,944
Al Gomes, Madera, Calif. 3,842

Steer Roping

Clark McEntire, Kiowa, Okla. 3,314
Jim Snively, Pawhuska, Okla. 3,175
J. T. Wilkinson, Lander, Wyo. 2,376
Everett Shaw, Stonewall, Okla. 2,116
Sonny Davis, Kenna, N.M. 2,093

STANDINGS—1959

All Around Cowboy

Jim Shoulders, Henryetta, Okla. 32,905
Jim Bob Altizer, Del Rio, Tex. 25,263
Guy Weeks, Abilene, Tex. 25,207
Harry Charters, Melba, Ida. 24,930
Dale Smith, Chandler, Ariz. 23,885
Benny Reynolds, Melrose, Mont. 22,724
Jim Tescher, Medora, N.D. 22,223
Jack Buschbom, Cassville, Wis. 22,184
Tom Nesmith, Bethel, Okla. 20,820
Bob A. Robinson, Rockland, Ida. 20,420

Saddle Bronc Riding

Casey Tibbs, Ft. Pierre, S.D. 17,485
Winston Bruce, Calgary, Alta. 14,250
Enoch Walker, Cody, Wyo. 12,625
Jim Tescher, Medora, N.D. 12,157
Marty Wood, Bowness, Alta. 12,125

Bareback Riding

Jack Buschbom, Cassville, Wis. 17,611
John Hawkins, Twain Harte, Calif. 16,176
Jim Shoulders, Henryetta, Okla. 14,885
Ralph Buell, Sheridan, Wyo. 12,489
Walt Mason, Las Vegas, Nev. 9,679

Bull Riding

Jim Shoulders, Henryetta, Okla. 17,021
Bob Wegner, Ponca City, Okla. 15,714
Bill Rinestine, Amarillo, Tex. 10,409
Joe Green, Sulphur, Okla. 10,226
Ed LeTourneau, Davis, Calif. 8,600

Calf Roping

Jim Bob Altizer, Del Rio, Tex. 24,728
Dale Smith, Chandler, Ariz. 18,421
Dean Oliver, Boise, Ida. 18,104
Olin Young, Albuquerque, N.M. 17,732
Sonny Davis, Kenna, N.M. 15,678

Steer Wrestling

Harry Charters, Melba, Ia. 18,636
Don Feddersen, Sidney, Nebr. 12,940
Danny Daniels, Dallas, Tex. 11,256
Tom Nesmith, Bethel, Okla. 10,362
Willard Combs, Checotah, Okla. 10,132

Team Roping

Jim Rodriguez, Jr., Castroville, Calif. 6,184
Joe Glenn, Benson, Ariz. 6,120
Gene Rambo, Shandon, Calif. 6,087
John Glem, Chandler, Ariz. 5,449
Art Arnold, Buckeye, Ariz. 5,260

Steer Roping

Everett Shaw, Stonewall, Okla. 5,155
Shaot Webster, Lenapah, Okla. 3,753
Jim Snively, Pawhuska, Okla. 3,280
Sonny Davis, Kenna, N.M. 2,756
Troy Fort, Lovington, N.M. 2,695

STANDINGS—1960

All Around Cowboy

Harry Tompkins, Dublin, Tex. 32,522
Bob A. Robinson, Rockland, Ida. 29,213
Guy Weeks, Abilene, Tex. 25,459
Duane Howard, Minnewaukan, N.D. 25,367
Jim Shoulders, Henryetta, Okla. 23,368
Benny Reynolds, Melrose, Mont. 22,168
Freckles Brown, Lawton, Okla. 19,838
Alvin Nelson, Sentinel Butte, N.D. 19,553
Jack Buschbom, Cassville, Wis. 19,064
Harry Charters, Melba, Ida. 18,360

Saddle Bronc Riding

Enoch Walker, Cody, Wyo. 20,832
Alvin Nelson, Sentinel Butte, N.D. 17,509
Winston Bruce, Calgary, Alta. 16,048
Guy Weeks, Abilene, Tex. 15,517
Marty Wood, Bowness, Alta. 14,221

Bareback Riding

Jack Buschbom, Cassville, Wis. 16,997
Harry Tompkins, Dublin, Tex. 15,379
John Hawkins, Twain Harte, Calif. 13,875
Jim Shoulders, Henryetta, Okla. 11,847
Buddy Peak, Tucson, Ariz. 9,661

Bull Riding

Harry Tompkins, Dublin, Tex. 17,143
Duane Howard, Minnewaukan, N.D. 16,274
Bob Wegner, Ponca City, Okla. 12,291
Pete Crump, Green Acres, Wash. 11,688
Jim Shoulders, Henryetta, Okla. 11,521

Calf Roping

Dean Oliver, Boise, Ida. 28,841
Glen Franklin, House, N.M. 20,081
Sonny Davis, Kenna, N.M. 15,226
Don McLaughlin, Ft. Worth, Tex. 13,953
Olin Young, Albuquerque, N.M. 13,562

Steer Wrestling

Bob A. Robinson, Rockland, Ida. 13,768
Harley May, Oakdale, Calif. 13,469
Jim Bynum, Forreston, Tex. 11,917
Jim Painter, McAlester, Okla. 11,569
Bill Linderman, Red Lodge, Mont. 10,668

Team Roping

Jim Rodriguez, Jr., Castroville, Calif. 10,408
Gene Rambo, Shandon, Calif. 9,111
Harold Mattos, Newman, Calif. 6,411
Les Hirdes, Turlock, Calif. 5,893
E. V. Dorsey, Sonoma, Calif. 4,961

Steer Roping

Don McLaughlin, Ft. Worth, Tex. 4,178
John Dalton, Cheyenne, Wyo. 3,068
Bill Harlan, Bueyeros, N.M. 2,735
Shoat Webster, Lenapah, Okla. 2,694
Joe Snively, Pawhuska, Okla. 2,394

STANDINGS—1961

All Around Cowboy

Benny Reynolds, Melrose, Mont. 31,309
Dean Oliver, Boise, Ida. 28,062
Guy Weeks, Abilene, Tex. 26,255
Tom Nesmith, Bethel, Okla. 25,497
Freckles Brown, Lawton, Okla. 22,652
Tex Martin, Meridian, Tex. 19,456
Dale Smith, Chandler, Ariz. 19,425
Harry Charters, Melba, Ida. 19,010
Sonny Davis, Kenna, N.M. 18,747
Alvin Nelson, Sentinel Butte, N.D. 18,725

Saddle Bronc Riding

Winston Bruce, Calgary, Alta. 20,833
Enoch Walker, Cody, Wyo. 17,608
Alvin Nelson, Sentinel Butte, N.D. 15,837
Kenny McLean, Okanagan Falls, B.C. 14,648
Marty Wood, Bowness, Alta. 13,558

Bareback Riding

Eddy Akridge, Midland, Tex. 15,029
Jack Buschbom, Mobridge, S.D. 13,519
Paul Templeton, San Jose, Calif. 11,844
Pete Fredericks, Halliday, N.D. 10,807
Benny Reynolds, Melrose, Mont. 10,315

Bull Riding

Ronnie Rossen, Broadus, Mont. 13,392
Bob Wegner, Ponca City, Okla. 12,974
Freckles Brown, Lawton, Okla. 12,850
Del Hataway, Snyder, Tex. 11,192
Billy Hand, Loxahatchee, Fla. 11,170

Calf Roping

Dean Oliver, Boise, Ida. 28,015
Sonny Davis, Kenna, N.M. 16,318
Tom Nesmith, Bethel, Okla. 16,111
Glen Franklin, House, N.M. 15,873
Jim Bob Altizer, Del Rio, Tex. 15,649

Steer Wrestling

Jim Bynum, Forreston, Tex. 15,565
C. R. Boucher, Burkburnett, Tex. 14,312
Benny Combs, Checotah, Okla. 13,587
Billy Deussen, San Antonio, Tex. 10,656
Benny Reynolds, Melrose, Mont. 10,279

Team Roping

Al Hooper, Escalon, Calif. 6,346
R. D. Rutledge, Tulare, Calif. 6,166
Harold Mattos, Newman, Calif. 6,047
Les Hirdes, Turlock, Calif. 5,850
Ben Jacobs, Oracle, Ariz. 5,031

Steer Roping

Clark McEntire, Kiowa, Okla. 3,877
Joe Snively, Pawhuska, Okla. 3,783
Shoat Webster, Lenapah, Okla. 3,771
Sonney Wright, Alto, N.M. 2,756
Don McLaughlin, Ft. Collins, Colo. 2,701

STANDINGS—1962

All Around Cowboy
Tom Nesmith, Bethel, Okla. 32,611
Dean Oliver, Boise, Ida. 29,989
Benny Reynolds, Melrose, Mont. 24,058
Harry Charters, Melba, Ida. 22,694
Harley May, Oakdale, Calif. 21,517
Tex Martin, Meridian, Tex. 21,384
Freckles Brown, Lawton, Okla. 20,483
Kenny McLean, Okanagan Falls, B.C. 18,370
Bernis Johnson, Cleburne, Tex. 17,699
Mark Schricker, Sutherlin, Ore. 16,759

Saddle Bronc Riding
Kenny McLean, Okanagan Falls, B.C. 18,204
Marty Wood, Bowness, Alta. 16,821
Winston Bruce, Calgary, Alta. 16,759
Larry Kane, Big Sandy, Mont. 11,654
Guy Weeks, Abilene, Tex. 10,137

Bareback Riding
Ralph Buell, Sheridan, Wyo. 16,720
Don Mayo, Grinnell, Ia. 15,189
Buddy Peak, Tucson, Ariz. 11,948
Walt Mason, Las Vegas, Nev. 10,138
Paul Templeton, San Jose, Calif. 9,567

Bull Riding
Freckles Brown, Lawton, Okla. 18,675
Bill Rinstine, Amarillo, Tex. 14,042
Bob Wegner, Ponca City, Okla. 12,042
Billy Hand, Loxahatchee, Fla. 11,648
Pete Crump, Green Acres, Wash. 11,597

Calf Roping
Dean Oliver, Boise, Ida. 27,756
Glen Franklin, House, N.M. 16,242
Tom Nesmith, Bethel, Okla. 15,822
Olin Young, Albuquerque, N.M. 15,412
Bob Ragsdale, Wilder, Ida. 15,117

Steer Wrestling
Tom Nesmith, Bethel, Okla. 16,789
Harry Charters, Jr., Melba, Ida. 16,016
Harley May, Oakdale, Calif. 12,331
Wilbur Plaugher, Prather, Calif. 11,380
Mark Schricker, Sutherlin, Ore. 11,287

Team Roping
Jim Rodriguez, Jr., Castroville, Calif. 9,623
Dale Smith, Chandler, Ariz. 6,545
Gene Rambo, Shandon, Calif. 6,392
Frank Ferreira, Fresno, Calif. 5,985
Les Hirdes, Turlock, Calif. 5,470

Steer Roping
Everett Shaw, Stonewall, Okla. 4,308
Sonny Davis, Kenna, N.M. 4,131
Don McLaughlin, Ft. Collins, Colo. 3,688
Joe Snively, Pawhuska, Okla. 2,594
Jim Bob Altizer, Del Rio, Tex. 2,475

STANDINGS—1963

All Around Cowboy
Dean Oliver, Boise, Ida. 31,329
Guy Weeks, Abilene, Tex. 28,717
Tom Nesmith, Bethel, Okla. 26,271
Harry Charters, Melba, Ida. 25,149
Dale Smith, Chandler, Ariz. 23,984
Bernis Johnson, Cleburne, Tex. 23,220
Tom Tescher, Medora, N.D. 20,904
Benny Reynolds, Melrose, Mont. 19,303
Jim Bausch, Rapid City, S.D. 19,040
Bob Ragsdale, Chowchilla, Calif. 18,973

Saddle Bronc Riding
Guy Weeks, Abilene, Tex. 19,372
Marty Wood, Bowness, Alta. 19,128
Jim Tescher, Medora, N.D. 15,099
Bill Martinelli, Oakdale, Calif. 13,722
Larry Kane, Big Sandy, Mont. 13,322

Bareback Riding
John Hawkins, Twain Harte, Calif. 16,388
Buddy Peak, Tucson, Ariz. 15,655
Bernis Johnson, Cleburne, Tex. 12,891
Jim Bausch, Rapid City, S.D. 12,693
Clyde Frost, Lapoint, Utah 10,243

Bull Riding
Bill Kornell, Palm Springs, Calif. 15,452
Dickey Cox, McKinney, Tex. 13,180
Carl Natzger, Olton, Tex. 13,010
Joe Green, Sulphur, Okla. 12,047
Bob Wegner, Ponca City, Okla. 11,452

Calf Roping
Dean Oliver, Boise, Ida. 28,375
Bob Wiley, Porterville, Calif. 18,180
Olin Young, Albuquerque, N.M. 15,334
Bob Ragsdale, Chowchilla, Calif. 15,116
Dale Smith, Chandler, Ariz. 15,101

Steer Wrestling
Jim Bynum, Waxahatchie, Tex. 18,252
Billy Hale, Checotah, Okla. 15,635
C. R. Boucher, Burkburnett, Tex. 15,363
Don Huddleston, Talihina, Okla. 14,460
Tom Nesmith, Bethel, Okla. 13,352

Team Roping
Les Hirdes, Turlock, Calif. 13,266
Al Hooper, Escalon, Calif. 12,186
Dale Smith, Chandler, Ariz. 8,885
Billy Hamilton, Phoenix, Ariz. 7,642
Frank Ferreira, Sr., Fresno, Calif. 7,374

Steer Roping
Don McLaughlin, Ft. Collins, Colo. 3,792
Sonny Davis, Kenna, N.M. 3,529
Shoat Webster, Lenapah, Okla. 3,018
Troy Frost, Lovington, N.M. 2,681
Everett Shaw, Stonewall, Okla. 2,638

STANDINGS—1964

All Around Cowboy
Dean Oliver, Boise, Ida. 31,150
Benny Reynolds, Dillon, Mont. 27,413
Jim Tescher, Medora, N.D. 25,644
Mark Schricker, Sutherlin, Ore. 23,323
Kenny McLean, Okanagan Falls, B.C. 23,233
Ronnye Sewalt, Chico, Tex. 22,831
John W. Jones, San Luis Obispo, Calif. 22,674
Jim Houston, Omaha, Nebr. 21,822
Ken Stanton, Weiser, Ida. 20,492
Guy Weeks, Abilene, Tex. 19,282

Saddle Bronc Riding
Marty Woods, Bowness, Alta. 22,148
Jim Tescher, Medora, N.D. 21,577
Kenny McLean, Okanagan Falls, B.C. 19,760
Enoch Walker, Cody, Wyo. 18,083
Shawn Davis, Whitehall, Mont. 13,289

Bareback Riding
Jim Houston, Omaha, Nebr. 20,897
Jim Mihalek, Broomfield, Colo. 15,086
Jim Bausch, Rapid City, S.D. 14,070
John Hawkins, Twain Harte, Calif. 14,069
Malcolm Jones, Lethbridge, Alta. 11,168

Bull Riding
Bob Wegner, Auburn, Wash. 20,757
Bill Kornell, Palm Springs, Calif. 19,012
Delbert Hataway, Roby, Tex. 14,129
Ken Stanton, Weiser, Ida. 12,899
Ronnie Rossen, Broadus, Mont. 11,014

Calf Roping
Dean Oliver, Boise, Ida. 23,591
Ronnye Sewalt, Chico, Tex. 22,374
Barry Burk, Wagoner, Okla. 17,180
Olin Young, Albuqerque, N.M. 16,886
Bob Wiley, Porterville, Calif. 16,012

Steer Wrestling
C. R. Boucher, Burkburnett, Tex. 19,716
John W. Jones, San Luis Obispo, Calif. 19,021
Billy Hale, Checotah, Okla. 14,543
Benny Reynolds, Dillon, Mont. 12,742
Walter Wyatt, Bakersfield, Calif. 11,280

Team Roping
Bill Hamilton, Phoenix, Ariz. 12,394
Gary Gist, Lakeside, Calif. 11,652
Jack Gomez, Reno, Nev. 8,647
Ted Ashworth, Tulare, Calif. 8,337
Jim Rodriguez, Jr., San Luis Obispo, Calif. ... 6,066

Steer Roping
Sonny Davis, Kenna, N.M. 6,558
Jim Bob Altizer, Del Rio, Tex. 4,792
Joe Snively, Pawhuska, Okla. 4,492
Kelly Corbin, Delaware, Okla. 4,006
Shoat Webster, Lenapah, Okla. 3,700

STANDINGS—1965

All Around Cowboy
Dean Oliver, Boise, Ida. 33,163
Mark Schricker, Sutherlin, Ore. 30,696
Glen Franklin, House, N.M. 29,701
Shawn Davis, Whitehall, Mont. 25,949
Ken Stanton, Weiser, Ida. 25,787
Paul Mayo, Grinnell, Ia. 25,494
Winston Bruce, Cochrane, Alta. 24,602
Larry Mahan, Brooks, Ore. 24,000
Jim Houston, Omaha, Nebr. 23,603
Harry Tompkins, Dublin, Tex. 20,357

Saddle Bronc Riding
Shawn Davis, Whitehall, Mont. 25,599
Winston Bruce, Cochrane, Alta. 23,575
Enoch Walker, Cody, Wyo. 19,350
Marty Wood, Bowness, Alta. 14,319
Bill Smith, Cody, Wyo. 12,661

Bareback Riding
Jim Houston, Omaha, Nebr. 17,631
Paul Mayo, Grinnell, Ia. 16,990
Malcolm Jones, Lethbridge, Alta. 14,136
Clyde Vamvoras, Lake Charles, La. 14,019
Jack Buschborn, Mobridge, S.D. 14,015

Bull Riding
Larry Mahan, Brooks, Ore. 18,105
Ronnie Rossen, Broadus, Mont. 17,084
Ken Stanton, Weiser, Ida. 15,823
Bob Wegner, Auburn, Wash. 14,635
Bob Sheppard, Tucson, Ariz. 11,974

Calf Roping
Glen Franklin, House, N.M. 29,646
Dean Oliver, Boise, Ida. 23,687
Lee Farris, Sebastopol, Calif. 16,154
Ronnye Sewalt, Chico, Tex. 16,111
Mark Schricker, Sutherlin, Ore. 15,604

Steer Wrestling
Harley May, Oakdale, Calif. 16,817
Mark Schricker, Sutherlin, Ore. 15,021
Billy Hale, Checotah, Okla. 14,720
Don Huddleston, Talihina, Okla. 13,492
C. R. Boucher, Burkburnett, Tex. 12,124

Team Roping
Jim Rodriguez, Jr., Paso Robles, Calif. 11,050
Ken Luman, Merced, Calif. 10,029
Billy Hamilton, Phoenix, Ariz. 8,660
Al Hooper, Fallon, Nev. 6,912
Joe Glenn, Phoenix, Ariz. 6,807

Steer Roping

Sonney Wright, Alto, N.M.	4,817
Joe Snively, Pawhuska, Okla.	4,202
Kelly Corbin, Delaware, Okla.	3,783
Don McLaughlin, Ft. Collins, Colo.	3,751
Everett Shaw, Stonewall, Okla.	2,954

STANDINGS—1966

All Around Cowboy

Larry Mahan, Brooks, Ore.	40,358
Dean Oliver, Boise, Ida.	34,290
Paul Mayo, Grinnell, Ia.	30,339
Bob Ragsdale, Chowchilla, Calif.	26,764
Jim Houston, Omaha, Nebr.	24,067
Ken Stanton, Weiser, Ida.	23,904
Jack Roddy, San Jose, Calif.	23,037
Ronnie Rossen, Broadus, Mont.	21,498
Benny Reynolds, Dillon, Mont.	21,467
Walt Linderman, Belfry, Mont.	20,449

Saddle Bronc Riding

Marty Wood, Bowness, Atla.	20,319
Bill Smith, Cody, Wyo.	18,802
Winston Bruce, Cochrane, Alta.	18,135
Hugh Chambliss, Albuquerque, N.M.	14,575
Shawn Davis, Whitehall, Mont.	12,970

Bareback Riding

Paul Mayo, Grinnell, Ia.	25,473
Jim Houston, Omaha, Nebr.	17,159
John Edwards, Cheyenne, Wyo.	17,027
Larry Mahan, Brooks, Ore.	16,255
Clyde Vamvoras, Burkburnett, Tex.	13,150

Bull Riding

Ronnie Rossen, Broadus, Mont.	18,072
Bob Wegner, Auburn, Wash.	17,560
Freckles Brown, Soper, Okla.	16,393
Billy Minick, Medora, N.D.	14,358
Ken Stanton, Weiser, Ida.	11,929

Calf Roping

Junior Garrison, Marlow, Okla.	24,304
Dean Oliver, Boise, Ida.	24,208
Ronnye Sewalt, Chico, Tex.	23,338
Bob Ragsdale, Chowchilla, Calif.	20,414
Jim Bob Altizer, Del Rio, Tex.	17,274

Steer Wrestling

Jack Roddy, San Jose, Calif.	22,405
Walt Linderman, Belfry, Mont.	19,358
Roy Duvall, Boynton, Okla.	13,593
Billy Hale, Checotah, Okla.	13,440
Walter Wyatt, Lakeview Terrace, Calif.	12,220

Team Roping

Ken Luman, Merced, Calif.	11,343
Jack Branham, Tuscon, Ariz.	8,817
Jim Rodriguez, Jr., Paso Robles, Calif.	8,329
Joe Glenn, Phoenix, Ariz.	7,425
Art Arnold	6,311

Steer Roping

Sonny Davis, Kenna, N.M.	5,089
Olin Young, Peralta, N.M.	4,923
Don McLaughlin, Ft. Collins, Colo.	4,471
Shoat Webster, Lenapah, Okla.	4,291
Kelly Corbin, Delaware, Okla.	3,331

STANDINGS—1967

All Around Cowboy

Larry Mahan, Brooks, Ore.	51,996
Mark Shricker, Sutherlin, Ore.	31,076
Barry Burk, Duncan, Okla.	31,299
John W. Jones, San Luis Obispo, Calif.	29,105
Shawn Davis, Whitehall, Mont.	25,406
Olin Young, Peralta, N.M.	24,984
Jim Bob Altizer, DelRio, Tex.	24,302
Paul Mayo, Grinnell, Ia.	23,679

Bob Ragsdale, Chowchilla, Calif.	22,163
Tony Haberer, Muleshoe, Tex.	21,054

Saddle Bronc Riding

Shawn Davis, Whitehall, Mont.	25,277
Marty Wood, Diamond, Mo.	19,907
Larry Mahan, Brooks, Ore.	16,326
Bill Smith, Cody, Wyo.	13,652
John McBeth, Atlanta, Kans.	12,636

Bareback Riding

Clyde Vamvoras, Burkburnett, Tex.	24,228
Paul Mayo, Grinnell, Ia.	20,555
Bob Mayo, Grinnell, Ia.	14,556
Larry Mahan, Brooks, Ore.	14,017
Jim Mihalek, Broomfield, Colo.	13,970

Bull Riding

Larry Mahan, Brooks, Ore.	21,653
Bill Stanton, Amboy, Wash.	20,877
Myrtis Dightman, Houston, Tex.	16,014
George Paul, DelRio, Tex.	14,666
Freckles Brown, Soper, Okla.	14,098

Calf Roping

Glen Franklin, House, N.M.	31,268
Barry Burk, Duncan, Okla.	24,832
Junior Garrison, Marlow, Okla.	24,011
Olin Young, Peralta, N.M.	20,412
Jim Bob Altizer, Del Rio, Tex.	19,457

Steer Wrestling

Roy Duvall, Boynton, Okla.	30,715
John W. Jones, San Luis Obispo, Calif.	26,786
Mark Schricker, Sutherlin, Ore.	21,501
Jerry Peveto, Orange, Tex.	16,398
Leon Bauerle, Kyle, Tex.	15,518

Team Roping

Joe Glenn, Phoenix, Ariz.	11,084
Art Arnold, Buckeye, Ariz.	10,740
John Miller, Pawhuska, Okla.	9,632
Jim Rodriguez, Jr., Paso Robles, Calif.	8,518
Ken Luman, Merced, Calif.	7,195

Steer Roping

Jim Bob Altizer, DelRio, Tex.	5,696
Don McLaughlin, Ft. Collins, Colo.	3,621
Olin Young, Peralta, N.M.	3,415
Kelly Corbin, Delaware, Okla.	3,291
Tim Prather, Post, Tex.	2,797

STANDINGS—1968

All Around Cowboy

Larry Mahan, Salem, Ore.	49,129
Jim Houston, Burkburnett, Tex.	37,501
Glen Franklin, House, N.M.	33,468
Barry Burk, Duncan, Okla.	31,942
George Paul, Del Rio, Tex.	30,742
Jack Roddy, San Jose, Calif.	29,524
Paul Mayo, Grinnell, Ia.	29,228
Bob Ragsdale, Chowchilla, Calif.	28,378
Shawn Davis, Whitehall, Mont.	27,015
Mark Schricker, Sutherlin, Ore.	22,742

Saddle Bronc Riding

Shawn Davis, Whitehall, Mont.	22,697
Larry Mahan, Salem, Ore.	18,990
Bill Smith, Cody, Wyo.	16,604
Mel Hyland, Port Kells, B.C.	14,282
Kenny McLean, Okanagan Falls, B.C.	13,208

Bareback Riding

Clyde Vamvoras, Burkburnett, Tex.	25,832
Jim Houston, Burkburnett, Tex.	22,402
Bob Mayo, Grinnell, Ia.	21,715
Paul Mayo, Grinnell, Ia.	18,949
Gary Tucker, Carlsbad, N.M.	18,631

Bull Riding

George Paul, Del Rio, Tex.	27,822

Gary Leffew, Santa Maria, Calif.	17,027
Freckles Brown, Soper, Okla.	15,783
Myrtis Dightman, Houston, Tex.	15,348
Ronnie Rossen, Broadus, Mont.	14,095

Calf Roping

Glen Franklin, House, N.M.	33,252
Barry Burk, Duncan, Okla.	24,939
Junior Garrison, Marlow, Okla.	21,619
Dean Oliver, Boise, Ida.	19,733
Bob Ragsdale, Chowchilla, Calif.	18,577

Steer Wrestling

Jack Roddy, San Jose, Calif.	29,315
Roy Duvall, Boynton, Okla.	18,275
Billy Hale, Checotah, Okla.	17,093
John W. Jones, Morro Bay, Calif.	15,536
Jim Houston, Burkburnett, Tex.	15,098

Team Roping

Art Arnold, Buckeye, Ariz.	12,823
Joe Glenn, Phoenix, Ariz.	10,665
Jerold Camarillo, Oakdale, Calif.	8,801
John J. Miller, Pawhuska, Okla.	8,497
Jim Rodriguez, Jr., Shandon, Calif.	5,514

Steer Roping

Sonny Davis, Kenna, N.M.	6,438
Jim Bob Altizer, Del Rio, Tex.	3,748
Nick Harris, Gillette, Wyo.	3,429
Glenn Nutter, Thedford, Nebr.	2,750
Harry Lynn, So. Coffeyville, Okla.	2,731

STANDINGS—1969

All Around Cowboy

Larry Mahan, Salem, Ore.	57,726
Doug Brown, Silverton, Ore.	40,964
Dean Oliver, Boise, Ida.	39,081
Mark Schricker, Sutherlin, Ore.	32,982
Barry Burk, Duncan, Okla.	32,862
Bob Berger, Halstead, Kans.	31,264
Bob Ragsdale, Chowchilla, Calif.	30,621
Ronnie Sewalt, Chico, Tex.	25,947
Ken Stanton, Weiser, Ida.	25,612
Roy Duvall, Boynton, Okla.	24,460

Saddle Bronc Riding

Bill Smith, Cody, Wyo.	23,642
Larry Mahan, Salem, Ore.	20,730
Hugh Chambliss, Santa Rosa, N.M.	17,989
Bobby Berger, Halstead, Kans.	17,384
Buzz Seely, Roosevelt, Wash.	17,198

Bareback Riding

Gary Tucker, Carlsbad, N.M.	24,944
Jim Ivory, Pampa, Tex.	22,914
Royce Smith, Iona, Ida.	20,164
Larry Mahan, Salem, Ore.	18,375
Paul Mayo, Grinnell, Ia.	16,388

Bull Riding

Doug Brown, Silverton, Ore.	27,610
Larry Mahan, Salem, Ore.	18,621
Gary Leffew, Santa Maria, Calif.	17,516
Bill Stanton, Oakdale, Calif.	15,577
Randy Magers, Ft. Worth, Tex.	15,032

Calf Roping

Dean Oliver, Boise, Ida.	38,118
Barry Burk, Duncan, Okla.	22,540
Junior Garrison, Marlow, Okla.	22,455
Bob Ragsdale, Chowchilla, Calif.	20,622
Ronnye Sewalt, Chico, Tex.	20,427

Steer Wrestling

Roy Duvall, Boynton, Okla.	24,362
Jerry Peveto, Orange, Tex.	23,172
Walt Linderman, Belfry, Mont.	21,589
John W. Jones, Morro Bay, Calif.	15,687
Mark Schricker, Sutherlin, Ore.	14,804

Team Roping

Jerold Camarillo, Oakdale, Calif.	11,532
John Paboojian, Fowler, Calif.	10,813
Bill Darnell, Animas, N.M.	10,759
John Miller, Pawhuska, Okla.	10,594
Jim Rodriguez, Jr., Shandon, Calif.	9,216

Steer Roping

Walter Arnold, Silverton, Tex.	5,460
Sonny Davis, Kenna, N.M.	5,005
Olin Young, Peralta, N.M.	4,488
Don McLaughlin, Ft. Collins, Colo.	4,407
Tim Prather, Post, Tex.	3,206

STANDINGS—1970

All Around Cowboy

Larry Mahan, Brooks, Ore.	41,493
Warren Wuthier, Banner, Wyo.	35,080
Bob Berger, Norman, Okla.	34,084
Paul Mayo, Ft. Worth, Tex.	33,973
John W. Jones, Morro Bay, Calif.	28,019
Ace Berry, Modesto, Calif.	27,799
Barry Burk, Duncan, Okla.	27,463
Mark Schricker, Sutherlin, Ore.	25,330
Bob Ragsdale, Chowchilla, Calif.	22,941
Mel Hyland, Surrey, B.C.	22,716

Saddle Bronc Riding

Dennis Reiners, Scottsdale, Ariz.	25,384
Mel Hyland, Surrey, B.C.	22,453
Larry Mahan, Brooks, Ore.	14,737
Bob Berger, Norman, Okla.	14,442
Hugh Chambliss, Santa Rosa, N.M.	14,228

Bareback Riding

Paul Mayo, Ft. Worth, Tex.	26,644
Gary Tucker, Carlsbad, N.M.	25,919
Clyde Vamvoras, Devol, Okla.	23,082
Ace Berry, Modesto, Calif.	20,808
Joe Alexander, Cora, Wyo.	17,831

Bull Riding

Gary Leffew, Santa Maria, Calif.	23,583
Bob Berger, Norman, Okla.	19,642
Lee Markholt, East Tacoma, Wash.	18,129
Bill Kornell, Salmon, Ida.	16,902
Randy Magers, Ft. Worth, Tex.	16,326

Calf Roping

Junior Garrison, Duncan, Okla.	24,311
Barry Burk, Duncan, Okla.	22,443
Warren Wuthier, Banner, Wyo.	21,930
Ronnye Sewalt, Chico, Tex.	21,423
Stan Harter, Phoenix, Ariz.	17,705

Steer Wrestling

John W. Jones, Morro Bay, Calif.	25,934
Walt Linderman, Belfry, Mont.	19,482
Roy Duvall, Warner, Okla.	19,196
Ed Galemba, Stratford, Conn.	17,522
Billy Hale, Checotah, Okla.	14,882

Team Roping

John Miller, Pawhuska, Okla.	11,658
Jim Rodriguez, Jr., Shandon, Calif.	10,830
Jerold Camarillo, Oakdale, Calif.	10,647
Ken Luman, Winton, Calif.	9,744
Bill Darnell, Rodeo, N.M.	9,101

Steer Roping

Don McLaughlin, Ft. Collins, Colo.	6,331
Billy Frank Good, Caprock, N.M.	4,986
Olin Young, Peralta, N.M.	4,977
Randy Burchett, Pryor, Okla.	4,325
Allen Keller, Olathe, Colo.	3,397

STANDINGS—1971

All Around Cowboy

Phil Lyne, George West, Tex.	49,245
Bob Berger, Norman, Okla.	46,746
Paul Mayo, Ft. Worth, Tex.	35,780
Bill Nelson, San Francisco, Calif.	34,442
Larry Mahan, Brooks, Ore.	33,732
Barry Burk, Chandler, Okla.	27,223
Warren Wuthier, Banner, Wyo.	25,650
Doug Brown, Silverton, Ore.	23,548
Jay Himes, Beulah, Colo.	23,507
Bob Ragsdale, Chowchilla, Calif.	23,237

Saddle Bronc Riding

Bill Smith, Cody, Wyo.	26,378
J.C. Bonnie, Hysham, Mont.	21,064
Mel Hyland, Surrey, B.C.	18,374
Shawn Davis, Whitehall, Mont.	17,471
Bill Martinelli, Oakdale, Calif.	17,400

Bareback Riding

Joe Alexander, Cora, Wyo.	28,669
Paul Mayo, Ft. Worth, Tex.	24,227
Jay Himes, Beulah, Colo.	23,291
T. J. Walter, Watkins, Ia.	20,943
Clyde Vamvoras, Devol, Okla.	17,488

Bull Riding

Bill Nelson, San Francisco, Calif.	21,200
Bob Berger, Norman, Okla.	20,776
Bob Steiner, Austin, Tex.	17,999
John Quintana, Eugene, Ore.	17,931
Randy Magers, Comanche, Tex.	16,084

Calf Roping

Phil Lyne, George West, Tex.	28,220
Richard Stowers, Madill, Okla.	22,393
Barry Burk, Chandler, Okla.	22,137
Ernie Taylor, Hugo, Okla.	21,970
Junior Garrison, Duncan, Okla.	18,783

Steer Wrestling

Billy Hale, Checotah, Okla.	23,504
Walt Linderman, Belfry, Mont.	15,871
Tommy Puryear, Austin, Tex.	15,636
Nathan Haley, Hanna, Okla.	14,828
Roy Duvall, Warner, Okla.	14,822

Team Roping

John Miller, Pawhuska, Okla.	9,613
John Rodriguez, Castroville, Calif.	8,429
Leo Camarillo, Donald, Ore.	8,071
Ken Luman, Salinas, Calif.	7,461
Gary Gist, Lakeside, Calif.	7,322

Steer Roping

Olin Young, Peralta, N.M.	6,190
Walter Arnold, Silverton, Tex.	5,652
Don McLaughlin, Ft. Collins, Colo.	4,867
Sonny Savis, Kenna, N.M.	4,531
James Allen, Santa Ana, Tex.	3,884

STANDINGS—1972

All Around Cowboy

Phil Lyne, George West, Tex.	60,852
Bob Ragsdale, Chowchilla, Calif.	36,435
Larry Mahan, Salem, Ore.	34,799
Barry Burk, Duncan, Okla.	33,064
Leo Camarillo, Donald, Ore.	31,811
Mel Hyland, Surrey, B.C.	26,854
Kenny McLean, Vernon, B.C.	26,113
Sandy Kirby, Greenville, Tex.	26,032
Ronnye Sewalt, Chico, Tex.	25,803
Ernie Taylor, Hugo, Okla.	24,429

Saddle Bronc Riding

Mel Hyland, Surrey, B.C.	26,812
J.C. Bonine, Hysham, Mont.	24,925
Bill Smith, Cody, Wyo.	22,127
Ivan Daines, Innisfail, Alta.	21,306
John McBeth, Burden, Kans.	18,620

Bareback Riding

Joe Alexander, Cora, Wyo.	32,126
Rusty Riddle, Mineral Wells, Tex.	24,123
Jim Dix, N. Collie, W. Aust.	23,321
Gary Tucker, Carlsbad, N.M.	21,120
Royce Smith, Challis, Ida.	17,688

Bull Riding

John Quintana, Creswell, Ore.	23,054
Phil Lyne, George West, Tex.	19,577
Larry Mahan, Salem, Ore.	18,480
Gary Leffew, Arroyo Grande, Calif.	17,629
Jack Kelley, Deer Lodge, Mont.	17,411

Calf Roping

Phil Lyne, George West, Tex.	32,216
Barry Burk, Duncan, Okla.	27,886
Dean Oliver, Boise, Ida.	25,358
Bob Ragsdale, Chowchilla, Calif.	24,126
Ronnye Sewalt, Chico, Tex.	23,412

Steer Wrestling

Roy Duvall, Warner, Okla.	24,327
Frank Shepperson, Midwest, Wyo.	21,649
Tom Elliott, Peyton, Colo.	21,475
Bob Marshall, San Martin, Calif.	18,256
Fred Larson, Sheridan, Wyo.	17,154

Team Roping

Leo Camarillo, Donald, Ore.	17,587
Bucky Bradford, Lakeside, Calif.	16,137
Gary Gist, Lakeside, Calif.	13,598
Jim Rodriguez, Paso Robles, Calif.	12,679
Ken Luman, Visalia, Calif.	12,232

Steer Roping

Allen Keller, Olathe, Colo.	7,593
John Miller, Pawhuska, Okla.	5,923
Olin Young, Peralta, N.M.	5,213
Walt Arnold, Silverton, Tex.	4,370
James Allen, Santa Ana, Tex.	3,605

STANDINGS—1973

All Around Cowboy

Larry Mahan, Dallas, Tex.	64,447
Tom Ferguson, San Martin, Calif.	45,447
Ernie Taylor, Hugo, Okla.	39,154
Doug Brown, Silverton, Ore.	38,978
Leo Camarillo, Donald, Ore.	38,538
Bob Ragsdale, Chowchilla, Calif.	37,078
Jack Ward, Odessa, Tex.	31,881
Barry Burk, Duncan, Okla.	31,114
Bob Berger, Norman, Okla.	29,349
Don Gay, Mesquite, Tex.	27,318

Saddle Bronc Riding

Bill Smith, Cody, Wyo.	26,069
Larry Mahan, Dallas, Tex.	22,153
John McBeth, Burden, Kans.	21,903
Darryl Kong, Kaycee, Wyo.	21,882
J.C. Bonine, Hysham, Mont.	21,707

Bareback Riding

Joe Alexander, Cora, Wyo.	37,021
Rusty Riddle, Mineral Wells, Tex.	30,744
Ace Berry, Modesto, Calif.	22,031
Jack Ward, Odessa, Tex.	20,279
Jim Dix, N. Collie, W. Aust.	20,149

Bull Riding

Bobby Steiner, Austin, Tex.	28,099
Don Gay, Mesquite, Tex.	26,889
Larry Mahan, Dallas, Tex.	24,439
Doug Brown, Silverton, Ore.	20,974
Pete Gay, Mesquite, Tex.	19,284

Calf Roping

Ernie Taylor, Hugo, Okla.	38,772
Barry Burk, Duncan, Okla.	27,849
Ronnye Sewalt, Chico, Tex.	23,231
Bob Ragsdale, Chowchilla, Calif.	22,391
Tom Ferguson, San Martin, Calif.	20,655

Steer Wrestling

Bob Marshall, San Martin, Calif.	31,817
Billy Hale, Checotah, Okla.	25,854
Tom Ferguson, San Martin, Calif.	23,604
Walt Linderman, Belfry, Mont.	17,715
Frank Shepperson, Midwest, Wyo.	17,327

Team Roping

Leo Camarillo, Donald, Ore.	20,693
H.P. Evetts, Hanford, Calif.	15,557
Bucky Bradford, Sylmar, Calif.	15,365
Jerold Camarillo, Oakdale, Calif.	14,581
Reg Camarillo, Oakdale, Calif.	13,551

Steer Roping

Roy Thompson, Tulia, Tex.	6,259
John Miller, Pawhuska, Okla.	6,136
Irv Alderson, Birney, Mont.	4,996
Nick Harris, Gillette, Wyo.	4,605
Charley Lynn, So. Coffeyville, Okla.	4,254

STANDINGS—1974

All Around Cowboy

Tom Ferguson, Miami, Okla.	66,929
Leo Camarillo, Oakdale, Calif.	34,786
Bob Berger, Norman, Okla.	34,743
Don Gay, Mesquite, Tex.	33,314
Sandy Kirby, Greenville, Tex.	31,426
Larry Mahan, Dallas, Tex.	30,943
Jack Ward, Odessa, Tex.	29,696
Barry Burk, Duncan, Okla.	27,402
Monty Henson, Mesquite, Tex.	24,922
H.P. Evetts, Hanford, Calif.	24,697

Saddle Bronc Riding

John McBeth, Burden, Kan.	36,730
J.C. Bonine, Hysham, Mont.	30,304
Monty Henson, Mesquite, Tex.	21,505
Bill Smith, Cody, Wyo.	20,749
Dennis Reiners, Scottsdale, Ariz.	20,431

Bareback Riding

Joe Alexander, Cora, Wyo.	36,073
Rusty Riddle, Weatherford, Tex.	27,747
Chris LeDoux, Kaycee, Wyo.	25,740
Jack Ward, Odessa, Tex.	25,193
Jim Dix, North Collie, W. Australia.	23,423

Bull Riding

Don Gay, Mesquite, Tex.	32,917
John Davis, Homedale, Ida.	24,720
Butch Kirby, Greenville, Tex.	21,769
Jerome Robinson, Brandon, Nebr.	20,883
Marvin Shoulders, Henryetta, Okla.	16,491

Calf Roping

Tom Ferguson, Miami, Okla.	40,839
Dean Oliver, Boise, Ida.	23,697
Barry Burk, Duncan, Okla.	23,571
Jeff Copenhaver, Seaside, Ore.	21,837
Gary Ledford, Comanche, Okla.	21,813

Steer Wrestling

Tommy Puryear, Norman, Okla.	26,253
Tom Ferguson, Miami, Okla.	25,893
Frank Shepperson, Midwest, Wyo.	24,554
Bob Marshall, San Martin, Calif.	21,372
Mike Ring, Toppenish, Wash.	17,703

Team Roping

H.P. Evetts, Hanford, Calif.	23,018
Leo Camarillo, Oakdale, Calif.	18,510
Jerold Camarillo, Oakdale, Calif.	16,368
Jim Wheatley, Hughson, Calif.	12,675
Les Hirdes, Turlock, Calif.	12,207

Steer Roping

Olin Young, Peralta, N.M.	12,416
Kenny Call, Blanco, Tex.	6,858
Sonny Davis, Kenna, N.M.	6,100
Ed Becker, Ashby, Neb.	4,541
Jim Moore, Gillette, Wyo.	4,290

STANDINGS—1975

All Around Cowboy

Leo Camarillo, Oakdale, Calif.	50,300+
Tom Ferguson, Miami, Okla.	50,300+
Larry Mahan, Dallas, Tex.	47,425
Jack Ward, Springdale, Ark.	41,579
Larry Ferguson, Miami, Okla.	39,635
Don Gay, Mesquite, Tex.	39,234
Sandy Kirby, Greenville, Tex.	38,492
Barry Burk, Duncan, Okla.	35,014
Jeff Copenhaver, Spokane, Wash.	34,670
Bobby Berger, Norman, Okla.	34,445
Doug Brown, Silverton, Ore.	32,286
Monty Henson, Mesquite, Tex.	30,831
Kaye Kirby, Woodstown, N.J.	28,748
H.P. Evetts, Hanford, Calif.	26,562
Ronnye Sewalt, Chico, Tex.	25,355

Saddle Bronc Riding

Monty Henson, Mesquite, Tex.	29,788
Tom C. Miller, Faith, S.D.	21,345
Doug Brown, Silverton, Ore.	21,141
Sammie Groves, New Deal, Tex.	21,139
John Forbes, Kaycee, Wyo.	20,354
Melvin Coleman, Pierceland, Sask.	19,936
Bill Smith, Cody, Wyo.	19,537
Bobby Berger, Norman, Okla.	18,415
Joe Marvel, Battle Mt., Nev.	18,346
Mel Hyland, Surrey, B.C.	16,942
Larry Mahan, Dallas, Tex.	16,884
Bill Pauley, Miles City, Mont.	15,469
Mike Marvel, Battle Mt., Nev.	15,432
Bobby Brown, Adrian, Tex.	14,459
Chancy Wheeldon, Jackson, Wyo.	12,892

Bareback Riding

Joe Alexander, Cora, Wyo.	41,184
Rusty Riddle, Weatherford, Tex.	38,767
Jack Ward, Springdale, Ark.	37,848
Jim Dix, N. Collie, W. Aust.	33,219
Royce Smith, Challis, Ida.	28,261
Bruce Ford, Greeley, Colo.	24,990
Scotty Platts, Lyman, Wyo.	23,035
Chick Elms, Stephenville, Tex.	20,031
Sandy Kirby, Greenville, Tex.	19,092
Larry Mahan, Dallas, Tex.	18,511
Kaye Kirby, Woodstown, N.J.	18,228
T. J. Walter, Eastland, Tex.	15,596
J. C. Trujillo Santa Fe, N.M.	14,800
Ike Sankey, Rose Hill, Kans.	13,610
Ben Calhoun, Bryan, Tex.	12,820

Bull Riding

Don Gay, Mesquite, Tex.	34,850
Randy Magers, Comanche, Tex.	24,422
Marvin Shoulders, Henryetta, Okla.	21,858
Jerome Robinson, Brandon, Nebr.	20,578
Butch Kirby, Greenville, Tex.	19,199
Denny Flynn, Springdale, Ark.	18,888
John Davis, Homedale, Ida.	18,681
Mike Bandy, Adkins, Tex.	17,395
Sandy Kirby, Greenville, Tex.	16,938
Don Graham, Troup, Tex.	16,547
John Gloor, Jr., Damon, Tex.	16,072
Bobby Berger, Norman, Okla.	15,027
Charlie Underwood, Tucson, Ariz.	14,971
A. J. Swaim, Portland, Ore.	14,610
Leander Frey, Eunice, La.	14,040

Calf Roping

Jeff Copenhaver, Spokane, Wash.	34,628
Barry Burk, Duncan, Okla.	32,057
Junior Garrison, Elgin, Okla.	24,057
Tom Ferguson, Miami, Okla.	23,963
Bobby Goodspeed, High Ridge, Mo.	23,952
Ernie Taylor, Hugo, Okla.	23,756
Terry Davidson, Wayne, Okla.	23,719
Ronnye Sewalt, Chico, Tex.	22,494
Bob Ragsdale, Chowchilla, Calif.	21,543
Willard Moody, Elmore City, Okla.	20,913
Greg Winham, Rush Spgs., Okla.	20,307
Don W. Smith, Kiowa, Okla.	20,229
Billy Doenz, Big Horn, Wyo.	20,201
Gary Ledford, Comanche, Okla.	17,654
Larry Ferguson, Miami, Okla.	16,419

Steer Wrestling

Frank Shepperson, Midwest, Wyo.	34,863
Tommy Puryear, Kyle, Tex.	25,836
Tom Ferguson, Miami, Okla.	25,662
Larry Ferguson, Miami, Okla.	22,516
Bob Marshall, San Martin, Calif.	22,119
Roy Duvall, Warner, Okla.	21,954
Mike Ring, Toppenish, Wash.	18,401
Carl Deaton, Hampshire, Tex.	16,625
Bob Christophersen, Glendive, Mont.	16,456
Fred Larsen, Decker, Mont.	15,702
Leon Bauerle, Kyle, Tex.	14,418
C. R. Jones, Lakeside, Calif.	13,645
Gary Walker, Brentwood, Calif.	13,038
Casper Schaefer, Miles City, Mont.	12,897
Darrel Sewell, Lucile, Ida.	12,837

Team Roping

Leo Camarillo, Oakdale, Calif.	28,102
H. P. Evetts, Hanford, Calif.	25,393
Reg Camarillo, Oakdale, Calif.	18,363
Jerold Camarillo, Oakdale, Calif.	18,248
Julio Moreno, Bakersfield, Calif.	11,880
Bucky Brandford, Jr., Sylmar, Calif.	11,330
John Rodriguez, Castroville, Calif.	10,605
Ken Luman, Merced, Calif.	9,893
David Motes, Mesa, Ariz.	9,553
Dennis Watkins, Taft, Calif.	9,162
Jim Wheatley, Hughson, Calif.	8,844
Jim Rodriguez, Jr., San Luis Obispo, Calif.	8,773
Ed Hirdes, Turlock, Calif.	8,378
J. D. Yates, Pueblo, Colo.	8,218
Ace Berry, Knights Ferry, Ca.	7,814

Steer Roping

Roy Thompson, Tulia, Tex.	6,121
Eldon Dudley, Perryton, Okla.	5,651
Dewey Lee David, Riverton, Wyo.	5,547
Charlie Lynn, S. Coffeyville, Okla.	4,723
Olin Young, Peralta, N.M.	4,625
Walt Arnold, Silverton, Tex.	4,574
Kenny Call, Blanco, Tex.	4,242
Eddie Becker, Ashby, Neb.	4,174
James Allen, Santa Anna, Tex.	3,975
J. R. Kvenild, Pavillion, Wyo.	3,464
John Dalton, Cheyenne, Wyo.	3,161
Jim Moore, Gillette, Wyo.	3,160
Don McLaughlin, Ft. Collins, Colo.	3,115
Charles Good, Elida, N.M.	2,890
Bud Upton, San Angelo, Tex.	2,878

STANDINGS—1976

(Beginning with the 1976 National Finals, championships are awarded to the contestant who wins the most money in his event at the Finals—previous winnings are not counted.)

All Around Cowboy

Tom Ferguson, Miami, Okla.	9,005
Sandy Kirby, Greenville, Tex.	7,777
Jim Rodriguez, Jr., Fowler, Calif.	2,376
Bobby Berger, Norman, Okla.	1,462

Saddle Bronc Riding

Monty Henson, Mesquite, Tex.	4,473
Mel Hyland, Surrey, B.C.	4,473
Tom Miller, Faith, S.D.	3,655
Joe Marvel, Battle Mt., Nev.	3,070
Mel Coleman, Pierceland, Sask.	3,011
J.C. Bonine, Hysham, Mont.	2,865

Doug Brown, Silverton, Ore.	2,427
Bobby Brown, Adrian, Tex.	2,193
Howard Hunter, Kyle, S.D.	2,193
Bill Pauley, Miles City, Mont.	1,900
Lyle Sankey, Rose Hill, Kans.	1,316
John Forbes, Kaycee, Wyo.	1,169
Jim Kelts, Consort, Alta.	1,023
Wilf Hyland, Surrey, B.C.	731
Bobby Berger, Norman, Okla.	585

Bareback Riding

Chris Le Doux, Kaycee, Wyo.	4,912
Jack Ward, Springdale, Ark.	3,742
Chick Elms, Stephenville, Tex.	3,216
Sandy Kirby, Greenville, Tex.	3,157
Rusty Riddle, Weatherford, Tex.	3,011
Mickey Young, Wellington, Utah	3,011
Bruce Ford, Greeley, Colo.	2,924
Joe Alexander, Cora, Wyo.	2,631
Royce Smith, Challis, Ida.	2,485
T. J. Walter, Eastland, Tex.	1,462
Sam Perkins, Chadron, Nebr.	1,316
Jim Dix, N. Collie, W. Aust.	1,316
Ike Sankey, Rose Hill, Kans.	1,023
J. C. Trujillo, Santa Fe, N.M.	877
Glen Ford, Greeley, Colo.	0

Bull Riding

Don Gay, Mesquite, Tex.	5,496
Sandy Kirby, Greenville, Tex.	4,619
Brian Claypool, Saskatoon, Sask.	4,035
Randy Magers, Comanche, Tex.	4,035
Denny Flynn, Charleston, Ark.	3,596
Wacey Cathey, Big Spring, Tex.	2,485
John Gloor, Beaumont, Tex.	2,047
Gary Leffew, Santa Maria, Calif.	1,608
Pete Gay, Mesquite, Tex.	1,462
Mike Bandy, Adkins, Tex.	1,169
Bob Robertson, Yellow Grass, Sask.	1,023
Bobby Berger, Norman, Okla.	877
John Davis, Homedale, Ida.	585
John Bland, Trent, Tex.	585

Bob Blandford, San Antonio, Tex.	585

Calf Roping

Roy Cooper, Durant, Okla.	5,789
Tom Ferguson, Miami, Okla.	4,970
Bobby Goodspeed, High Ridge, Mo.	4,035
Kim Gripp, Hereford, Tex.	4,035
Jeff Copenhaver, Spokane, Wa.	3,450
Kyle Ditto, Coahoma, Tex.	3,157
John Rothwell, Hyannis, Nebr.	1,754
Terry Davidson, Wayne, Okla.	1,462
Gary Ledford, Comanche, Okla.	1,462
Edd Workman, Mineral Wells, Tex.	1,169
Dean Oliver, Boise, Ida.	1,169
Larry Cohorn, Las Cruces, N.M.	1,169
Butch Bode, Milano, Tex.	877
Barry Burk, Duncan, Okla.	585
Billy Doenz, Big Horn, Wyo.	0

Steer Wrestling

Rick Bradley, Burkburnett, Tex.	5,496
Tommy Puryear, Leander, Tex.	5,058
Frank Shepperson, Midwest, Wyo.	4,824
Danny Torricellas, Eugene, Ore.	4,678
Tom Ferguson, Miami, Okla.	4,035
Carl Deaton, Hamshire, Tex.	1,900
Larry Ferguson, Miami, Okla.	1,754
Pat Nogle, Grass Valley, Ore.	1,696
Stan Christian, Sarcoxie, Mo.	1,608
Roy Duvall, Checotah, Okla.	1,169
Bob Marshall, Chowchilla, Calif.	1,111
Larry Dawson, Gruver, Tex.	731
R. G. Kekich, Sheridan, Wyo.	585
Russ Dolven, Wickenburg, Ariz.	439
Bill Busch, Council Bluffs, Ia.	0

Team Roping

Ronnie Rasco, Lakeside, Calif.	4,512
Bucky Bradford, Jr., Sylmar, Calif.	
Leo Camarillo, Oakdale, Calif.	4,360
Reg Camarillo, Oakdale, Calif.	

Doyle Gellerman, Oakdale, Calif.	3,902
Frank Ferreira, Sr., Fresno, Calif.	
Jeff Barmby, Acampo, Calif.	3,597
Ed Hirdes, Turlock, Calif.	
Arnold Felts, Woodward, Okla.	3,292
Ray Lapan, Riverside, Calif.	
Jim Rodriguez, Jr., Fowler, Calif.	3,201
Ken Luman, Windsor, Calif.	
Jim Wheatley, Hughson, Calif.	2,896
John Rodriguez, Castroville, Calif.	
Dennis Watkins, Taft, Calif.	2,744
Julio Moreno, Bakersfield, Calif.	
John Paboojian, Fowler, Calif.	2,439
David Motes, Mesa, Ariz.	
Gary Gist, Oakland, Calif.	1,982
Joe Murray, Oakdale, Calif.	
Les Hirdes, Turlock, Calif.	1,524
Stan Melshaw, Patterson, Calif.	
Bob McClelland, Lockeford, Calif.	762
Walt Woodward, French Camp, Calif.	
Jack Gomez, Janesville, Calif.	762
John Wheatley, Elk Grove, Calif.	
H. P. Evetts, Hanford, Calif.	610
Jerold Camarillo, Oakdale, Calif.	
Dick Yates, Pueblo, Colo.	0
J. D. Yates, Pueblo, Colo.	

GRA Barrel Racing

Connie Combs, Comanche, Okla.	3,665
Colette Graves, Hardtner, Kans.	2,696
Jimmie Gibbs, Valley Mills, Tex.	2,108
Kay Vamvoras, Valentine, Nebr.	1,995
Marion Gramith, Urbana, Mo.	1,354
Dammy Johnson, Norco, Calif.	1,354
Gail Petska, Tecumseh, Okla.	1,283
Dottye Goodspeed, High Ridge, Mo.	855
Marilyn Camarillo, Oakdale, Calif.	499
Lila Glade, Ekalaka, Mont.	315
Cindy, Witcher, Urbana, Mo.	285
Darla Higgins, Cortez, Colo.	113
Renee Sutherland, Gate, Okla.	0
Pam Ross, Silmar, Calif.	0
Lorraine Alexander, Newton, N.J.	0

ACKNOWLEDGMENTS

Special Appreciation: To the late Frank Reece, my friend who liked cowboys, late bull sessions, and helped me with a number of good ideas for this book.

I express my very special thanks to Randy Spears of the Mesquite Rodeo, and Dave Knight, Winston's man on rodeo, for their untiring help and interest in this book. Without their assistance in contacting and putting me in touch with various people, it would have taken a great deal longer to write this book. My warmest appreciation to Neal Gay and his family, who are always helpful and kind—especially Pete and Don. And to Ted Hornick for getting the whole thing started. I also wish to thank Henry and Iris Stowers for their help and understanding and appreciate the counsel of John Anders and Pat Evans, who in a way are cowboys whether they know it or not. The Cowboy Hall of Fame in Oklahoma City was helpful when I needed it, as was the PRCA. There are, of course, many, many others, but I hope what they see and read on these pages will best express my thanks. Of course, I also appreciate the help and guidance I got from the rodeo cowboys, though mostly I appreciate them for being them.

This book is not meant to be a history or a bringing to life of statistics. It is only meant to tell of people, as they are and as they were.

—THE AUTHOR

The photographs that I took for this book were shot at the National Finals Rodeo in Oklahoma City, the Calgary Stampede, the Snow Mass, Colorado, Rodeo, and the Cheyenne Frontier Days. I would like to extend my sincere appreciation to the public relations departments of these events; most particularly, to Dave Paulsen of the Calgary Stampede and Gene Bryan of the public relations firm of Bryan, Bryan and Black in Cheyenne, Wyoming. Thank you to Randy Witte, Publicity Director for the Professional Rodeo Cowboys Association in Denver, Colorado, and George Williams of The National Cowboy Hall of Fame in Oklahoma City for generously providing historical photographic material for this book.

Diane Vanek, Marilyn Stark, and Lois Martin of the Spectra-Action staff deserve mention for their vigilance during my six weeks' absence and their tireless labor in organizing the enormous number of photographs from which the contents were chosen. Special recognition is due Spectrum Professional Color Laboratories for their handling of the color film and to Bob Bishop, Steve Goldstein, and Chip Maxwell for their many hours spent processing film and making the fine black and white photographs herein reproduced.

Thank you to Ken Stemmler, Vice President of Marketing for Frontier Airlines, and to Dave Knight, Publicity Manager–Winston Rodeo Awards for the R.J. Reynolds Tobacco Company, for their support of my interest in professional rodeo. Thank you to my wife, Judee, and our family for their many tolerances.

To the men of the Professional Rodeo Cowboys Association and to the women of the Girls' Rodeo Association, a special vote of gratitude and appreciation for a most exciting photographic adventure.

—LEWIS PORTNOY

"Ride Me Down Easy," by Billy Joe Shaver. © 1973 by Return Music. Used by permission of the publishers. All rights reserved.
"Willie, the Wandering Gypsy, and Me," by Billy Joe Shaver. © 1972 by Return Music. Used by permission of the publishers. All rights reserved.
"Rhinestone Cowboy," by Larry Weiss. © 1974 and 1975 by Twentieth Century Music Corporation and House of Weiss Music Company. All rights reserved. Used by permission of the publishers.
"Bandy, the Rodeo Clown," by Sanger D. Shafer and Lefty Frizzell. © 1975 by Acuff Rose Publications, Inc. Used by permission of the publishers. All rights reserved.
"Mr. Bojangles," by Jerry Jeff Walker. © 1968 by Cotillion Music, Inc., and Danel Music Corporation, Inc. Used by permission of the publishers. All rights reserved.
"Crazy," by Willie Nelson. Used by permission of the author.
"Freckles Brown," by Red Steagall. Used by permission of Otter Creek Music.

Photo credits   All photography by Lewis Portnoy except for the following:

Larry Burgess, courtesy PRCA: **123 top.** Ferrell Butler: **123 bottom right, 177, 200 bottom left.** Foxie Photo: **175 bottom.** Bern Gregory: **125.** DeVere Helfrich: **37 bottom, 173, 178, 200 top.** Randy Huffman, Bryan, Texas: **208.** Al Long: **25, 123 bottom left.** Dozier Mobley, Winston: **44 right, 203–5, 223, 226 bottom right.** Professional Rodeo Cowboys Association: **37 top and center, 175 top, 179, 200 bottom right.** Rodeo Historical Society: **16 bottom, 172.** John A. Stryker, courtesy PRCA: **124.** Western History Collections, University of Oklahoma Library: **13, 16 top, 32.**